The Executive Director's Guide to
Thriving as a Nonprofit Leader

The Executive Director's Guide to Thriving as a Nonprofit Leader

SECOND EDITION

Mim Carlson
Margaret Donohoe

JOSSEY-BASS
A Wiley Imprint
www.josseybass.com

Published by Jossey-Bass
A Wiley Imprint
989 Market Street, San Francisco, CA 94103–1741—www.josseybass.com

Jossey-Bass books and products are available through most bookstores. To contact Jossey-Bass directly call our Customer Care Department within the U.S. at 800–956–7739, outside the U.S. at 317-572-3986, or fax 317-572-4002.

Jossey-Bass also publishes its books in a variety of electronic formats. Some content that appears in print may not be available in electronic books.

Library of Congress Cataloging-in-Publication Data
    Carlson, Mim, 1950-
        The executive director's guide to thriving as a nonprofit leader / Mim Carlson, Margaret Donohoe.—2nd ed.
          p. cm.
        Includes bibliographical references and index.
        ISBN 978-0-470-40749-3 (pbk.)
       1. Nonprofit organizations—Management. 2. Associations, institutions, etc.—Management.
  3. Chief executive officers.   I. Donohoe, Margaret, 1954- II. Title.
       HD62.6.C266 2010
       658.4'22—dc22

                           2010001205

Printed in the United States of America
SECOND EDITION

PB Printing   10 9 8 7 6 5 4 3 2 1

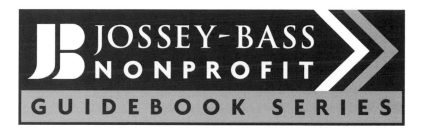

The Jossey-Bass Nonprofit Guidebook Series

The Jossey-Bass Nonprofit Guidebook Series provides new to experienced nonprofit professionals and volunteers with the essential tools and practical knowledge they need to make a difference in the world. From hands-on workbooks to step-by-step guides on developing a critical skill or learning how to perform an important task or process, our accomplished expert authors provide readers with the information required to be effective in achieving goals, mission, and impact.

Other Titles in The Jossey-Bass Nonprofit Guidebook Series

Strategic Communications for Nonprofits: A Step-by-Step Guide to Working with the Media, Second Edition, *Kathy Bonk, Emily Tynes, Henry Griggs, and Phil Sparks*

Winning Grants: Step by Step, Third Edition, *Mim Carlson, Tori O'Neal-McElrath, and The Alliance for Nonprofit Management*

How to Write Successful Fundraising Letters, Second Edition, *Mal Warwick*

The Budget-Building Book for Nonprofits: A Step-by-Step Guide for Managers and Boards, Second Edition, *Murray Dropkin, Jim Halpin, and Bill La Touche*

CONTENTS

EXHIBITS

PREFACE

Our society is blessed with hundreds of thousands of nonprofit, public benefit, and nongovernmental organizations, led by an incredible cadre of paid or unpaid leaders known by such varied titles as Executive Director, Chief Executive Officer, or President, depending on the size and culture of the organization.

No matter what title they assume, these individuals are passionate, committed, resourceful, and creative people. They believe that the work their organization performs makes a significant difference in the lives of those they serve. And they are right. The contributions these organizations make to society provide solid evidence that clearly supports this belief.

The reality that we and many of our nonprofit colleagues see among this inspirational group of men and women is that, despite their enviable role and their tremendous contribution to society, nonprofit leaders tend to struggle with the complexity of the job. The paradox is that Executive Directors can make life better for others while their own lives become increasingly difficult. Why does this happen?

UNCOVERING THE PARADOX

What we have seen in our work as Executive Directors, and what many others have shared in their stories, is that nonprofit leaders are exposed to and must juggle countless external and internal pressures. They wrestle with the competing internal priorities of staff and volunteer development, financial management, program effectiveness, resource development, and Board relations. At the same time, they look beyond the organization's walls to monitor the changing nonprofit environment, form strategic partnerships, and be responsive to stakeholders' demands for accountability. With these pressures, work-life balance is difficult. Rarely has anyone the time or energy to focus effectively on all these priorities. Long days are the norm, and quite often there is no such thing as a weekend. Burnout and fatigue are common.

Many Executive Directors don't know where to turn for support to prevent burnout or to get their most basic questions answered. Over time some begin to feel overwhelmed and distracted by yearnings for a better quality of life.

Recent studies of Executive Directors have revealed some alarming statistics. The average tenure has declined to less than six years. The majority of current Executive Directors indicate that they do not want to be an Executive Director in their next job. This data underscores the significant retention issues in holding onto leadership talent in nonprofits.

Some experts in the field suggest that new Executive Directors require at least three to five years before they can make significant achievements in an organization. If this is so, then almost half of Executive Directors leave their position prior to reaching their full potential. Not only is organizational capacity being severely compromised, the entire nonprofit sector is wasting a major resource of talent.

Additionally, the new generations of leaders say they expect a life that is balanced. Work is important but so are family, friends, and fun. These twenty- and thirty-year-olds have the same passion, commitment, values, and motivation that their older Executive Director colleagues have, but they are equally committed to a balanced life. We say, "Good for you!"

We hope that if you are an Executive Director, or are thinking about becoming one, you will see the challenges that Executive Directors face as a call to reform and to rally around the need for anyone in this profession to have a healthy, balanced life. For the nonprofit sector to thrive and continue to provide important and necessary programs, we all must acknowledge the paradox. We must look for ways to help Executive Directors survive longer in their positions and ultimately thrive as leaders.

FINDING YOUR OWN PATH TO SUCCESS AS EXECUTIVE DIRECTOR

The nonprofit sector is awash in Web sites, blogs, literature, support organizations, and academic research expounding a variety of theories about what it takes for nonprofits to succeed. They all agree that the Executive Director, whether paid or volunteer, is one of the most critical factors to an organization's success. Our premise is that an effective Executive Director is the primary factor in nonprofit success. Without the right leader, few organizations ever truly achieve their stated mission or potential.

We also believe that a nonprofit must have strong systems (finance, HR, technology, communication, and governance, for example) in place for a nonprofit leader to succeed. All too often, we have seen Executive Directors struggle valiantly to move their organizations forward, only to fail because the systems infrastructure of the nonprofit was not there to support the effort.

Thus the nonprofit depends on a highly effective Executive Director to be successful, and the ED depends on a well-functioning nonprofit to succeed.

This book was written to encourage the heart and passion that brought Executive Directors to their leadership roles in the first place. The focus is on helping them strengthen and further develop personal, interpersonal, and organizational effectiveness while keeping shifting societal changes within their peripheral vision. We called the first edition *The Executive Director's Survival Guide* to highlight the complex cultural and relationship-based environment that EDs must navigate. This second edition has been renamed *The Executive Director's Guide to Thriving as a Nonprofit Leader* because this book will do more than help you survive. The practical advice, the encouragement, and real-world examples will increase your resilience, help you explore new ways of managing and leading your unique organization, develop strong systems in your nonprofit, find your own path to personal and organizational balance, and thrive fully as a nonprofit leader.

This book differs from most other books on the market. It doesn't try to compete with the many excellent publications for Executive Directors on managing staff, working with the Board, raising money, and the like, or the insightful books that discuss the unique nature of the nonprofit sector and key benchmarks for success. As we listen to both new and seasoned Executive Directors, we hear them say again and again that simply learning specific skills and academic theory is not enough. Their main struggle isn't really with how to do all the tasks that must be done by an Executive Director. Instead, they are challenged daily with how to put all the pieces together to create a well-functioning organization, be an effective leader, and still have time for themselves.

We understand this to mean that Executive Directors have a need to more fully comprehend and integrate multiple roles, relationships, and resources so that their specific work can take root in their organizations and their communities.

So we see this guidebook as a companion to the many excellent how-to books in the marketplace; instead of how-to, it offers practical insight, motivating quotes, tips for success, stories from the field, and answers to some of the real-life issues EDs face. It provides insight into emerging trends in the nonprofit sector and the important role that organizational culture plays. It is about understanding and balancing internal and external roles and relationships so as to lead more inclusively. It is about developing strong organizations to support the ED. It is about building community and managing resources. It is about encouraging and managing organizational and personal change. It is about helping Executive Directors find their own way as nonprofit leaders.

WHO THIS BOOK IS FOR—WAYS TO USE THIS BOOK

First and foremost, the guidebook is for Executive Directors. We wrote for all the remarkable individuals who lead their organizations.

- If you are new to the field, you can use this book as

    1. An introduction to the exciting and challenging position of Executive Director

    2. A reference for you, your Board of Directors, and others who may want to know more about your job

    3. A guide to turn to when you need answers, practical tips, or other help for everything from developing better communication systems to setting a visionary course for the future for your organization, and to find time for yourself

- If you are already familiar with the questions and answers raised on these pages, you can use this book as

    1. Encouragement or new tools to bring to your role

    2. Talking points and cases to demonstrate your role as leader, manager, and supporter

    3. A guide when you are evaluating the decision to stay or move on to a new organization or career

    Many others will also find valuable information to help them:

- Executive coaches, consultants, and technical assistance providers can use this book as information to share with nonprofit leaders at all levels and others who may wish to become an ED.

- Funders can use this book as

    1. A guide to help explore the role of the Executive Director as the leader in an organization

    2. An evaluation tool to measure whether an organization has the staff leadership and Board-ED partnership to make effective use of its funds

- Board members who work with Executive Directors can use this book as

    1. A resource to support and rejuvenate the Executive Director they work with

    2. A tool to help them work as a partner with their ED and to evaluate that individual's progress

- Anyone who has ever contemplated becoming an Executive Director can use this book as

    1. An aid to help determine what skills they already have for the position, and those they need to develop

    2. A reference to decide if an ED position is the job for them

For everyone, the *Executive Director's Guide to Thriving as a Nonprofit Leader* was written to serve as an inspiration, and as encouragement along the path of creating a better society. As you will see, the Executive Director's role is an extraordinary job for extraordinary people.

HOW TO GET THE MOST FROM THIS BOOK

Throughout the book we use the terms *nonprofits* or *organizations* and *Executive Directors (EDs)* or *nonprofit leaders* as inclusive terms for the sector and its leadership.

We use a question-and-answer format for each chapter. The questions are practical ones that have been raised by new as well as experienced Executive Directors. The answers are designed to be quickly assimilated into the day-to-day work of an ED.

Stories are scattered through most chapters to illustrate a variety of responses to complex issues. While some of the stories are based on our own experience, others reflect the journeys of colleagues and clients. To respect their confidentiality and candor, we have allowed the organizations and the people to remain anonymous.

Some chapters have practical materials that Executive Directors can use for themselves and for others in their organizations, including exercises designed to promote discussion and reflection. You will find useful tips for success at the end of the chapters, to emphasize key messages. At the end of the book, a set of resources for each chapter will help you explore the various topics further if you so desire.

The book is divided into parts to make it easy for readers to move to the topic that most interests them. Since most Executive Directors have little time for contemplative reading, this book encourages you to go quickly to the chapter or topic where you need assistance and find the specific help you want.

Part One provides a foundation to help EDs address the ultimate question: How to succeed and thrive on the job. Included is information about the essential roles and responsibilities, the characteristics required to be successful, the ways to broaden your skills, and last but not least, the way to maintain some semblance of personal and professional balance. If you skip over this section initially, please come back.

Part Two starts by examining the importance that culture plays in creating the roles and relationships that define each organization. The next chapters emphasize the ED's leadership role in creating shared values, a powerful vision, a solid plan, and ways to determine organizational effectiveness. If your organization is seeking to understand the underlying impact of its culture or defining its vision, or in need of tools to measure its success and accountability, you will find helpful information here.

Part Three explores the emerging trends facing the nonprofit sector, the changing nature of organizations as they move through their life cycle, and the ED's role in embracing changes necessary to keep an organization responsive and viable. Turn to this section if you find yourself leading an organization with systems, roles, and programs that are no longer in sync with the community or broader nonprofit sector.

Part Four focuses on the importance of building and maintaining a vast array of internal partnerships. Go to this section if you are working to build, understand, or repair relationships. For an Executive Director, nothing is more important than being well connected with Board, staff, and volunteers. And since the influence of the person who started or defined an organization is often so strong and prevalent in nonprofits, we have devoted a chapter to Founders alone. Many of the topics in this chapter can be shared with staff and Board as a way to strengthen these partnerships, which are critical to the success of Executive Directors.

Part Five discusses the role of external stakeholders, partnerships, and broad representation as the foundation for creating community to achieve the organization's mission. In these chapters you will find insight into the benefits and barriers inherent in acquiring and nurturing stakeholders and building strategic partnerships.

In Part Six we move into the practical demands for resource wizardry. Turn to these pages if you want some quick ideas on building systems for the business or financial side of the organization, and if you want to develop a team-based approach to fundraising.

Finally, Part Seven raises the emotional yet often-overlooked subject of your own career transition. Although many nonprofits would like their Executive Director to stay forever, long tenures (fifteen years or more) are rarely healthy for the organization. If you are feeling the urge for new opportunities, this last section will prove timely.

Whatever section you turn to for support in your job, enjoy it, learn from it, and remember that, as an Executive Director, you have chosen one of the world's most rewarding and challenging careers.

SHARE YOUR STORIES

We recognize that a significant percentage of an Executive Director's job is listening to others in order to understand their needs and expectations. This book is our gift to you. We are committed to listening to your needs and experiences. We hope you will continue to share your stories, your insights, your successes, your questions, and your challenges with us. You can reach us at mimcarlson@comcast.net, and we look forward to hearing from you!

February 2010

Mim Carlson
Kensington, California
Margaret Donohoe
San Jose, California

ACKNOWLEDGMENTS

It takes a village to raise a child, lead a nonprofit organization, and compose a book worthy of the nonprofit sector. Many people made this book possible, and all deserve special recognition.

We appreciate the guidance, patience, and excitement for the project that Dorothy Hearst, senior editor at Jossey Bass, gave us in the first edition, and Jesse Wiley has given us in the second edition. From the early concepts and evolving focus, they have been a consistent voice for the need for this type of book.

The first edition was enriched by the creative thinking, compelling questions, solid reasoning, and brilliant editing of Judi MacMurray. Much of her wisdom remains in the second edition. We are indebted to the tireless hours she gave in helping us.

Another individual who made significant contributions is Elizabeth Norton-Schaffer, financial guru extraordinaire, who wrote the chapter on financial management for both editions. Our own efforts at this topic would never have matched her wisdom and insight.

The second edition has benefited enormously from the guidance of Vince Hyman, who did a brilliant review of the first edition and added his suggestions to make this one a strong tool for Executive Directors.

Cindy Loveland's breadth of experience in the nonprofit sector was invaluable in identifying and screening many of the valuable resources you will find at the end of the book.

The first and second editions received an incredibly thorough and thoughtful copyedit from Hilary Powers, ably directed by Rachel Anderson. Nothing is more important to a successful book than having a high-quality production crew, and we are grateful that we had the best.

Numerous individuals read early drafts of the first edition and gave us their counsel and wisdom. Others inspired our writing with their experience and ideas. We are grateful to Emily Goldfarb, Tim Wolfred, Kathleen Quinlan, Donna Wilson, Anna Cwieka, Pam Van Orden, Lynn Myhal, Marge Lantor, Lisa Breen Strickland, Robert Freiri, Patty Wipfler, Roni Posner, Jeannie Labozetta, Amari Romero Vorwerk, Kathi Gwynn, Barry Posner, Kitty Lopez, Molly Polidoroff, Jane Dies, Terry Temkin, Kimberly Hsieh, Carol Evans, Katherine Hatcher, J.R. Yeager, Tom Adams, Kerry Enright, Mary Hiland, Bill Coy, David La Piana, and Susan Egmont. The second edition revisions are the result of continuing conversations with these people and the reviews and guidance of Holly Ross, Executive Director of Nonprofit Technology Network, and Katie Winterbottom, former Interim Executive Director at Grassroots.org, for making this book a more powerful resource for Executive Directors.

Countless Executive Directors provided the framework for questions and the responses that you see in the book. Our heartfelt thanks go to Katherine Toy, Holly Van Houten, David Stegman, Jane Hammoud, Mandi Billinge, Miriam Gordon, Michael Williams, Nancy Tivol, Christa Gannon, Janet Knipe, Angie Helstrup Alverez, Shamina Hasan, Judith Steiner, Reed Holderman, Mary Simon, George Archambeau, Joseph Smooke, Diane Harrington, Jenny Nicholas, Poncho Guevara, and Susanne Mulcahy—and to the many other Executive Directors we have met and supported.

And last but not least we thank our respective husbands, Bob and Dennis, our families, and our animal companions for their support and encouragement throughout the journey.

THE AUTHORS

Mim Carlson and Margaret Donohoe have focused their experience, insight, and energy on helping the new generation of nonprofit leaders navigate the many opportunities and challenges of this career choice. The insight they provide is not just academic or theoretical—it comes from their own careers in the sector. They each draw on over twenty-five years of hands-on experience as Executive Directors, interim Executive Directors, and Board members, as well as in a variety of other leadership positions, to inform the content of this guidebook.

Mim Carlson consults and coaches in the area of organizational leadership with nonprofit organizations. She has worked for small community-based groups as well as large national nonprofits. In these organizations, she has served as an Executive Director and in other leadership positions. As a consultant, Mim specializes in Board and Executive Director development, staff leadership transitions, strategic planning, and restructures. She also works as an Interim Executive Director in nonprofits that are without a person in this critical position on a permanent basis. She is the author of two books, *Winning Grants Step by Step* and *Team-Based Fundraising Step by Step,* both published by Jossey-Bass.

Margaret Donohoe guides nonprofit organizations through the opportunities and challenges of leadership, Board, and organizational transitions. Her experience as an Executive Director and her active participation on a variety of nonprofit Boards and task forces, along with her MBA from Santa Clara University and ongoing professional development in areas of critical importance to the sector, have provided her with a broad foundation of skills and insight to help Executive Directors, Boards, and their organizations not just survive but thrive in these changing times.

The Executive Director's Guide to
Thriving as a Nonprofit Leader

PART ONE

Finding Your Way as Executive Director

The leader beyond the millennium will not be the leader who has learned the lessons of how to do. . . . The leader of today and the future will be focused on how to be . . . how to develop quality, character, mind-set, values, principles, and courage.

—Frances Hesselbein

A career in the nonprofit sector equates to an unspoken calling for many. You have a strong desire to make your community and world a little better or brighter. You are driven to explore the good as well as the bad that humankind has to offer. You want to manifest your lifelong focus and interest—your vocation—to the benefit of others.

Wrapped around these qualities is a new breed of servant-leader, manager, visionary, change agent, relationship builder, and resource wizard.

The nonprofit CEO—the Executive Director—is someone who appears to effortlessly juggle multiple responsibilities, relationships, and stakeholder interests while keeping both eyes fixed on the mission and bottom line. If you allow the nonprofit leader position to consume your life, it will. There is no end to the challenges and opportunities of being an Executive Director.

The reality is that nonprofit leadership is one of the most personally rewarding yet professionally complex career opportunities to be found. It is not for the weak of heart. Those looking to leave behind the politics of government work or the changing economic whims of the business sector will find no safe haven here. As a colleague recently paraphrased the old saying, "The ED job isn't rocket science; it is much harder than that. Rocket science at least comes with precise formulas, mathematics, and laws of physics that result in a visible outcome."

Can any Executive Director handle all the important tasks of the position effectively and still hope to have a life beyond the nonprofit? We believe that the answer is yes, and the chapters in Part One uncover some of the ways to make this possible. In Chapter One we take a close look at the unique job of the Executive Director and identify the characteristics critical to doing that job well. Chapter Two offers ways for Executive Directors to increase their effectiveness through professional development—and find the time to do so. Chapter Three offers insights and possibilities for leading a balanced life as an Executive Director. We know this is an unheard-of concept for many, but we believe wholeheartedly that a balanced life is possible!

Understanding This Big Job

Leaders at all levels and in all situations must pay close attention to situations in which their most effective option is to follow . . . because performance requires them to rely on the capacities and insights of other people.

—Douglas K. Smith, "The Following Part of Leading,"
Leader of the Future

Executive Directors have a very big job! If you are currently working as an Executive Director, or have done so in the past, you surely know just how big and complex the position is. You converse with funders and donors, inspire and manage staff, keep Board members informed and involved, listen to clients, raise money, review (and often worry about) finances, and articulate the case for your programs and the organization's accomplishments; you often serve as an accidental technology expert, facilities manager, or HR specialist, and sometimes you even clean the office. Your responsibilities seem to change depending on who needs what. You must be able to prioritize a variety of stakeholders in a multitude of different ways. And no matter how well you plan and prioritize your day or week, something unexpected always occurs to draw your attention.

Because of all these responsibilities, Executive Directors must lead, manage, and support others to be successful. We believe that by knowing when to be a leader, manager, or supporter, you can more efficiently focus your efforts, and in many cases delegate to others. As a result you can make more time for a life beyond the nonprofit. In this chapter, we answer these questions:

- What are the roles and responsibilities of an Executive Director?
- What is the difference between a leader and a manager?
- When should an Executive Director lead, manage, or support others?

WHAT ARE THE ROLES AND RESPONSIBILITIES OF AN EXECUTIVE DIRECTOR?

All Executive Directors (paid or unpaid) share one universal role, regardless of where they work. The Board always hires the ED as a temporary caretaker of the mission, entrusting the organization to the ED with the expectation that it will thrive in that person's care. So the Executive Director does not own the nonprofit but is charged by the Board with controlling its operations and course while making it thrive. The Executive Director is the key caretaker of the nonprofit.

To perform this central caretaker role, an Executive Director must have five important characteristics. The strength of each will differ from person to person, but every Executive Director needs all of the following in some combination:

- Visionary
- Change agent
- Relationship builder
- Community creator
- Resource wizard

These characteristics will look different in each person—and in each non-profit. In some nonprofits, all five characteristics may need to be in evidence all the time, while in others they ebb and flow in the Executive Director depending on the needs of the organization.

Throughout the remainder of the book, we will be describing these characteristics in great detail and offering you ideas on how to apply them in your nonprofit. First, though, to understand them more fully, it's helpful to look at the five in terms of the Executive Director's responsibilities.

The characteristics of an Executive Director are manifested and become apparent in the responsibilities of the position. These responsibilities generally are listed in the job description or work plan for the ED. They vary from person to person and nonprofit to nonprofit, depending on the size and culture of the organization and where it is in its life cycle. Exhibit 1.1 highlights the key responsibilities of an Executive Director and should be viewed as an illustration of what most EDs are responsible for in most organizations. You may find it helpful to use this chart to create a more specific list of responsibilities for you in your own nonprofit.

Exhibit 1.1
Responsibilities of an Executive Director

As a *visionary,* an Executive Director is responsible for

- Motivating internal and external stakeholders with a shared picture of the greatness of their nonprofit.
- Inspiring passion to achieve what is possible.
- Discovering and articulating the values that form the guiding principles of the nonprofit.
- Bringing focus to the vision with a strategic plan.
- Thinking strategically about the best way to meet community needs.
- Evaluating, on an ongoing basis, the effectiveness of the nonprofit in fulfilling its mission.

(Continued)

As a *change agent,* an Executive Director is responsible for

- Monitoring trends in the nonprofit sector and keeping the organization responsive to changing community needs, shifting revenue sources, emerging competition, and ever-increasing public scrutiny.
- Boldly moving the organization in a new direction with programs and resources if community trends dictate a change.
- Providing the skills needed to lead, manage, and support the organization at any point in its life cycle.
- Managing internal change processes by working with stakeholders to set goals and outcomes, create plans, and make the change happen.
- Persuading and motivating others to accept change as part of the daily routine in the organization, while also acknowledging people's natural resistance to change.
- Taking risks to try new ideas and take new approaches to achieving the mission.

As a *relationship builder,* an Executive Director is responsible for

- Communicating successfully with internal stakeholders—staff, volunteers, and Board.
- Managing staff and volunteers in a manner that fosters a healthy culture to ensure that everyone's role on the team is valued and recognized.
- Providing an open and transparent organizational culture that appreciates and respects differences.
- Supporting and at times leading the Board of Directors to ensure it adds value to the organization.
- Carrying on the wisdom of the organization's Founder while implementing bold new ideas.

As a *community creator,* the Executive Director is responsible for

- Creating a visible organization with broad stakeholder support.
- Communicating with external stakeholders to ensure continuing interest and involvement in the mission.

- Building partnerships that further the mission through cooperative efforts and strategic relationships.

As a *resource wizard,* an Executive Director is responsible for

- Recruiting, mentoring, and recognizing people who will raise funds that allow the organization to thrive.
- Communicating and building relationships with funders and donors to gain interest in the mission and support for it.
- Building a strong resource portfolio that secures the organization with funding during economic downturns and other financial lean times.
- Stewarding and managing funds received so well that the organization's trustworthiness is unquestionable.

The list of responsibilities in the exhibit may seem daunting to anyone who has not experienced the job of an Executive Director. The list is long, particularly when you think about the specific tasks needed for each responsibility. Remember, though, that not all responsibilities have highest priority on any given day.

In some smaller organizations that have no paid staff, the Executive Director may struggle to accomplish any of the indicated responsibilities because of the need to handle routine tasks normally performed by others in larger organizations. In this case, an ED needs to remember the core responsibilities as listed here, and work diligently to delegate as much of the other work as possible to volunteers. As an example, one Executive Director who was the only employee in her nonprofit was struggling to keep donors informed of the innovations taking place in programs. Her role as "community creator" was hampered by poor external communication systems. She enlisted two volunteers who had a background in marketing communications, and they redesigned the Web site, opened a Facebook page, set up the nonprofit on Twitter, and agreed to update and manage these communication tools so the ED could do other tasks.

Being a successful Executive Director is a learned role—no one starts out in the position as the "perfect ED." In fact, successful Executive Directors are always improving themselves and taking time to build and strengthen the skills most needed to fulfill their responsibilities and lead their nonprofit to greater success. Remember this if you find yourself doubting your capabilities or feeling inadequate.

The very big job of an Executive Director requires an ongoing process of learning and development. We discuss this further in Chapter Two and throughout the book.

It is also important to realize that, most often, the job is not about you. For instance, an ED working at 150 percent and still struggling to juggle all the responsibilities of the position is probably doing an excellent job—but simply has too much to do, or the organizational systems are not in place to support the position. This is actually true for most Executive Directors, and too many choose to find some fault with themselves for their inadequacy. Understand that you are not inadequate, the position is just enormous. Much of Chapter Three will give you ideas of balancing this very big job you have undertaken. Other action steps you can take:

- Remind yourself that the job is not about you.
- Talk with other EDs—help each other remember the challenges of this position and that each of you is extraordinary for being an Executive Director.
- Identify ways others in the organization (Board, staff, volunteers) can support you.
- Evaluate what organizational systems and processes need updating to help you be effective.

Remember that you have been given the job of serving as caretaker for your organization—to be truly effective, the people within the organization must also take care of you, and the infrastructure must be there to support you.

WHAT IS THE DIFFERENCE BETWEEN A LEADER AND A MANAGER?

These days people constantly speak and write about leadership and management styles. How often have you heard someone described as "a great leader but a weak manager" or "a great manager of people but not a very good leader"? What do those comments mean? The lines between the definitions of manager and leader have blurred to the point that people often use the words interchangeably. But being a successful manager and being a great leader are two very different roles—and both are required of Executive Directors on a daily basis if they are to fulfill the broader role of caretaker for the organization.

The challenge is twofold: knowing the difference between leadership and management, and discerning when to use one or the other.

A manager focuses on efficiency, effectiveness, and making sure the right things happen at the right time. This is an essential role for every Executive Director.

You are in a manager role when you set performance objectives with staff, prepare budgets, review cash flow projections, develop action plans, design new communication systems, and evaluate programs or fundraising strategies or any other aspect of the nonprofit. Managing may also include doing hundreds of other tasks that require focused and logical attention to the good health of the organization.

On the other hand, a leader is a strategist, a visionary, and someone who inspires others to greatness. This is the most critical role for Executive Directors in any organization. You are leading when you bring stakeholders together to decide on the organization's vision or values, or when you bring staff and volunteers together to design a program or develop a strategy or resolve a problem. Leaders motivate staff and volunteers, serve as role models, inspire donors to give generously, build community and capacity inside and outside the nonprofit, and create learning environments in which people can grow and develop themselves without fear. A strong leader will display all of the characteristics discussed in this chapter.

One of our Executive Director colleagues expressed the difference between leader and manager this way: "When you are a leader, you work from the heart. As a manager, you work from the head." Although it is probably more complex than that, the point to remember is the difference between what you do as a leader and what you do as a manager—and the constant need to be able to do both. Furthermore, the head and heart need to be partners, not independent operators.

An exercise you might wish to do is make a list of your key activities for a day or a week. Then separate them into leadership tasks and management tasks based on the descriptions given here. As you look at your list, do you find yourself doing primarily one or the other? Or is there a balanced division between leader and manager? There is no "right answer" to this exercise. But knowing if you are focusing your attention primarily on leadership or management tasks can help you understand your job and role in the organization. It sometimes can help you make changes in your job if you feel you need to be doing more leader or manager tasks.

One Executive Director's list looked like the example in Exhibit 1.2.

The Executive Director who prepared this list did not include other tasks she did that week, as they were neither managerial nor leadership activities.

Exhibit 1.2
Sample Task List

TASKS FOR WEEK OF _____

Leader	Manager
Held vision meeting with Board	Interviewed candidates for Finance Manager
Meeting with collaboration peers	Reviewed monthly financial data
Spoke at Rotary Club luncheon	Set quarterly benchmarks with managers
Meeting with volunteers for input on programs	Reviewed last quarter's benchmarks and addressed successes and improvements
Designed new public relations strategy	Disciplinary meeting with staff member
Conducted staff recognition event	Called 5 major donors to thank them
	Reviewed monthly newsletter draft
	Called and discussed 2 clients' complaints
	Renewed annual liability insurance

Examples of these tasks would be answering general questions from the public about programs, handling staff or volunteer general concerns about programs, saying daily thank-yous to staff and volunteers, and doing routine facilities tasks. This particular Executive Director decided her work was balanced appropriately for herself and the organization. However, she also realized she did the exercise during a relatively quiet time for the nonprofit and decided to re-do the exercise in a few months when the nonprofit was in its busiest quarter of the year.

WHEN SHOULD AN EXECUTIVE DIRECTOR LEAD, MANAGE, OR SUPPORT OTHERS?

Executive Directors generally understand they have the roles of leading and managing in the nonprofit. Supporting others to allow them to lead is sometimes more challenging. There seems to be an unwritten rule that new Executive Directors absorb through their pores—that to be a good Executive Director, you always have be in charge and responsible for every aspect of the organization. You can throw idea out the window now, because it just isn't true. As a matter of fact, the best and most successful Executive Directors are those that seek out and develop leadership and management qualities in paid and unpaid staff and Board members. In addition, they enjoy empowering others, giving them the responsibility and authority to lead the organization. By supporting paid and unpaid staff and Board members, you can try out new ideas, learn new practices, and grow as an Executive Director. At the same time, you will give others the opportunity to take leadership or management roles, to be innovative, and to grow into their own personal style, deepening your organization's leadership reserves so you can concentrate on the parts of your job that matter most—and even develop the breathing room to take some time off.

Another important reason for playing the supporting role is that Executive Directors should be preparing others in the nonprofit for someday becoming EDs too. Supporting and mentoring those staff and volunteers who aspire to become an Executive Director is especially crucial as a growing number of EDs make plans for retirement. New generations of nonprofit leaders need the training and experience necessary so they can also succeed in this very big job.

Exhibit 1.3
Executive Director as Leader, Manager, Supporter

You will lead when your nonprofit needs direction and focus for relationships that create unity within the nonprofit and stronger communities outside, an inspiring vision to generate passion and excitement, resources that support and enhance success, increased capacity to fulfill the mission, and change to stay effective and true to the community.

You will manage when the nonprofit needs tactical plans to keep programs on track and funds coming in, processes and procedures to keep staff and volunteers accountable, budgets and finance reports to ensure sustainability, and written materials to promote the organization and satisfy stakeholders.

You will support others when your nonprofit has Board members, staff, or volunteers interested and skilled (or willing to develop skills) in building and sustaining relationships, planning and carrying out programs, making the organization visible, ensuring financial stability and growth, managing internal changes, or tracking external trends.

To discern when to lead, manage, or support, think about your role as ED as outlined in Exhibit 1.3.

The lists in the exhibit are not exhaustive and will of course be different for each Executive Director. The main point is that no one person, not even you, can single-handedly juggle all the required activities effectively. Your primary responsibility to your nonprofit is leadership, and that leadership must include the wisdom to know when to become a manager and a supporter. You must know when to seek out and ask for help and when to take time to develop support that will ensure success for you, your nonprofit, and the community you serve. The following story from the field illustrates this point.

STORY FROM THE FIELD

After graduating from college with a degree in sociology (and a desire to save the world!), Susan applied for her first Executive Director's job at a family health community clinic. In the interview, she was told that the ten staff people worked together as a collective with equal rights and equal pay, and they only gave anyone the title of Executive Director because their federal contracts mandated it. Bravely, she accepted the position and quickly became immersed in issues of authority, decision making, communication, and control.

Susan understood that the clinic needed a manager who could achieve the level of efficiency required by federal contracts. On a much more vague level she understood that the clinic needed a leader who had a vision and could inspire its independent-minded and passionate people.

Susan began her work at the clinic believing that as an Executive Director, she was in charge of everything, responsible for everything and everyone, had little room for mistakes, and could not allow others in the organization to provide leadership or management.

The toughest lesson for Susan was recognizing that leadership sometimes includes supporting others while they take on this role. Because this was a collective of equals, Susan had to learn that effectiveness as a manager and a leader depended on her willingness to be a supporter—to let other staff people take the lead with their ideas and take responsibility for them. It was frightening at first, especially when she found herself clashing with a few of these capable people. However, when the clinic's Nurse Practitioner came back from a conference with new information on clinic best practices, Susan asked this individual to lead the effort to integrate those best practices into their organization. As a result, Susan and everyone else saw the clinic's programs becoming more innovative and effective in the community due to the Nurse Practitioner's leadership.

Susan realized she was not the only leader in the nonprofit. Staff, volunteers, Board members, and community stakeholders had expertise in areas and a desire to bring their expertise to the clinic. The creative and innovative people around her had great ideas that they were quite capable of implementing, and they were willing to be held accountable for them.

Fortunately, she recognized the value of these resources. She saw the fallacies of her initial perceptions of what a good Executive Director was and learned the value of supporting other leaders. Her relationships with staff improved and she became a much more effective leader and manager as the staff progressed toward a collective shared vision.

Susan was able to support other leaders in her clinic because they had a shared vision for their organization and were implementing proven best practices, and they developed metrics to evaluate success. In another example, an Executive Director chose to support two aspiring staff leaders who nearly brought the organization to financial ruin! These two well-meaning individuals did not bother to research best practices prior to implementing a new program strategy, and they did not work with the Executive Director to determine success criteria for the program changes they were making. The result was a failed program that should have been the cornerstone of the organization's mission. In this case, the Executive Director learned the best way to support staff leadership is to make sure they are set up to be successful. Having a clear plan based on best practices and a set of quantifiable objectives helps to make sure that both emerging staff leaders and the organization thrive.

Believing that the Executive Director always has to know the right thing to do in any situation is guaranteed to make the job more difficult than it already is. It's an unfair expectation that too many Executive Directors put on themselves, to the ultimate detriment of everyone. Very often, the best leadership practice is to identify knowledgeable, trustworthy individuals to whom you can delegate and then follow them.

The big job of being an Executive Director has its challenges with the overall role of caretaker and the numerous responsibilities assigned to it. However, the rewards you receive often far outweigh these challenges. Under your care, the nonprofit's programs, staff, Board, and community can thrive. Your own growth as a leader, manager, and supporter can also be viewed as a huge reward on both a personal and professional level.

TIPS FOR SUCCESS

In this chapter, we provide information to help you understand the magnitude and complexities of the Executive Director position. In summary, here are a few tips for success.

- It is important to remember that the Executive Director's role is to be the caretaker of the organization. Everything you do as ED should fulfill this role.

- The very big job of Executive Director takes great confidence, plus a clear understanding that this job is not about you—be dedicated and passionate, but also be objective about the fact that the organization is separate from you.

- Keep focused on your leadership and managerial activities, especially being a leader. Prioritize your days and weeks to keep leadership tasks at the forefront.

- Know who the other leaders in your organization are and support them in implementing their ideas while holding them responsible.

- Feel free to ask for help when you need it. Being a successful Executive Director requires you to lead, manage, and support others inside and outside the organization. But you should fulfill these roles with advice and assistance from others.

Developing as an Executive Director

Apart from learning from books and experiences, leaders learn by self-reflection. . . . They also learn from mentors. . . . Most of all, they learn by personal experimentation, often putting themselves in challenging situations that require tenacity, courage, and personal growth.

—Burt Nanus and Stephen Dobbs,
Leaders Who Make a Difference

Executive Directors, like all leaders, need development opportunities to inspire them and keep them in touch with the best practices of their profession. This chapter addresses the following questions that Executive Directors ask about ways to develop themselves:

- What can Executive Directors do to self-reflect on skills they wish to develop on the job?
- How does an Executive Director find the time for professional development, and what opportunities are available?
- When are executive coaches helpful to an Executive Director?
- When the going gets really tough, how does an Executive Director stay inspired?

WHAT CAN EXECUTIVE DIRECTORS DO TO SELF-REFLECT ON SKILLS THEY WISH TO DEVELOP ON THE JOB?

One of the fundamental truths of being Executive Director of a nonprofit organization is that there are always more skills to learn, more ways to develop yourself, and more opportunities to do so. Successful Executive Directors have a natural curiosity about ways to develop their own competencies as well as ways to develop others in the organization. You will find a useful tool to develop yourself in Exhibit 2.1. This tool is for you to use—not an evaluation tool for your Board of Directors or others to determine your level of competency. This is an exercise you can do for yourself to determine your level of skill in these areas, so you can make a plan to further develop those areas where you feel you need to gain competency. We recommend you do the skills competency exercise early in your career as an ED, and repeat it annually as a way to show yourself how you are growing in your position.

As with all the exercises and examples in this book, this one has no "right" answer. Executive Directors will all choose their competency level differently. The point of the exercise is to determine for yourself what areas of competency you feel should be developed further, and to take the first steps in planning for that development. For example, one Executive Director did the skills competency review exercise after six months in her position. She scored herself in the green and yellow ranges for all but three skill areas, which she scored as red. Those three areas were understanding the organization's culture, building partnerships outside the organization, and having a professional development plan. Doing the exercise helped this busy and slightly overwhelmed new Executive Director realize that she was doing fine in many parts of her job, but she needed to begin building her competency in these three areas that she considered important to her and to her organization.

Exhibit 2.1
Executive Director Skills Competency Worksheet

Purpose: To help Executive Directors understand and develop core competencies to aid professional development

#	Competency	Red	Yellow	Green	Improvement Plan
1	**Visionary:** Leads with a vision, articulates it with passion, and inspires others to achieve it				
2	**Planner:** Leads organization with a mission focus; keeps mission in line with community needs				
3	**Planner:** Provides leadership to and engages stakeholders in the organization's strategic planning process; communicates plan to stakeholders				
4	**Planner:** Understands and communicates the organization's culture; if needed, oversees the process for changing the culture				
5	**Evaluator:** Develops organization and program benchmarks; manages evaluation and review process				
6	**Relationship Builder:** Communicates regularly with stakeholders to identify community issues and needs				
7	**Relationship Builder:** Provides leadership, management, and support to staff, Board of Directors, and volunteers				
8	**Relationship Builder:** Ensures organization is visible and respected in the community				

(Continued)

#	Competency	Red	Yellow	Green	Improvement Plan
9	**Relationship Builder:** Creates partnerships to expand the organization's ability to achieve the mission and vision				
10	**Advocate:** Presents community and organization needs to agencies, funders, partners				
11	**Change Agent:** Leads internal change process to keep organization vital and thriving				
12	**Change Agent:** Maintains awareness of internal and external changes needed to best serve clients				
13	**Financial Manager:** Reviews, understands, and communicates organization's financial condition to Board of Directors and key stakeholders				
14	**Fundraiser:** Develops and leads a team-based fundraising strategy with Board, staff, volunteers				
15	**Nurturer:** Defines work-life balance and ensures this value is an organizational and personal priority				
16	**Nurturer:** Has professional development plan and serves as role model to staff and Board for their professional development				

Green = satisfaction with competency level; Yellow = minor improvements needed; Red = major improvements needed

HOW DOES AN EXECUTIVE DIRECTOR FIND THE TIME FOR PROFESSIONAL DEVELOPMENT, AND WHAT OPPORTUNITIES ARE AVAILABLE?

Part of the answer to this question involves time management, balancing and prioritizing your workload to include time for professional development. Most Executive Directors know this is important, but for various reasons, self-development never makes it to the top of the priority list. We recommend you put this task right up at the top with your other key priorities. Here are some ideas of what you can do to make time for professional development:

- Include in your work plan each year ways you want to develop professionally, budget funds for them, and make sure the Board discusses this area of your work plan with you.
- Discuss your professional development ideas with your Board Chair or Executive Committee, and obtain their commitment to supporting you.
- Make staff development a norm of the organization's culture so that all staff have a priority of growing in their position.
- Set aside thirty minutes or more every week to read online articles related to your organization's mission or leadership.
- Send one or more of your managers to conferences you'd like to attend if you had time, and have them do short presentations for you and other staff to tell what they learned. Make sure they bring back handouts to copy for other staff.
- Plan far in advance for classes, conferences, and other activities, trying to find those that occur during times when your organization's activity level is likely to be relatively low.
- Take the necessary time to reflect on what you have learned and envision ways to apply your new knowledge to your work.

These are simple, basic ideas that will work if you have a commitment to professional development. But what happens if you have done everything right to find the time necessary, and in spite of your best efforts an unexpected crisis looms over your organization on the day you have committed to a development activity for yourself?

When that happens (as it probably will), there is a simple but highly effective management prioritizing tool you can use to help determine if you must forgo your professional development activity. The prioritizing tool presented in Exhibit 2.2 can be used in many other situations faced by EDs; this is just one example to demonstrate its use.

If you do this priority decision tree and decide you must or should handle the situation, then by all means do so. Notice though, that the examples given are

---

Exhibit 2.2
Management Prioritizing Decision Tree

Crisis Occurs → Is this a life-or-death situation for the organization → Yes → ED must handle? → Yes

   Examples of life-or-death situations that an ED probably must handle:

• A fire at the organization the previous evening has destroyed much of the building.

• A major natural disaster has struck the community and the organization provides essential disaster relief activities.

• All staff walk out (or threaten to do so immediately).

• Any other activity occurs that would result in all regular services of the organization coming to an abrupt halt.

Crisis Occurs → Does it have major political or appearance and reputation repercussions? → Yes → ED must handle? → Yes

   Examples of crises that an ED should handle:

• An unexpected news report on financial mismanagement involving the ED appears.

• An unexpected funder (or other extremely important person) visits for a major project and demands the ED be present for the visit (negotiations with this visitor might allow the ED to attend most of the scheduled professional development activity).

• Any other activity occurs that would result in the ED being fired or organization's mission being severely hampered if the ED was absent for a day.

---

of fairly catastrophic events, not everyday occurrences. Most of the time, there will be someone in the organization (staff, volunteer, Board member) who can handle less major crises to allow you to attend a professional development activity. Empowering other individuals to step in and handle the crisis for you while you are gone enhances their development in the process.

Executive Directors interested in professional development have endless activities to choose from. Exhibit 2.3 lists some of the more popular ones, but is not exhaustive. The quickest way to access specific professional development information is via the Internet. Numerous Web sites give you useful and helpful tips and tools. Depending on the type of service you provide, you may also find e-mail discussion lists with fellow Executive Directors. Such lists can provide a wonderful virtual support group as well as giving great professional development advice.

To find interesting and relevant opportunities in your area, search the Web for related professional associations, colleges and universities, Chambers of Commerce, and local or regional nonprofit management support organizations.

Exhibit 2.3
Professional Development Activities for Executive Directors

- Look for workshops and conferences related to your various roles:

    Management-related workshops on budgeting, supervision, fund-raising, strategic planning, and numerous other topics

    Leadership development workshops on team building, Board–ED partnership development, diversity in the workplace, or community partnerships

    Conferences sponsored by local or regional nonprofit management assistance organizations, where you can network and share experiences and resources with other professionals in your field

- Find an ED support group, either online or in your community, and attend regularly.

- Find a coach to work with you.

- Enroll in a college or university nonprofit certificate or degree program. Some of these programs are online, making them easier to handle for the time-crunched executive.

- Conduct Web searches for books and articles related to ED professional development. Then take time to obtain and read them!

Depending on your budget size, you can pick and choose from a catalogue of development activities. Some, like participating in an informal online discussion list or face-to-face support group, generally don't cost money. Others, such as online courses, getting a nonprofit degree or certificate, or attending a conference, may be more expensive and may stretch budget resources. The critical point to understand is that the growth and long-term health of your organization require commitment to the ongoing growth and development of its leadership. An Executive Director who actively participates in professional development is essential to sustainable organization growth.

WHEN ARE EXECUTIVE COACHES HELPFUL TO AN EXECUTIVE DIRECTOR?

Working with an executive coach is becoming increasingly popular in the nonprofit sector. The practice started in the corporate sector and it is now common for a for-profit company to have one or more coaches working with managers and executives on a variety of issues. Some of these include leadership development, building departmental teams, skills development, and leadership transitions.

There is no standard definition of an executive coach, but they generally provide the space and guidance Executive Directors need to make changes that impact their own development as well as their organization. Coaches can help in many ways, including these:

- Giving performance feedback to EDs and supporting those wanting to build leadership or management skills
- Increasing problem-solving capabilities so an ED can resolve personal, professional, and organizational issues
- Building confidence in an ED to work through tough situations and have a more sustainable job
- Providing tools and guidance so EDs can manage fast-paced changes in their organization
- Guiding Boards of Directors to develop a strong partnership with their ED and give value to their organization
- Assisting EDs to find other leaders in their organization and helping them with their leadership development

- Working with an ED to align the organization's mission, vision, and goals
- Helping an ED determine the time for a leadership transition and develop a sustainable plan for it

It is also important to understand what coaches will not do for you. They are not psychotherapists. They are concerned about your present and future life, not your past. Coaches are also not problem solvers, though by working with a coach, you will solve many problems. The coach's job is to support you as you find your own solutions to problems. This may be done through mentoring, or by challenging your theories, or with other methods of facilitating your learning.

There are some situations where a coach will not be helpful in improving performance. For instance, an Executive Director with no interest in obtaining skills in an area essential to the success of an organization will not benefit from having a coach. A coach also should not be brought in after the Board of Directors has already made the decision to fire an ED or the ED has made the decision to fire a manager. Coaches should not be used to deliver the hard messages to staff. While a coach may be useful in helping EDs make the changes necessary to stabilize an organization, they are generally not useful if poor systems have caused the instability. For example, if an organization has been operating with deficit spending for several years, the Board and Executive Director would be wiser to change their business model rather than hire a coach to help improve the ED's performance.

So how do you know if a coach is right for you and your organization? A good start is to answer the following questions:

On a personal level:

- Do you want a change in your life, for instance, to become more conscious or competent in some area?
- Are you willing to think beyond your own mind-set or mental model to explore new perspectives?
- Are you willing to look deeply inside yourself at your values, beliefs, personal strengths, and limitations?
- Are you curious about what possibilities your future may hold? Can you be open to dreaming about and envisioning those possibilities for yourself?

On a professional level:

- Are there leadership or management skills you want to develop?

- Would you like to have greater impact in your organization or to have your organization have greater impact in the community you serve?

- Do you need individualized assistance to help your organization move through a tough change or transition?

- Are there other staff in the organization with leadership potential who could benefit from a coach?

- Would you like better communication with your Board of Directors and staff to ensure everyone is working toward a common vision?

These are some questions to ask yourself as you think about the advantages of hiring a coach. If you want to find a professional coach, or if you just want more information about coaching, your local management assistance organization may have a program that matches coaches with Executive Directors. In addition, numerous Web sites provide valuable information about and referrals to coaches, and some are listed in the Resource section at the end of this book. Talk also with other Executive Directors in the community. They may have used a good coach or know of others who have.

One of the most powerful features of having a coach working with you is that you have individualized attention for on-the-job leadership development. The coach is there for you, and is your guide to meet whatever goals you need to meet. However, your organization is usually also a partner in this relationship—if (as is usually the case) the organization is paying for the coaching sessions, it therefore has some input into the goals and outcomes.

The partnership of coach, Executive Director, and organization needs to be grounded in specific expectations of each party along with written goals and indicators of success. Otherwise, you may never know if the coaching investment was a success. Ideally, as the Executive Director, you will determine your own goals and expectations that you believe are needed to build your own leadership capacity while also building organizational capacity. This information should be presented to the Board of Directors (and in some cases, the management team) to add their own expectations and goals. You should then select the coach you believe will have the most success in fulfilling your needs and those of the organization.

One word of caution to Boards of Directors: choosing the executive coach for your ED is unwise. If the ED does not agree with your coach selection, a trusting relationship cannot develop, and the partnership is doomed.

The next story from the field shows how one successful ED-coach-organization partnership was developed.

STORY FROM THE FIELD

As a new Executive Director, Sam found himself struggling in his organization. Although he had a great deal of management experience and was knowledgeable (and passionate) about the organization's mission of immigrant rights, Sam lacked confidence in his new leadership role. He was open with the Board of Directors about his struggles, and also about his interest in leadership development. Fortunately, the Board saw the leadership potential in Sam. He was respected by people inside and outside the organization. In his short tenure, he had already brought new focus and energy to the staff with an important campaign that had also created excellent media exposure for the organization. The Board felt this was an ED they could not afford to lose.

A strategic planning consultant working with the organization suggested they hire an executive coach to build Sam's leadership capacity. Since Sam was unaware of the field of executive coaching, he did some research and developed a leadership development plan for himself that included confidence-building goals and increased competency in the areas of communication and cross-cultural relationship building. Sam discussed his leadership development plan with the Board and explained why the plan would help him as well as building organizational capacity for the future. The Board initially balked at the anticipated time of one hour per week coaching sessions with Sam, the realization that they would also have to participate in some coaching sessions, and the cost of having a coach. Wisely, the Board also saw the benefits of the individualized attention a coach would bring and what a more confident Executive Director could do for their organization.

After gaining the Board's approval, Sam developed a summary of the attributes he was looking for in a coach. First and foremost, he wanted someone who had experience with developing confidence in leaders. He also wanted a coach who understood the unique challenges of being an Executive Director in a nonprofit organization. He knew he was looking for someone who he could trust with confidential information. And he wanted a coach who made him comfortable while also challenging him to develop his potential. Finally, Sam wanted someone who could provide guidance and tips to increase competency in the areas he and the Board had identified.

Finding a coach with all these attributes was not easy. Sam and his Board members asked for referrals from colleagues and searched online for people in the community who offered the type of services he was looking for. After three months of searching and a few interviews, Sam finally found the perfect match.

Happily, Sam is still with the organization after six years. His weekly coaching sessions ran for six months with a monthly check-in for another three months. Both Sam and the Board felt the result was well worth the money they spent. Because of the investment of money and time, this organization has a more confident Executive Director who is building and sustaining a much-needed service in the community.

An alternative to having an individual coach is to join a peer group or leadership circle. Most of the groups we are familiar with are geared to professional development and are an excellent resource for learning and growing in the profession. They are, of course, also good for networking. The groups may meet in person on a regular basis, or via an e-mail discussion list or a conference call for those busy professionals who struggle to leave the office.

Sometimes, a peer group will develop for Executive Directors of mission-similar organizations, such as environmental nonprofits or youth services. Other groups are formed with Executive Directors from different backgrounds in order to gain a broader perspective.

The value of belonging to a peer group is that you have structured time to talk about achievements, problems, new learning, and other important topics. You receive support from individuals who have hands-on experience with situations like the ones that are new to you and can give you ideas, reality checks, a sounding board, or a vehicle for safely venting frustration. Belonging to a support group is also a great way to reduce that lonely-at-the-top feeling reported by many Executive Directors.

Finding an Executive Director peer support group in your community can be challenging. If you have an organization in your community that provides training or other technical assistance to nonprofits, that's usually a good place to start. These organizations may have already formed a peer group for Executive Directors or may know of some that exist in the community. Sometimes funders will know of Executive Director peer support groups as well. Word of mouth is often the most reliable source of information. Call other Executive Directors in your area and find out if they know of any peer support groups. If your efforts to locate an existing group fail, then perhaps you can use your leadership skills to get one formed!

WHEN THE GOING GETS REALLY TOUGH, HOW DOES AN EXECUTIVE DIRECTOR STAY INSPIRED?

It is not unusual to find an Executive Director who is feeling overwhelmed and losing all inspiration for the job. When individuals tell us they are losing their passion, focus, inspiration, or whatever word they use to describe an essential quality of job connection, we immediately wonder what barrier has developed. Have job pressures gotten in the way? Are the organizational systems not there to support the ED? Is the struggle for funding just too much to handle right now? Have external or internal criticisms reduced self-esteem? Has there been a loss of personal purpose? All these factors and many more can cause a loss of inspiration.

More than people in any other profession, Executive Directors take on this difficult job because of some passion or inspiration that sustains them through good times and bad. When you feel your passion and inspiration, you feel alive, energetic, and productive. By contrast, when a barrier comes between you and your passion and inspiration, you can feel overwhelmed, lethargic, guilty, bored, or just plain negative.

We cannot emphasize enough the importance of taking time to reflect on what lies beneath any loss of inspiration. It is equally important to ask yourself what you need to regain that passion. Since these questions may clearly be easier to ask than to answer, a beginning strategy for coping with that sense of "it just doesn't matter anymore" is to get up from your desk—even in the middle of a busy, chaotic day—especially when you feel like you are crumbling under the weight of some huge burden—and break away for even a few minutes. Dare to take a fifteen-minute walk around the block or spend an even longer period of time in a park or garden—remove yourself from interaction with the immediate job circumstances. We know of one Executive Director who takes naps to regain inspiration!

Here are some other ideas on ways to pinpoint the barriers to your inspiration and begin to regain it:

- Take yourself on a day-long retreat with an agenda that has you answering questions like these:

    What inspires me?

    What is blocking my ability to be inspired?

    What can I do to remove those barriers?

    What can I ask others to do to help me remove them?

    What will keep me inspired today, tomorrow, and in the future?

- Have a staff retreat where people can talk about what inspires, motivates, and empowers them. Share your own thoughts, and benefit from the group's inspiration.

- Take some time (an hour or whatever you can afford) to focus on your vision for your organization. Is the vision still inspiring to you or is it time to revisit it and make it bolder?

- Remember those individuals who have been mentors to you, or who inspired you with their work as an Executive Director. Think about what these people might do if they were in your shoes right now, and let them inspire you again.

- Find a coach to support you and help you rediscover your inspiration.

- Give yourself recognition for being an incredible person doing an amazing job that is making a difference. If you are unable to give yourself recognition, then find someone to do it for you.

- Form a personal Board of Directors or Advisory Council that is filled with people who have shared your passion and vision, and are inspired by many of the things you are. Go to them when you find yourself drained of inspiration and let them fill you back up.

Chapter Nineteen returns to this point, offering further thoughts on reconnecting with your passion as well as considering whether it's time for a new career.

Executive Directors who have been on the job for more than five years should seriously consider a sabbatical. That is, completely leave your organization for a period (not shorter than three months, and generally not longer than six months) and take time for reflection, travel, family, or whatever will provide you with the inspiration and energy to return to your position with your passion restored. Some U.S. foundations are supporting organizations to allow their leaders to take time off. The California Wellness Foundation is a good example. There are also an increasing number of specialized retreat facilities where nonprofit professionals can go for several weeks and be among others who, like themselves, are needing a time-out from their very big jobs. For instance, the Windcall Institute in Bozeman, Montana, has a specific program for social activist professionals, including Executive Directors, needing to get away and revitalize themselves.

This chapter highlights the value and importance of developing professionally as an Executive Director. By purchasing and reading this book, you have demonstrated an interest in your development and success in this very big job! The following tips for success will help you take the steps needed to succeed and stay inspired.

TIPS FOR SUCCESS

- On-the-job professional development makes you feel good about yourself and helps your organization. Make learning opportunities part of your annual work plan.

- Take a skills self-reflection analysis and determine ways to help yourself grow in your position.

- Look around you for a mentor, coach, peer group to help you. Professional development is not a task you need to do by yourself.

- It may seem counterintuitive, but getting away from your job and taking time for yourself will help you when you are feeling overwhelmed and uninspired.

Finding Balance in the Role of Executive Director

*Have fun in your command. Don't always run at breakneck pace.
Take time when you've earned it and spend time with your
family. Surround yourself with people who take their
work seriously, but not themselves.*

—General Colin Powell

Much has been written about balance and how elusive that goal is for Executive Directors. The job of an ED is composed of numerous and ever-changing roles and responsibilities. You are required to be accountable to a complex, diverse, and often demanding array of stakeholders from your Board of Directors and staff to your funders and community. In addition, there is seldom enough staff or volunteer help to accomplish all that needs to be done. As a result, balance tends to seem out of reach, leading to personal burnout for the Executive Director—and paralysis for an entire organization.

Are any of the following classic signs of overstress or burnout familiar to you?

- Difficulty making decisions
- Negative feelings about people you work with
- Loneliness at the top
- Avoidance of tasks that need to be done
- Feeling overwhelmed most of the time
- Believing you need to work days, nights, and weekends
- Fear and despair that you aren't doing a good enough job

If so, you are not alone. Finding balance and avoiding burnout were two of the most frequently cited challenges among the Executive Directors we interviewed prior to developing the first edition of this book. At times, all Executive Directors feel overwhelmed. It goes with the territory. But no Executive Director should allow life to become so unbalanced that symptoms of burnout make it difficult to lead effectively. As the caretaker for your organization, you must also take care of yourself so you can do your job well.

This chapter focuses on some self-reflection techniques and steps you can take to avoid burnout and develop a mind-set that encourages a balanced life while still having a rewarding career as an Executive Director. The questions we address here are simple but critical to your success:

- Why are Executive Directors so susceptible to burnout?
- How can I find balance as an Executive Director?
- How do I set boundaries on my work life so I still have a personal life?
- Where do I find the time to do everything an Executive Director has to do?
- How can an Executive Director delegate when everyone is already busy?

WHY ARE EXECUTIVE DIRECTORS SO SUSCEPTIBLE TO BURNOUT?

The potential for burnout increases dramatically depending on who you are, where you work, and what your job is. Thus the road to burnout is paved with good intentions, and good EDs have flocked down it. Most agree that if you're a hard worker who gives 110 percent—an idealistic, self-motivated achiever who thinks anything is possible if you just work hard enough—you are a candidate for burnout.

The same is true if you're a rigid perfectionist with unrealistically high standards and expectations. And in a job with frequent meetings or deadlines, you advance from a candidate to a probable victim.

There's certainly nothing wrong with being an idealistic, hardworking perfectionist or a self-motivating achiever. There's nothing wrong with having high aspirations and expectations. Indeed, these are admirable traits often cited in job announcements for Executive Directors.

The problem is in unrealistic job descriptions and annual work plans, and in internally driven expectations. While you may not have a lot of control over the day-to-day issues that create stress in your organization and your job, you do have some control over setting realistic goals and expectations with your Board. You also have control over how you respond to those daily stresses of the job. Thus it is important for all EDs to recognize the underlying personal and organizational sources of pressure and take conscious steps toward working with their Boards to establish realistic expectations while creating their own personal and professional balance and boundaries.

If you are susceptible to burnout—or, worse yet, feel overwhelmed by the stress of the job—seek help. Do not isolate yourself or think it will go away. A coach or counselor can help you tease apart the various causes of stress and take steps to identify and improve upon those that are controllable. Your colleagues may have experienced some or all of the same symptoms of burnout as you. Talk to them and learn from their experiences—that will help you take more control of your job, and ultimately your life.

It's very important to realize that most Executive Directors experience burnout at some point in their career. It is common to have these feelings, but it can also be temporary if you take the time to create a more balanced life.

HOW CAN I FIND BALANCE AS AN EXECUTIVE DIRECTOR?

Finding balance isn't a single outcome or goal—it's an ongoing process and sometimes a lifelong journey. The definition of balance is unique to each person's values and life situation. Balance is a gift you have to create for yourself, as no one can do it for you. A balanced life is something you strive for over a long time. It is your vision of yourself as you ultimately hope to be. One Executive

Director's vision of a balanced life was to get married, have a child, and reduce her work hours to the point she could give equal attention to her partner, her child, and her work. It took her a few years to achieve the balance she wanted (and she continues ongoing reflection to maintain the balance), but she has realized her vision of a balanced life.

And you must do it too. An Executive Director who is consistently overwhelmed by competing priorities cannot be an effective leader. Society is rich in approaches, theories, books, and self-help seminars about the need to negotiate the increasingly complex demands of work and personal life to feel fulfilled, balanced, in control of your life, and generally healthier. It takes work—and mental energy that is hard to find once you start down the slide toward burnout—to find the ones that are right for you.

A simple approach to the question of balance begins with awareness and self-reflection. It's essential to consider trade-offs between your personal values and your organization's priorities in light of your individual perception of consequences.

The exercise in Exhibit 3.1 is aimed at helping you clarify your individual values versus the reality of where you spend your time. It will help you locate your own imbalances and explore options for juggling or negotiating balance back into your life.

Exhibit 3.1
Life Balance Reflection

Priorities	Life in Balance (Percentage)	Reality of Where I Spend My Time (Percentage)	Discrepancies (Percentage of Goal)
Work	40	75	+ 88
Family	25	10	− 60
Health	5	0	−100
Home	5	2	− 60
Friends	10	3	− 70
Relationships	5	2	− 60
Hobbies	5	0	−100
Professional development	5	3	− 40

1. Using the chart in Exhibit 3.1 as a model, identify your own priorities—what you want for your life right now—and list them in the first column. Include any or all of the ones in the exhibit, and add others if necessary to produce your own unique list.

2. Envision your life as balanced, and estimate the percentage of your time you would spend on average on each of these priorities if that were the case. Place the percentages in the second column.

3. Now for a reality check. How do you really spend your time? Estimate percentages for what a typical week or month looks like, and post them in the third column.

4. Where are the greatest discrepancies between reality and balance? In the exhibit, the fourth column is calculated by taking the difference between the goal and the reality and figuring it as a percentage of the goal. Looking at the numbers may well be enough—you probably won't have to go through the math to see what you need to work on first.

5. List some realistic, small steps you could take in order to feel more satisfied and fulfilled.

6. Look at the steps you've listed. What is blocking you from taking these steps right now? Are these steps or changes things you have control of or do you need to negotiate some changes with your Board, your family, and your staff?

7. Think about the implications of the choices you face. What are the consequences of not taking these steps toward balance? What are the immediate and long-term rewards or benefits of greater balance?

As an example, one Executive Director created a chart that looks like this:

Priorities	Vision of Balance	Current Reality	Discrepancy
Work	40%	75%	+88%
Family	35%	15%	−27%
Exercise	15%	2%	−88%
Friends	10%	8%	−20%

When she reviewed the results, she realized that time with her friends was pretty close to her vision. If she took some of the time she spent with her friends and they exercised together, she could find more balance in that priority area, and feel physically better. She felt that was one realistic small step she could take soon.

The other priorities of work and family were more difficult to tackle. She set a goal for herself of focusing only 65 percent of her time on work in one year with 10 percent more time focused on family. Two small steps she took within the first few weeks were to stop checking and responding to work e-mail from home, and to make Sundays an absolute family-only day. These small steps helped her feel mentally more balanced, and her family was thrilled.

As you can see from the example, the process of defining and achieving balance is a personal one. You have to make it a priority, set realistic goals, and *do it.* Everyone has some sort of barrier or blockage that stands in the way of achieving personal goals. Understanding what might be blocking your way to leading a more balanced life is not easy. In the example, the Executive Director felt she had to be connected with her organization every day in case issues arose that she had to address. It took some time and honest self-reflection for her to understand that she could let others in the organization handle many of the daily issues, and that making the staff dependent on her to handle even the most minor of problems was not healthy for the organization or for the staff or for her.

If you are feeling burned out as an Executive Director, and your work is taking far more mental, physical, and emotional energy than you prefer, ask yourself why this is happening. What do you get from overworking? How is this helping or hurting you? Is this helping your organization or hurting it? Your answers to these questions may surprise you, and start you on your journey toward a more balanced life. Clearing these blockages is a significant step and may require outside support from a colleague or friend, a mentor, or a professional coach.

HOW DO I SET BOUNDARIES ON MY WORK LIFE SO I STILL HAVE A PERSONAL LIFE?

One most important step in gaining balance in your life is to set some self-prescribed work boundaries. When you have your vision of your own balanced life and have begun taking steps to realize it, you will likely find the need to set some clear boundaries at work and stick to them. Establishing work boundaries is a mental activity more than anything else. Most people who become Executive Directors are highly motivated, driven by an important mission, and full of desire to succeed for the community being served. American society has produced a work ethic for the Baby Boomer generation that measures success through how hard people work. Those in this generation who choose the profession of Executive Director seem to have this work ethic soul-deep. Some even believe that if their organization is not achieving its mission, they have failed as an Executive Director. They are driven to work hard for organizational success, thinking it is their own.

Nothing could be further from the truth. Many external and internal influences, beyond any Executive Director's control, can hinder progress toward an organization's mission. Understanding this and learning to focus on what is within your control will help you be more effective and more satisfied.

Fortunately, the generations of leaders following the Baby Boomers have a better understanding of the importance of work-life balance and place it as a higher priority. These generations of Xers and Yers question the need to be a workaholic and are looking for a new way to help their organizations succeed without burning out in the process. This is good, and gives hope that the Executive Director profession will become more reasonable and balanced.

The fact is that it isn't how hard you work that really matters. It's how effectively you work and having good systems in place to support you—that's what really matters. In addition to focusing on what you can control and measuring success, part of being effective is allowing time on a regular basis for non–work-related activities, and believing this is okay. For most people, the most creative and strategic thoughts do not happen in the office, they come in the middle of doing something else— exercising, conversation, on vacation, reading a book. To have downtime from work, it is necessary to have set boundaries that are clearly stated and always upheld. It is also important to have a work plan with quantifiable measurements that you can use to demonstrate your success to yourself and others.

Executive Director work plans are generally developed by the ED with the guidance of the Board of Directors. The Board may set the priorities for the year, or it may be a combination of the ED and Board developing those priorities. When that is completed, the ED drafts the work plan and submits it to the Board for review and approval. Every work plan is different based on the organization's priorities.

Executive Director work plans should also tie to the position's job description. If the Board and Executive Director find that a newly developed work plan has responsibilities that are not included in the ED job description, then revisions are needed to either update the job description or modify the work plan to make the two a better fit.

All ED work plans should have measurable performance objectives that state what the Executive Director must do to be successful in the Board's collective mind.

Exhibit 3.2 shows an example of an Executive Director's work plan with performance objectives. It comes from an organization that has a few staff people with program responsibilities, as well as a support staff person.

Exhibit 3.2
Sample Executive Director Work Plan and
Performance Objectives

PLAN TIME FRAME _____

Fundraising Performance Goals

- Increase grant revenues by 15 percent by fiscal year end.

- Increase nongovernmental revenues by 10 percent this fiscal year.

- Receive major donor level gifts from five people (with Board leadership).

   Professional development needs: A course in proposal writing

Staff Management Performance Goals

- Improve supervisor skills in evaluating their staff with two training sessions by HR specialists.

- Conduct an evaluation of staff morale and report results to Board.

   Professional development needs: Coaching on managing diverse staff and volunteers

Board Development Goals

- Support the recruitment of four new Board members.

- Develop a Board orientation program.

- Schedule a program manager to speak at quarterly Board meetings.

Vision Goals

- Lead Board and staff in a process to redefine organizational vision.

- Communicate the organizational vision to constituency audiences through a minimum of five speaking engagements.

Clear performance objectives and defined responsibilities make good communication much easier. Board members understand what the Executive Director is doing and what communication is needed to help ensure success. Progress toward the ED performance objectives should be reviewed on a regular basis—we recommend a quarterly review at a minimum. This should be a written summary distributed to all Board members with a listing of performance objectives achieved, progress toward others, and those that are lagging. There is almost always a good explanation for objectives that are lagging and the explanations should be part of the report. Allowing time for healthy discussions of the ED's performance on a regular basis reduces the possibilities of a surprise attack during the annual performance review. Since the annual review is based on the agreed upon performance objectives, it should be a fairly straightforward process that is fair and objective.

In addition to a clear work plan to set work boundaries, you may need to educate your staff and Board of Directors, persuading them that it is important to set boundaries for themselves, as well as modeling the new behavior patterns. The first step is to acknowledge that the culture of excessive hours is unhealthy and help your staff begin to move toward one that rewards new behaviors and realistic work boundaries. Many times we have heard complaints from disgruntled staff and Board members who tell us their Executive Director isn't doing the job well. The problem? The ED dares to take a lunch hour or leave the office regularly at 5 PM. And there is no work plan to show the Board and staff that the job is being done very well. We've stopped being surprised by these comments and now spend time helping people understand why it is important for everyone to set these boundaries and have a work plan. In the long run, it's better for the agency because the Executive Director is not burning out and can be more effective for a longer tenure.

Talk to your Board Chair and jointly establish some important boundaries in your work to allow you to find the balance you need to continue to be an effective leader. Work with your Board to develop a realistic work plan that allows you to have the boundaries you want. The boundary you set may be a schedule boundary, or it may be a task boundary such as only attending two evening meetings or events in a week and delegating Board members, volunteers, or staff to attend any others. If your vision of a more balanced life is related to health issues, you may need a work boundary that has you eating healthier meals in a quiet location or even negotiating a flexible or reduced work schedule to achieve or regain your vision of balance. In Chapter Twelve we discuss the concept of establishing a social contract with each new Board Chair that may also help you define some professional and personal boundaries.

WHERE DO I FIND THE TIME TO DO EVERYTHING AN EXECUTIVE DIRECTOR HAS TO DO?

This question immediately raises the priorities flag for us and we look to see if the Executive Director has been given clear directives from the Board of Directors regarding performance priorities and expectations. Is there a work plan that both the Board and ED have agreed upon? Are there established metrics that help an Executive Director know when expectations are being met? Usually, we find that the Board has failed to develop the ED's job description or metrics-based work plan and has defaulted to the slogan, "Just do it." Unfortunately, that's not very specific or helpful.

So the first step toward finding time is to work with your Board of Directors to clarify and establish some jointly developed priorities. You may already have some tools to help guide this negotiation.

If you have a job description, this is a good starting point. Is it up-to-date and relevant to the job that you actually do? If not, work with your Board to update it so that it accurately reflects the job you have today, not the job you were hired into five years ago—or your predecessor's predecessor a decade before that. A well-crafted job description goes a long way toward clarifying your roles and responsibilities.

One example of a job description follows in Exhibit 3.3.

Some organizations will take an added step to emphasize each key area of responsibility in the job description and indicate with a percentage figure its relative importance. For example, one organization that was launching a capital campaign broke out its priorities as follows:

Administration and management	20 percent
Board of Directors	25 percent
Fund development and community relations	30 percent
Strategic planning and evaluations	25 percent

The reality was that administration and management currently accounted for about 60 percent of the ED's week. Rather than simply leave the ED to do everything and work longer hours, the Board and ED came up with a plan that

Exhibit 3.3
Sample Executive Director Job Description

The Executive Director is the Chief Executive Officer of _____.
The Executive Director reports to the Board of Directors, and is responsible for the organization's consistent achievement of its mission and financial objectives.

In program development and administration, the Executive Director will:

1. Ensure that the organization has a long-range strategy for achieving its mission, toward which it makes consistent and timely progress.

2. Provide leadership in developing program, organizational, and financial plans with the Board of Directors and staff, and carry out plans and policies authorized by the Board.

3. Promote active and broad participation by volunteers in all areas of the organization's work.

4. Maintain official records and documents, and ensure compliance with federal, state, and local regulations.

5. Maintain a working knowledge of significant developments and trends in the field.

In community building, the Executive Director will:

1. Publicize the activities of the organization and its programs and goals.

2. Establish sound working relationships and cooperative arrangements with community groups and organizations.

3. Represent the programs and point of view of the organization to agencies, organizations, and the general public.

In relationships, the Executive Director will:

1. See that the Board is kept fully informed on the condition of the organization and all important factors influencing it.

2. Be responsible for the recruitment, employment, and release of all personnel, both paid staff and volunteers.

(Continued)

3. Ensure that job descriptions are developed, that regular performance evaluations are held, and that sound human resource practices are in place.

4. See that an effective management team, with appropriate provision for succession, is in place.

5. Encourage staff and volunteer development and education, and assist program staff in relating their specialized work to the total program of the organization.

6. Maintain a climate that attracts, keeps, and motivates a diverse staff of top-quality people.

In resource development, the Executive Director will:

1. Be responsible for developing and maintaining sound financial practices.

2. Work with the staff, Finance Committee, and the Board in preparing a budget; see that the organization operates within budget guidelines, and provide timely financial reports to the Board of Directors.

3. Ensure that adequate funds are available from diversified funding sources to permit the organization to carry out its work.

4. Jointly with the President and Secretary of the Board of Directors, conduct official correspondence of the organization, and jointly with designated officers, execute legal documents.

promoted one of the organization's senior managers to Associate Director to take on added responsibilities for program oversight and administrative details, freeing up about ten to fifteen hours a week for the Executive Director to work on Board development, community relations, and fund development issues in order to build a strong foundation for the capital campaign. The new Associate Director thrived on the additional responsibilities.

The second place to look for clarity is the organization's strategic plan or annual goals. Whether it is a formalized plan carefully preserved in binders or simply a set of summary notes from a Board meeting, it is a start. The key question for you and the Board to ask is, Where do you need to focus your talents and time to help make these goals become reality?

We also encourage you to avoid one of the common weaknesses of such a discussion. Resist the temptation to develop a list with fifteen to twenty so-called priorities on it. While such a list may summarize a variety of issues facing the organization, it does nothing to provide clarity, direction, and focus. Don't let a list of priorities exceed five items, and three is better. The extra thought and attention it takes to whittle the list down forces you and the Board to carefully debate and negotiate what is most important among everything that needs to be done. The other items should not be discarded. They may become secondary priorities once the key three to five issues are addressed or they may be addressed by others in the organization. While the resulting priority list may be invaluable to you, the process or discussion the organization engages in is even more important, as it helps strengthen a unified vision and Board-ED partnership (a point discussed in more detail in Chapters Six and Eleven).

Even after you and the Board achieve clarity in defining the Executive Director position, you may well find there is still too much for one person to do. And, because the modern environment is changing so rapidly, new priorities emerge and need to be juggled with existing ones.

If you are feeling the pressure of competing priorities, we recommend asking yourself the following questions to help determine what issues really need your immediate attention. You may also want to involve others in your organization, such as key staff or volunteers and Board members.

- Which priorities are leadership-related and which are management-related? Of those that are management-related, can I delegate any to someone else to allow me to focus on the leadership priorities?

- Do I need information from someone else in order to undertake the priority? Is this person available now, or will I need to wait? If I need to wait, can I set up an appointment now so I feel I am making some progress toward achieving this priority?

- Which priorities on the list are life-and-death issues for my agency?

A life-and-death issue is one that requires something to be done soon or the clients or community may be harmed, the agency doors may close, or resources of funding or people may be lost—issues that threaten the immediate existence of the agency.

STORY FROM THE FIELD

Elizabeth renegotiated her Executive Director priorities with her Board by calling the twenty-member Board together for an evening planning session. The purpose of the planning session was to look at the growing list of agency issues and compare them with her work plan, which had been approved earlier that year.

The new priorities that had been added came primarily from the community. The organization is an active neighborhood association with a staff of four who listen to and speak for the neighborhood. Community members were always calling or dropping by and asking Elizabeth to please take care of something that was bothering them. As you can imagine, the to-do list became huge very quickly and Elizabeth began feeling pressure from her Board and the community to meet everyone's priorities.

At the planning session, the Board looked at the original work plan and the growing list from the community. Together with the staff, they determined which priorities were most related to the mission and long-range goals of the organization, which priorities were do-or-die activities or decisions for the community, and who on the Board and staff should have responsibility for meeting those mission-related, do-or-die priorities.

In one evening, an overwhelming list of issues became a more manageable set of clear priorities for Elizabeth and the organization. The group also discussed ways of receiving community ideas that respected everyone's opinion but did not give the impression that all ideas would receive equally high priority from the association.

It was decided that the community would be better informed through the existing newsletter regarding the mission, current priorities, and long-term goals of the association. The Board and the community-relations staff person also decided to hold a community forum twice a year to gather ideas and ask for input. Staff members were instructed to encourage community members to attend these forums to express their ideas and also to join Board committees that allowed non-Board members. Everyone agreed that if community members became more actively involved in finding solutions and taking ownership of their ideas, then the community would be better served.

In this neighborhood association the Executive Director struggled most with delegating to staff, to Board members as appropriate, and to community volunteers. Here is where the question "Is this a leadership priority or a management priority?" becomes a valuable one to ask.

HOW CAN AN EXECUTIVE DIRECTOR DELEGATE WHEN EVERYONE IS ALREADY BUSY?

We have found in our work that some Executive Directors think their staff or volunteers are already overburdened and should not be asked to take on any more work. At the same time, we have talked with staff who are looking for added responsibility and the opportunity to learn new skills. So if you feel you need help, ask—you may be doing people a favor rather than heaping burdens upon them. As you delegate new responsibilities, however, be sure to include some degree of added authority. When responsibilities are passed down without the required authority to get the job done, staff may become frustrated and may shrink away from further opportunities.

If you have established work plans and metrics for staff, you'll need to revisit these as you delegate new responsibilities to them. Just as you negotiate with the Board of Directors when new priorities are added, your staff should be able to negotiate with you to set aside current priorities and keep their workload within reasonable bounds. This is one key point to remember in successfully delegating tasks and responsibility to staff.

Other keys to success in delegation include clear communication and support. Don't simply adopt the "just do it" approach. Discussion should consider the purpose and importance of the task to be delegated in relationship to the employee's current priorities; plus understanding of the steps or process the task requires and a reasonable time frame for completing it.

Some Executive Directors believe that delegating a task that was originally stated as a priority by the Board means shirking their own responsibilities. Not so, especially if the priority is a management issue. As a Board and Executive Director develop or renegotiate a work plan for the year, clear communication about tasks the Executive Director may wish to delegate to others is essential. Delegation of management issues allows the Executive Director to maintain focus on the leadership priorities of the organization.

TIPS FOR SUCCESS

- There is no magic formula for leading a balanced life. Defining *balance* is a personal choice, and achieving it is a constant work in progress. Define what it means for you.

- Work hard on what is in your control to achieve organizational success, and realize that some influences will always be outside your control.

- Have a specific job description that you and the Board review at least annually while developing your work plan.

- Maintain clear communication with your Board of Directors and staff about what is reasonable and possible for yourself and the organization.

PART TWO

Executive Director as Visionary

You are not here merely to make a living. You are here in order to enable the world to live more amply, with greater vision, with a finer spirit of hope and achievement. You are here to enrich the world, and you impoverish yourself if you forget the errand.

—President Woodrow Wilson

An Executive Director is often the person that Board and staff look to for inspiration and motivation. As the ED, you have an invigorating passion for the cause you are serving, and you carry a vision of greatness for your organization. It is this vision that holds people together and inspires them to come to work each day, raise necessary funds, provide governance and oversight, and serve the community well. Without vision, an organization may flounder and struggle and never attain greatness.

The vision is not single-handedly created by the Executive Director. Nor should it ever be. To create, hold, and articulate a powerful vision, the Executive Director and others in the organization must understand the culture of the nonprofit. What are the underlying values, principles, beliefs, practices, and assumptions that guide the organization and are deeply rooted in it? No vision can ever take hold that isn't built on the nonprofit's culture.

A central core of the organization's vision is also the community's values and beliefs, practices, and assumptions. You need to understand who you are serving, what needs can be met by your organization, and how your vision is inspiring to your community. An Executive Director and Board of Directors should think and act strategically to keep the organization's vision relevant to the community.

Doing this will mean that the vision is shared by people inside and outside the organization. For an organization to be successful, its vision must be articulated, understood, massaged, and written down for all to see.

While having a vision of the future for a community and nonprofit is exciting, to actually achieve a vision, an organization must have a road map. Often this is a strategic plan that spans several years with goals and operational tasks that move the nonprofit ever closer to its vision.

Finally, for a vision to take hold and motivate everyone in the organization, people must believe that it is a fundamental element to the success of the nonprofit. The Executive Director and Board must be vigilant in defining what the word *success* means for their nonprofit in its efforts to achieve its vision, and must review progress toward this target regularly.

All these topics are covered in detail in this part of the book, starting first with understanding nonprofit culture in Chapter Four. Chapter Five digs deeper into the areas of values and guiding principles in a nonprofit. Chapter Six guides you toward defining a vision and describes the strategic planning process that helps your organization articulate a vision and plan for its achievement. Finally, Chapter Seven provides practical advice on measuring organizational effectiveness toward the vision's attainment.

Understanding Nonprofit Organizational Culture

It seems right that cultures are formed from an unusual point of view, refined and strengthened by external and internal challenges, and led by a portfolio of people with complementary skills.

—Regina E. Herzlinger, "Culture Is the Key,"
Leading Beyond the Walls

Just as nations and societies have characteristic cultures, all groups, large or small, develop an identifiable culture of their own. Doing things the HP way, the Ben and Jerry's way, or the Sun Microsystems way are examples of corporate cultures. Government cultures are expressed in the behavior of council members, public agency officials and employees, and national leaders. Family cultures are often dominated by one or more parental value systems. Service organizations and clubs such as the Kiwanis and your local soccer clubs all have established norms and traditions that express their cultures.

Nonprofit organizations are no exception. Within each nonprofit is at least one dominant culture, and most have several subcultures. Culture is frequently unseen and unarticulated, yet it is always operating at the heart of any organization. When things are going smoothly, the culture is revered and honored. Conversely, an organization's culture can become the scapegoat for discontent or dissatisfaction, or for individuals or ideas that don't fit.

In this chapter we explore the meaning of nonprofit culture and how the Executive Director's success in an organization depends upon understanding, defining, articulating, managing, and oftentimes changing this culture. We also describe how the Executive Director is generally the staff person who provides leadership in these areas—with the caveat that the ED is often not the creator of a nonprofit's culture. It is shaped by everyone in the organization, and by those who are served. As we explore nonprofit organizational culture, we address the following questions:

- What does *organizational culture* mean?

- How does understanding the organization's culture help the Executive Director be more effective?

- How does an Executive Director determine what the organization's culture is?

- What are some strategies for changing or moving an organization's culture to where it needs to be in order to be successful?

WHAT DOES *ORGANIZATIONAL CULTURE* MEAN?

The term *organizational culture* emerged in the 1950s, followed by such terms as *organizational characteristics* and *organizational identity.* Here are two commonly applied definitions:

DEFINITION

Organizational culture is the pattern of shared basic assumptions that the group learned as it solved its problems of external adaptation and internal integration, which has worked well enough to be considered valid and therefore to be taught to new members as the correct way to perceive, think, and feel in relation to those problems. (Edgar Schein)

DEFINITION

Organizational culture is the pattern of beliefs, values, rituals, myths, and sentiments shared by members of an organization. (Roger Harrison and Herb Stokes)

For the purposes of this book, we are using the following definition, which emerges from the similarities and differences expressed in the definitions just noted.

DEFINITION

Organizational culture is made up of the often-unspoken assumption of values, beliefs, and processes that underlie the goals, work habits, decision making, conflict resolution, management, and perceived success of any organization. The culture includes both the everyday patterns of work that have developed over time and the deeper hidden assumptions and beliefs that consciously and unconsciously drive that work.

In most nonprofits, the initial identity was established by the Founder and those working with the Founder to start the organization. Quite often, the Founder's viewpoint dominates the values, beliefs, and patterns of work during the early days. As new people come into the organization and the Founder becomes less influential, one or several new cultures may emerge.

As organizations mature and move through various life cycle stages (which are discussed in Chapter Nine), their cultures develop or evolve through strong assumptions and values that the Executive Directors, Board members, and staff bring from their respective communities and backgrounds. Executive Directors bring their leadership styles and management skills to the organization. If a facilitative-style Executive Director follows a strictly hierarchical one, then norms and processes will change over time. Board members from corporations sometimes encourage a nonprofit to change its culture to one that is more like that found in business by inserting some of their own corporate assumptions and practices into the organization. New staff will bring the culture of their previous employer into the organization and may try to impose the norms and values from their old workplace into their new one.

Clients served by a nonprofit, as well as the broader community in which the organization operates, also contribute to organizational culture. Values, beliefs, and practices from those outside the organization often have an impact on staff and volunteers. For example, in nonprofits serving disenfranchised populations it is a practice to hire these individuals as paid and volunteer staff. They bring many of the values and beliefs they hold into the organization, and over time, these can translate into program priorities and new ways of working with clients that eventually become integrated into the organization's culture. Whether this interweaving of a client culture into a nonprofit is an enhancement or a problem depends on the efforts of all who work in the organization to recognize and understand the cultural characteristics and to determine which elements contribute toward achieving the vision.

Through this process of integrating everyone's values, norms, beliefs, and practices, a nonprofit will have a dominant culture that is healthy or unhealthy. A healthy culture has Board, staff, and volunteers aligned with a set of organizational values, has procedures that align with the values, and has agreed-upon norms and processes to achieve the organization's vision. In these nonprofits, discussions and disagreements among the naturally occurring subcultures are viewed as opportunities for innovation and growth toward the vision. A healthy culture in a nonprofit can create a wonderful learning environment as people weave their values and beliefs together.

Alternatively, an organization with an unhealthy dominant culture has little alignment among those working there, and may not have an agreed-upon vision or values or processes for getting things accomplished. In these nonprofits, the disagreements among subcultures may throw the organization into chaos and major conflict as people try to impose their values and beliefs on others.

For an Executive Director to lead an organization successfully, there needs to be a healthy culture. You will need to understand as much as possible about the values, norms, and beliefs of the subcultures, and differences of opinion about all of these. It is part of your job to make your organization's culture as transparent as possible. But it is not just the Executive Director's job to make and maintain a healthy culture. That is something everyone—Board, staff, volunteers—must be committed to do.

HOW DOES UNDERSTANDING THE ORGANIZATION'S CULTURE HELP THE EXECUTIVE DIRECTOR BE MORE EFFECTIVE?

Almost everything you do as Executive Director is affected by the culture of the nonprofit where you work. The organizational vision, how people are or aren't recognized for good work, who makes what decisions and how they are made, the communication patterns and the bottlenecks, how conflicts are or aren't resolved, what is rewarded and punished, and how the organization responds to the larger community and client needs are all culturally based.

As Executive Director you have the option of reaffirming and building on the existing culture of your nonprofit or leading a change process in a culture that has become dysfunctional and is not serving the organization or community well. To accomplish either of these objectives, particularly as an Executive Director new to the nonprofit, you must spend time understanding the culture of the organization you lead and how it has evolved from its founding to the present. You can then determine where the organization might need to go in the future.

The consequences of not taking time to understand the organizational culture can be serious. One classic example is the "bad fit" phenomenon.

All too often Boards report that their Executive Director did not stay around very long: "It just wasn't a good fit," they say. We would suggest that a likely translation here is that the Executive Director didn't understand the organization's culture and tried to make changes in the nonprofit that ran into long-standing, deeply embedded norms and beliefs.

That you understand the nature of your fit with an organization is essential. In fact, those Executive Directors who report being happy and enjoying their work, and who have established strong partnerships with others in the organization, are the ones who have found the fit for themselves. To understand if you and your organization fit well together, ask yourself these questions:

- Is my vision for this organization shared by the staff and Board?
- Are my values the same as those of others in the organization? Do the articulated values match the behaviors of those working here?

- Are my ideas for changing practices and policies generally accepted rather than discarded?

- Do I have a positive relationship with people inside and outside the organization?

- Am I excited about my work most of the time, and am I committed to the mission?

If your answer is yes to these questions, then you probably have a good fit with your nonprofit. If you are unsure, then read the chapters in this book on vision, values, change processes, and relationship building to help yourself answer the questions. And if your answer is no to these questions, it may be time for a heart-to-heart conversation with yourself, trusted friends, and possibly your Board of Directors about what needs to be done to create a better fit—or to leave this organization.

All too often, organizations with an unhealthy culture will have a revolving door on the Executive Director's office—a string of new EDs who turn out to be a bad fit. If there is no clear vision or values, poor communication among Board and staff, lack of clear processes, and other factors that contribute to an unhealthy culture, then the Board may not have a clear picture of what is needed for successful executive leadership. For example, an environmental advocacy organization had a strong Founder in charge for several years. She led the organization in a very collaborative style with Board, staff, and volunteers working together, sharing ideas, and reaching consensus on vision and strategies. When she left, the Board decided that the new ED's focus should be on fundraising and marketing since organizational growth depended on new sources of funding. Little thought was given to the organization's healthy culture of collaboration. They hired someone very skilled in fundraising but with no interest in communicating with staff and Board about what he was doing. The collaborative culture began to deteriorate because of poor communication, and the Executive Director left within a year. The Board brought in an interim ED for six months to hold things together, and then hired someone with excellent communication skills but without the ability to bring people to consensus and build community. He worked hard to shift the organization to a hierarchical structure with new processes and procedures. He also left shortly after being hired and another interim was brought in. By this time, the Founder's collaborative culture had collapsed, and the organization had lost respect in its community and was no longer considered as a leader in its advocacy work. It had lost its effectiveness.

Had the Board of Directors and the Executive Directors who followed the Founder taken the time to understand the importance of the collaborative culture established by the Founder, it is likely the organization would still be thriving and successful. Instead, it is struggling to survive.

If you are an Executive Director who is new to an organization and you hear "but that's not how we do things around here," this is a good clue that you have just bumped into a cultural barrier. You will probably discover that processes developed in the early days by the Founder worked well back then and now have become the way people measure their success. Your idea threatens the security of the established culture. Pay attention to this and other clues to help avoid the "bad fit" syndrome.

As the organization just discussed illustrates, it is also important for boards of directors to pay attention to this syndrome. Choosing an Executive Director is the Board's job, and understanding your organization's culture helps you make a better choice when hiring a new Executive Director. The Board should always participate in, and provide leadership to, discussions of organizational vision, values, norms, and best practices. Ideally, the Board, staff, and other stakeholders will be aligned in understanding the culture. If not, and if there is a revolving door for Executive Directors, then the organization needs a healthier culture before any Executive Director can be a good fit and be successful.

In addition to the need for a good fit, understanding your organization's culture is important for a variety of reasons. It makes you more effective as a leader. It also allows you to build on the abilities of competent people around you, and on a bigger scale it ensures that your organization is fulfilling its mission and achieving its vision. When deeply felt and commonly shared values guide the work of an organization and underlie the vision, everyone tends to stay focused on what is possible for clients and community. In short, understanding the nonprofit's culture enables everyone in the organization to create priorities for the future and have an effective organization.

HOW DOES AN EXECUTIVE DIRECTOR DETERMINE WHAT THE ORGANIZATION'S CULTURE IS?

Regardless of how long you have been Executive Director of an organization, it's important to take some time to step back, take a deep breath, and attempt to define and articulate exactly what the culture is. First, realizing that no nonprofit has a culture exactly like any other, it is useful to understand what makes your nonprofit's culture unique and what it shares with others of similar background and outlook. Just as there may be similarities in the personalities of people, so too there may be similarities in the personalities of organizations, but regardless, each one is unique. A look at several key ingredients to organizational culture will help you to define yours.

The Founder's vision and beliefs: Nonprofits are typically started by someone who observes a community or societal problem that is not being resolved. This Founder generally plays a major leadership role in the early days of the organization, often as a Board Chair or Executive Director. Usually the Founder has a very strong vision and beliefs about what should be changed in society, and these perceptions will dominate the organization's culture.

The articulated learnings of paid and unpaid staff: People working in a nonprofit usually learn how to get something done from someone who has done the job before. Even when the organization has written policies or procedures, job tasks are most often just passed verbally along from one person to another. Learning originates from how people observe, assess, and implement any given task.

The common processes that remain in effect over time: Less apparent are communication and decision-making processes developed by a nonprofit's Founder and the first Board of Directors that may remain in effect years later. Who hears what information and who is involved in which decisions is often determined by the initially established processes for moving information through the organization to the designated people the original leadership group believed must have it.

The assumptions that have built up over time: Unquestioned assumptions usually guide the behavior of staff and volunteers in the organization, telling them how to think and feel about working there. Such assumptions can be found underlying all aspects of the culture, and they are usually not articulated. For example, staff may share the assumption that the Board of Directors is not in tune with the organization. This makes it difficult for Board members to build trust and credibility with staff, and puts the Executive Director into an awkward position of taking sides. The assumptions may have been established years ago and have nothing to do with the current members of the Board.

The values that shape and guide the organization's purpose: In a nonprofit, the values are likely to be deeply felt and altruistic. The people working in the organization will be passionate about these values whether they are spoken or not. Values will differ greatly from nonprofit to nonprofit. Staff in your organization may share the value of honoring differences in culture, or preserving open space for future generations, or ensuring dignity and choice for frail elders. Some of these values appear in the mission statement and are part of all programs and services in the organization. Others are more deeply felt and can be written in a Values Statement or some other document that provides transparency and understanding of the values.

An important question to reflect on is whether the values articulated by the organization match the behaviors of everyone in the organization. For instance, if your organization identifies collaboration as an important value, do you see staff working well with each other within and between departments? Does your organization have a positive reputation as a strong collaborator with others in the community? If not, the behaviors of those working in the nonprofit do not align with the values being articulated, ultimately creating a cultural confusion that grows over time if not addressed.

Some nonprofits seem to have no prevailing culture. This is seen in organizations with rapid turnover, especially in the leadership. It becomes difficult to build a shared experience and to articulate common learnings. Policies and procedures change depending on who has the loudest voice at the moment, and conflict is often pervasive because communication processes have broken down. The apparent absence of organizational culture usually indicates that several cultures are vying to be the strongest.

Exhibit 4.1 provides a list of questions to ask paid and unpaid staff and Board members to help define an organization's culture. When you have fully explored the answers, you can summarize the findings into a clear definition of your nonprofit's culture. Generally, there will need to be a reason for conducting this exercise. Telling Board and staff that you (as the ED) want to understand the organization's culture will likely not gain much enthusiasm from anyone. If you are relatively new to the nonprofit, or if a major change has occurred or is about to, or if the organization is about to transition to a new leader or merge with another nonprofit, these are great opportunities for serious culture reflection.

Ideally, this exercise will be conducted by a neutral party such as a consultant, organizational coach, or someone else. This allows for unbiased reporting and also allows the Executive Director to be an active participant. Depending on the size of your organization and the current level of team spirit and mutual respect of your Board and staff, you may want to do this exercise with Board and staff together or separately. In organizations with many staff members, several group meetings may be necessary or ask for staff to choose representatives to come to one meeting.

Ask the following questions:

1. What is our fundamental purpose in this community? What justifies this purpose?

2. What does our vision statement mean to you—what are we working to achieve in our community?

3. What organizational values are talked about most often? Do our behaviors align with these values? How do we reinforce these values in our work?

4. Does our organization have a set of shared goals? If not, why is that? If so, how well are we doing in meeting these goals and how do we articulate our success?

5. When a disagreement occurs between people here, what do you observe happen to resolve this disagreement? (Note: If people say there are no disagreements, dig deeper with the group! There are always disagreements in organizations and it's important to find out why people say there aren't.)

6. What sorts of behavior are expected, rewarded, or punished here?

7. What does rewarding behavior look like, and what does punishment look like? Do you know how well you are performing at your work?

8. How are decisions made in this organization? Are decisions based on opinions or facts? Who makes decisions? How transparent are these decisions to the people affected by them?

9. How would you describe this organization to others? Innovative, community focused, stuck, bureaucratic, effective, ineffective, exciting, other descriptors?

10. How would you rate this organization? A 10 means it is a highly effective, great place to work, and a 1 means it is highly ineffective and an unbearable place to work.

Take the time needed to gather as much input as possible. The questions will trigger a lot of discussion and reflection among those participating in the exercise.

When you have the answers to the questions in Exhibit 4.1, look for similarities and differences in the responses. Here are some tips to guide your analysis:

- As participants answer each question, watch for responses that differ and may conflict with one another.

- Is there a lot of consistency in responses to the vision and values questions?
- Are disagreements handled smoothly, professionally, and quickly?
- Are appropriate behaviors expected and rewarded?
- Do people involved with the organization feel good about it and what it is doing?

Grouping responses at the end of a discussion on each question can be helpful in discovering patterns that articulate different cultures. For instance, an all-volunteer animal rescue organization was deeply enmeshed in inexplicable conflict. After answering some of the questions in Exhibit 4.1, they grouped their responses and discovered two dominant cultures—one that felt the nonprofit needed to be more business oriented, and the other that felt that rescuing animals rose above everything else—including spending funds wisely. Clarifying these two distinct cultures helped the organization resolve some of its conflicts and improve its health.

A summary of the responses with analysis of the status of your organizational culture should be shared throughout the organization. Again, there will likely be more discussion as staff and Board members agree or disagree with the findings and conclusions.

Several tools and instruments for evaluating culture are on the market. These are noted in the Resources section for this chapter. While each of these tools has some value, a note of caution is needed because they all provide a set of criteria to enable you to neatly classify your organization with a specific label. In other words, if you answer the questions this way, then you are a certain type of nonprofit. Neither human personalities nor organizational personalities can be so easily categorized.

WHAT ARE SOME STRATEGIES FOR CHANGING OR MOVING AN ORGANIZATION'S CULTURE TO WHERE IT NEEDS TO BE IN ORDER TO BE SUCCESSFUL?

If you and others in the organization believe there is need to shift the culture to a healthier one, then realize it will take great patience and fortitude, and it will take a lot of time. Culture is embedded deep within an organization and is extremely difficult to change. Gaining allies within the organization through discussions of possible new ways to conduct the work is a necessary first step because it creates buy-in with those individuals who will work with you to shift the culture.

Changing organizational culture is not something an Executive Director should attempt alone. This absolutely requires many great minds working together.

Changing an organization's culture is no small task; it needs to be done attentively and gradually, allowing sufficient time for adaptation and integration. All too often, a decision will be made to shift the culture to become more healthy, a few steps will be taken, and then all will be abandoned because of the frustration of everything taking too long to change. The following story from the field gives an example of the lengthy process.

STORY FROM THE FIELD

Sally, the new Executive Director of a midsize regional nonprofit serving persons with disabilities, found she had staff members in her office every day complaining about other staff members and telling her to make things better. This was puzzling; the staff was full of bright and capable people, but they seemed completely unable to communicate with one another! It turned out that the culture as defined by the Founder—twenty-five years earlier—was one in which the Executive Director was expected to be "Mom" and take care of everyone in the organization. Even though several Executive Directors had come and gone since the Founder's time, the original culture was still dominant.

This cultural pattern was comfortable for the staff. They did not have to be accountable for their actions or work together as a team to get things accomplished. The organization was full of "lone rangers," and whoever spoke the loudest or displayed the most drama gained the most attention. This was how priorities were set and work got done. Unfortunately, the organization's ability to meet the needs of the clients and their families was below standards. An audit done by the regional licensing agency gave low marks to the facility, and Sally received their report a few weeks after she started as Executive Director.

She had experienced similar norms in other organizations she had led, so she knew what to do. She also knew that this culture was deeply embedded and could take years to fully shift it to a new culture that empowered staff to solve their own problems and work more closely with each other. She also knew that small steps would have to be taken, and that she would need allies along the way.

Her first step was to hold one-to-one meetings with her managers and tell them that she was most interested in their concerns and issues, but she expected them to bring her answers as well as problems. A few of the managers understood and appreciated this new approach, and became her allies. Others resisted, but Sally stood firm, and within a year, the managers were taking more responsibility for their departmental issues.

Another step she took was to create a management team with the six managers who reported to her. For the first few months, they were a team in name only. The monthly meetings were tense and often full of conflict. She realized the ED's job required her to add some structure to the team, so—using examples from other teams—she gave them the task of developing ground rules of how they were going to operate as a team, including how they were going to treat each other. This was their first team task together, and most of the managers got into it. It took them several months of discussion, but they came up with a good list of ground rules that were handed out as a reminder at each management meeting. A few of the managers began using the ground rules with their own staff in departmental meetings. Slowly but surely a new culture of cooperation and tolerance was being born!

Many more actions were taken by the Executive Director over the next few years. There were setbacks along the way, including a major rebellion among the two largest departments who tried to get her fired. Fortunately, the Board of Directors understood what Sally was doing and why it was important, so she had their support. Eventually, the managers of those departments left and were replaced with individuals who embraced the new culture the ED was trying to create. Additional steps taken over the years were making sure job descriptions were accurate, individual and departmental performance measures were in place, a strategic planning process was completed, and a zero tolerance rule among the managers for undermining and back-stabbing was established. Managers were expected to talk at each monthly meeting about their accomplishments in attaining their performance measures and some found that if their departments worked together, the goals were easier to achieve. As managers learned new behaviors of communication and cooperation, they began working with their department staff to change their behavior too.

Five years later, the organization was recognized by its licensing agency as having progressive and innovative programs for persons with disabilities. The hard work by Sally and her managers created a healthier culture, and also a more effective organization.

This story illustrates how one Executive Director used her understanding of her organization's culture to expand the capability of the staff and her organization to be more effective. In the process, she improved the general atmosphere and freed up her own time for other pressing obligations.

As Sally's story demonstrates, changing an organization's deeply embedded culture is not easy, and it takes time. But, with patience and firmness, it can be done. Here is a process an organization can use to start making a cultural change. Often, it is up to the Executive Director to begin the process, as in the example, but many others inside and outside the nonprofit need to keep the process alive and moving forward.

1. Acknowledge and put language around what is and isn't working well in your nonprofit by working through the questions in Exhibit 4.1.

2. Revisit the same set of questions in the exhibit, but this time have everyone answer them in terms of what they personally want or prefer for the organization, rather than what currently is.

3. Compare the two sets of answers and discuss them with Board and staff members.

If the first and second sets of responses are similar—in other words, people seem relatively satisfied—and if the organization is meeting community needs well, then it may not be time to make any major cultural shifts. Rather, you should articulate and celebrate your culture. On the other hand, if you notice significant differences between the two sets of responses, then you know that you need to gently introduce a process that will change some or all aspects of the culture that are dysfunctional.

One way to introduce this process is to meet with the Board of Directors and management team and describe the differences you found in the responses to the questions. Explain why these differences are creating some dysfunction in the organization and why you feel a change is needed. Have everyone discuss why they think these differences exist and what might be done about them. Get everyone's buy-in for making changes in the culture.

When you have buy-in, have the same conversation with other key staff and volunteers to help them understand the situation and get their support. You also might brainstorm with everyone about what a healthier culture for the nonprofit could look like.

After you have the all-important agreement of your Board, you can clearly articulate changes you would like to make to shift the culture from dysfunction to health. In the case of the animal rescue organization mentioned earlier, the Board President (also serving as the volunteer Executive Director) held a meeting with all interested volunteers during which he described the significant cultural conflict of some individuals wanting to run an efficient business model and others wanting to rescue all animals regardless of cost. He asked for individuals to help him shift the culture to one where the nonprofit could operate efficiently and still rescue those animals most in need. After several months of hard work, there was a noticeable shift in the culture as the conflict and tension in the organization was significantly reduced.

If you and others believe your organization's culture can use some strengthening, other chapters in this book can help you. Take a look at the chapters on vision and planning, managing change, and all the chapters in the relationship-building section. There are also many excellent resources online and in print that can help you. Some are listed in this chapter's section at the end of the book.

TIPS FOR SUCCESS

- Determine your organization culture's strengths and keep them as your cornerstones of a healthy culture. Determine your organization culture's weaknesses and change them.

- The analysis of your organization's culture should be done by the Board, managers, and other key staff along with you.

- Realize that understanding your organization's culture takes time and lots of discussion. Changing the culture may take years, and you will need allies to support you every step of the way.

- If your organization's culture is not a good fit for you and there is no interest in changing it, accept it and plan your transition.

Embracing Your Organization's Values

*Leaders must engage individuals in a discussion of what the values
mean and how their personal beliefs and behaviors are
influenced by what the organization stands for.*

—James Kouzes and Barry Posner,
Encouraging the Heart

An organization's values are deeply embedded in its culture. As
Executive Director, you will want to know what these values are
early in your tenure so you can determine if those values fit your personal ones. Discussions specific to organizational values are rarely held,
and you and others in your nonprofit will find the effort refreshing,
enlightening, and at times exhausting. But whatever the process and outcome, a discussion about your organization's values is crucial in attaining
the organization's mission and vision. Values are the guiding principles

that ground the organization in everything that is done, everything that is communicated, and in all efforts to measure effectiveness.

Realize though, that not all values in an organization are equal. Different levels of importance are usually given, and these levels of importance may change as the nonprofit evolves.

In this chapter, we help Executive Directors and other nonprofit leaders identify their organization's values and describe at what points they show themselves in all aspects of the nonprofit. We also take a look at one value that has gained increasing attention—that of cultural competency. Any nonprofit that understands this value and integrates it as a guiding principle will maximize its chance of garnering community support and achieving its mission and vision. Finally, we explore how an Executive Director provides strong leadership to an organization rich in values and diverse in culture. Specifically, we answer the following questions:

- What are organization values and how are they found within an organization's culture?
- How does an Executive Director establish values as the guiding principles in the organization?
- What is cultural competence and why is it so important?
- How does an Executive Director lead a culturally competent organization?

WHAT ARE ORGANIZATION VALUES AND HOW ARE THEY FOUND WITHIN AN ORGANIZATION'S CULTURE?

Organizational values are the guiding principles that inspire and inform the vision, mission, goals, and overall culture of any nonprofit. They are often intangible, generally subjective, and sometimes unarticulated. However, they are so important to any nonprofit that they should be discussed, written down, and reviewed often, because values inform all the actions in the organization.

For example, an organizational value could be *collaboration*. This value might show up in many types of organizational activity:

- Partnerships with other organizations on programs
- A team organization structure with shared decision making
- Regular discussions between Board and staff on issues facing the organization

- Regular discussions with community members to involve them in an organization's program

The following exhibit shows an example of one organization's values and the actions taken to support those values.

Exhibit 5.1
The Women's Foundation of California Values Chart

Statement of Values	Strategic Applications/ Implications	Internal/Operational Applications and Implications
Women's Rights Are Human Rights	Use a human rights framework in programs, grantmaking and positioning. Recognize the intersectionality of identities and interconnectivity of issues and rights in the lives of women and their families in all Foundation programs, grantmaking and positioning.*	Commit to continuing internal education of Board and staff with constituents and donors about human rights/women's rights.
Equity, Justice and Empowerment for Women & Girls • Foster opportunity to remove barriers and discrimination affecting low-income women and girls • Recognize the intersectional factors that limit opportunity and access • Value full participation of all women and girls in society	Utilize grantmaking, capacity building and policy advocacy training.	Structure grant review committees, Board and Board committees in a way that fosters the empowerment of women and girls in the state of California. *(Continued)*

Statement of Values	Strategic Applications/ Implications	Internal/Operational Applications and Implications
• Highly value the leadership of community-based women whose wisdom and insight based on first-hand experience helps create systemic solutions to inequity		
Inclusiveness • Find strength in honoring differences (race, class, religion, age, sexuality, etc.)	Consciously invest in organizations that exemplify diversity, including age diversity (engaging young women). Diversify marketing and fundraising to attract and build the confidence of donors across race, class and cultural lines. Seek likely (e.g., women-led organizations, women's funds and progressive donors) and unlikely partners (e.g., corporations, men, the public sector and faith-based communities).	Reflect inclusiveness and diversity at all levels, including leadership in both Board and staff. Develop hiring and recruitment practices that seek the broadest possible pool of applicants and Board members.
Self-determination • Physically, emotionally, mentally	Openly support the maximum choices in a woman's life and her ability to make them, particularly in her reproductive and childbearing life. Specifically support and fund pro-choice work. Recognize and fund sexual rights as human rights.	Institute family-friendly HR policies. Develop staff expertise on reproductive justice and sexual rights.

Statement of Values	Strategic Applications/ Implications	Internal/Operational Applications and Implications
Partnership & Collaboration • Donors • Community-based women and girls • Likely and unlikely allies • Public sector	Utilize our ability to convene diverse decision-makers as a way to inform our own work and to further partnerships within communities. Partner with likely and unlikely partners in policy advocacy, grantmaking, resource development and research. Utilize resources (funding and capacity building) to promote collaboration and partnerships that foster progressive/democratic movement building for social justice.	Develop and reward a staff team model that is collaborative. Encourage collaborative work on the part of the Board and Board committees. Engage donors in thinking about our strategies. Engage all staff and Board members in donor cultivation and stewardship.
Innovation and Risk-taking	Make grants for innovation and cutting-edge thinking and solutions. Invest resources in training advocates in the public policy-making process. Publish research on cutting edge issues, highlighting strategic solutions. Provide a public voice about cutting edge issues affecting women and girls.	Take more risks in hiring younger and older women and men and nurture their leadership. Create space, tolerance and learning processes for "failures." Develop streamlined decision-making practices which can accommodate risky ideas.
Effectiveness	Be willing to disclose grantmaking process and discuss grant decisions with applicants.	Conduct annual independent audit.

(Continued)

Statement of Values	Strategic Applications/ Implications	Internal/Operational Applications and Implications
• Transparency • Accountability • Credibility • Good planning & evaluation	Collect from grant partners documented outcomes of our work and funding that we can learn from and share with others. Meet the Nonprofit Integrity Act requirements. Publish credible reports.	Conduct annual staff evaluations. Conduct annual and ongoing planning and evaluation of all our work. Develop consistency between written policies and practices.

Source: Women's Foundation of California; used with permission.

*The concept of intersectionality recognizes that all individuals have a number of identities (e.g., gender, race/ethnicity, sexual orientation, class, age-related identities) and these identities intersect to make people who they are in the world.

Values are different from an organization's ground rules or code of conduct. The code of conduct enforces the values and holds people accountable to them. For instance, if your organization has a value of *respect,* the code of conduct to enforce this value would be zero tolerance for staff who trash fellow staff or the public, and there would be disciplinary action to enforce this value.

Executive Directors who help their organizations articulate values and create a code of conduct around them, and are vigilant in making sure that actions support the values, will find it easier to build a healthy organizational culture.

HOW DOES AN EXECUTIVE DIRECTOR ESTABLISH VALUES AS THE GUIDING PRINCIPLES IN THE ORGANIZATION?

The Executive Director generally plays a leadership role in discovering and establishing an organization's values. But everyone in the nonprofit is responsible for articulating them and working with them daily. The following exercise will help organizations determine their values, write them down, and apply them in the workplace.

It is very important to realize that an organization's values are not always easy to articulate, and there is often disagreement about what they are, how they are defined, and how they are or should be applied. Because the understanding and articulation of an organization's values is paramount to an Executive Director's ability to provide strong leadership, it is worth the time and patience to go through the exercise.

When there is a set of agreed-upon values and their applications, the leaders in the nonprofit will have their guiding principles for everything else—the organization's vision, its code of conduct, its programs and services, the basis for all communications, and much more.

WHAT IS *CULTURAL COMPETENCE* AND WHY IS IT SO IMPORTANT?

One of the organizational values that is receiving more and more attention as it becomes increasingly important is cultural competence. This is often a difficult value to understand, and there is no precise way it shows up in an organization. *Cultural competence* is defined as the guiding principle for a set of behaviors, attitudes, and policies that enable an organization to work effectively across cultures. As with all values, it is never achieved; it is always a work in progress.

Nonprofit leaders will often say their organizations are culturally competent because of the diversity of staff or clients served, or because of diversity training sessions, or a policy of transparent decision making. Indeed, these are elements of being a culturally competent organization. But a truly culturally competent organization has integrated an ability to evaluate and adapt services and internal policies readily and smoothly to be respectful to diverse populations.

For example, a hospice in the United States that chooses the value of cultural competence must learn and adapt the Western concepts of death and dying to the ethnicities, religions, ages, and so on of all persons served. There is ongoing learning involved with any organization that aspires to be culturally competent, and ongoing listening to people inside and outside the nonprofit for new ways to do so.

Exhibit 5.2
Values Exercise

We recommend having a facilitator lead the organization through this exercise. Having an outside person helps any group be more objective, and it allows the ED to participate on the same basis as any other person in attendance. The exercise is divided into steps to make it easier to understand and follow.

Step One: Gather all key staff, Board, and volunteers together for a daylong meeting with the intended outcomes of articulating the organization's values, defining them, and determining where they are or should be applied in the workplace.

Step Two: Define the word *values* for the group, and give some examples. Have people call out the values they believe are the guiding principles of the organization; write them down on a big sheet of paper.

Caution: Encourage people to call out values that can actually be attained such as transparency or inclusiveness or client-centeredness. Each will need to be reviewed in Step Five to determine the organization's ability to put the value into action.

Step Three: Define each of the listed values after reviewing them with the group. Depending on the size of the group, this might be more efficiently done in small groups. It isn't necessary at this point to have a full definition; bullet points will do. For instance, a tenants' rights group listed *compassion* as a value. The definition might include awareness for someone's difficult situation, concern for the welfare of the tenant and family, desire to relieve suffering.

Step Four: It is likely that as the group goes through the definitions, some values will overlap and can be blended together into one definition.

Caution: Expect a lot of discussion about these definitions and whether or not there is agreement on the values. Many times a group will spend hours, and sometimes weeks, on this part of the exercise. It is worth the time and effort to agree on what the values are and how they are defined.

Step Five: Take each of the values and have the group explain how it is applied or performed in the organization. For instance, the value *compassion* might be applied as follows:

- Listening to a client's tough situation without judgment or blame for the circumstances
- Focusing services on those at greatest risk of losing their housing
- Working with city officials to develop compassion-valued policies for tenants

Step Six: Write everything down and share the values and their applications with internal and external stakeholders. The document should be reviewed at least annually for discussion and updates.

The need for the value in organizations becomes increasingly important as we become a truly global society. In many areas of the United States, immigrant populations are growing faster than native-born. They bring a wonderful mixture of customs, values, languages, religions, and beliefs to this country. Additionally, the number of U.S.-born persons of color is exceeding the number of Caucasians in California and other states. Beyond the wide diversity of immigrant populations and ethnic cultures, nonprofits must also pay attention to the rich and broad attitudes, beliefs, values, and norms of the individuals working in the organization and those served by it.

The United States no longer has a dominant culture, and nonprofit leaders must all adapt their organizations to this reality. Those who are skeptical and slow will find they have lost their competitive advantage. Programs that are not designed based on cultural competence will lose clients, donors, funders, and community support. If they are not multicultural in their services, their quality and effectiveness will diminish. For example, a primary health care clinic watched its client population change from low-income Caucasians to low-income Vietnamese as more families moved into the clinic's service area. Instead of educating themselves on Vietnamese health care customs and practices, its staff required the families to adopt Western medicine practices. For several months, the clinic administrators and community leaders fought over the need for change. Meanwhile the quality of care was rapidly decreasing as families either did not understand the instructions given to them or their customs and beliefs prohibited them from following the medical orders. Finally, a new medical director was hired who embraced the value of cultural competence and began the big task of educating and training his staff to adapt to the needs of the Vietnamese families. In addition, the Vietnamese community leaders helped in creating new materials that would be understood by clients and they helped in hiring and training interpreters.

Executive Directors will also lose staff and volunteers if they are not adapting communication systems, decision-making styles, learning processes, and codes conduct based on cultural competency. Organizations with frequent turnover can rarely be effective and strong. On the other hand, the nonprofit leaders who embrace cultural competence will have organizations that are well-respected and effective in meeting the needs of their communities.

HOW DOES AN EXECUTIVE DIRECTOR LEAD A CULTURALLY COMPETENT ORGANIZATION?

To provide leadership, the Executive Director and other staff, volunteers, and Board leaders should have ongoing discussions about what *culturally competent* means, and how it is—and should be—applied in the organization. A definition for *cultural competence* has been given in this chapter—but what does it mean for your nonprofit? What other values does your organization have that contribute to this guiding principle? Some of these values might be equity, inclusion, parity, and empowerment. When you read your values statement or list of guiding principles, do you see any of these values somewhere? If not, a broader discussion with Board members and staff is needed to ensure that the values are fully applied in the organization and its code of conduct supports them. It is very important that everyone understands and accepts these values and that they have a shared meaning in your organization.

The workplace environment is also a part of being culturally competent. Ask yourself these questions:

- Do workplace signs, staff materials, and other written information meet the language needs of staff and people who are being served by them?
- Are there staff or volunteers who can speak the languages of our clients?
- Is the workplace fully accessible for persons with disabilities?
- Are holidays and vacation schedules sensitive to the religious and cultural needs of staff?

- Are the work processes of certain jobs adapted so that their essential functions can be successfully accomplished by individuals with disabilities?

- Do our policies address discrimination and harassment in the workplace?

- Do we have flexible work schedules to accommodate individuals who cannot work the traditional nine-to-five day?

- Is our technology accessible to all staff, even those who telecommute?

- Is our decision making transparent as possible at all levels of our organization?

- What is our plan for ensuring that the Board has broad representation? Does it include practices that ensure inclusiveness and respect for differing opinions?

If you can answer yes at all points, then you are creating a culturally competent organization. If not, then you and your Board have work to do. A good place to start is with a task force of staff and Board members to identify a vision of your ideal culturally competent workplace and a plan to achieve it. Then your leadership and that of others on the task force is needed to make sure that the plan is carried out and the vision is realized.

The Executive Director also needs to look at formal and informal relationships in the organization. Who talks to whom? In the halls, meetings, retreats, or other gatherings, do you see staff clustering based on their similarities, or is there a comfortable atmosphere where everyone interacts with everyone else regardless of differences?

Another way to be a positive role model is to encourage staff and Board members to join and participate in the activities of other nonprofits or membership groups that promote the values of cultural competency. These groups offer learning opportunities as well as opportunities to share information about your own organization. These learnings can be brought back and discussed with staff, volunteers, and Board members to help them expand their knowledge as well.

In this chapter, we look at organizational values and how critical they are for focused leadership and organizational effectiveness. The values are part of an organization's culture, as described in the preceding chapter. They are also essential to the organization's vision for itself and the community it serves. The next chapter provides you with the essential ingredients for translating values into vision.

TIPS FOR SUCCESS

- Compare articulated values to behaviors within the organization to make sure they are well aligned.

- Ensure the values that are developed are actually possible to achieve. Tie each value to actions within the organization that exemplify it.

- Make it clear to all that some values have a higher ranking, or higher priority, than others. Also make it clear to all when there is a change needed in the ranking of values.

- Expect the discussion with staff and Board to take awhile before reaching agreement and clarity on values.

Creating a Vision and Plan

*Unimpeded on a daily basis by the concern for survival, free from the
generalized assumption of scarcity, a person [that is, a visionary]
stands in the great place of possibility in a posture of openness,
with an unfettered imagination for what can be.*

—Rosamund and Benjamin Zander,
The Art of Possibility

Being a visionary requires someone to have imagination and to dream about what is possible. Martin Luther King Jr. was one of this society's greatest visionaries. His "I have a dream" speech reflected his passion for the future; it has inspired greatness in generations of people committed to social change.

Organizational vision comes from the collective voices of people who dream of what is possible for their nonprofits and their communities. They bring ideas, passion, and imagination to shape the vision, and they are inspired by it.

Executive Directors are the keepers of the vision in their organizations. They often lead the process to develop it, manage the process to communicate it in an inspirational way, and support others as they work to achieve it.

To succeed at achieving an organizational vision, there must be a plan. In today's fast-paced, ever-changing environment, strategic plans have become more flexible, with the mission, vision, and values holding the organization steady. The road to achieve these is built with short-term objectives, work plans, and benchmarks that are reviewed at least annually and modified to keep them relevant. Executive Directors often lead the process to develop a strategic plan, and are often responsible for ensuring the relevance of the objectives to achieve the vision. But everyone in the organization has a role in developing a strategic plan, making progress on the objectives, and achieving the vision.

This chapter addresses the concept of vision and planning by way of the following questions:

- What is a vision and why is it important?
- How does the Executive Director lead the way to having a shared organizational vision?
- Why is planning important to an organization's vision, and what is the Executive Director's role in this process?
- If you're always in crisis or catch-up mode as an Executive Director, how do you find time to plan?

WHAT IS A VISION AND WHY IS IT IMPORTANT?

In *The Leadership Challenge* James Kouzes and Barry Posner define the word *vision* as "an ideal and unique image of the future." That is, a vision is your picture of what is possible for your organization to accomplish within the community it serves.

Visions are never negative! They always picture hope and greatness, aiming at changing the world for those you serve. Kouzes and Posner give the following characteristics for vision:

- Vision suggests future orientation.
- Vision connotes a standard of excellence, an ideal. It implies a choice of values.
- Vision has the quality of uniqueness. It hints at what makes something special.

Vision statements articulate how your community is changed if you successfully fulfill your mission. It is your image of your organization making a profound difference in your community.

For instance, the American Humane Association states, "American Humane envisions a nation where no child or animal will ever be the victim of abuse or neglect." Another organization states its vision is "an end to HIV/AIDS in our community." The Smithsonian Museum of Natural History's vision statement is "understanding the natural world and everything in it." All these statements speak to a future and the organization's success in making its community (however big or small) a better place.

Having a vision and a written vision statement is important for an organization because, without it, no one in the organization—including the Executive Director—ever feels inspired to move beyond the daily grind and create new opportunities for fulfilling the nonprofit's mission.

Often, the lack of vision can mean a lack of focus for the organization as well. The famous saying "if you don't know where you are going, then anywhere will do" speaks to this lack of focus and direction. When there is vision, there is focus, which in turn helps the nonprofit expend resources wisely and channel the energy of staff, volunteers, and Board members in a single direction toward the future.

HOW DOES THE EXECUTIVE DIRECTOR LEAD THE WAY TO HAVING A SHARED ORGANIZATIONAL VISION?

When an organization is forming, the people creating it often informally discuss and agree on the vision. The organization is being created in response to some need that the Founder and others feel must be addressed. They have a picture of what should be different, and that is their vision. As organizations evolve and community needs change, the vision often does too so that it stays relevant and inspirational.

Changing an organization's vision should not be a regular process that happens with every change of leadership or new funding source that might be pursued. Inspirational visions are true big-picture thinking and must be grounded in the purpose of the organization, its values, and the needs of the community. Everyone inside and outside an organization owns its vision, and it is changed only when it has been attained, or when what is grounding the vision has changed.

An organization's vision is most often written down as a vision statement. There is a lot of confusion about the difference between mission and vision statements. Both are important to have because they offer big-picture perspectives that guide the programs and services in any nonprofit. Here is an easy way to remember the differences between them:

- A *mission statement* describes the purpose of an organization and its business. Example: The mission of XYZ nonprofit is to provide children and their families in ABC community with counseling, education, and support to prevent childhood diabetes.

- A *vision statement* is the future picture if the XYZ organization achieves its mission. Example: The XYZ organization envisions the ABC community as home to healthy, active children who are all free of the risks of diabetes.

There are many ways to create a vision statement for your organization. It should be a group process involving Board members, staff, volunteers, and others who have a role in moving the organization toward the vision. In some cases, an Executive Director will have a clear vision of the future and can use this as a starting point for discussion. There is a risk, of course, that others in the organization may not share this vision. So look for some level of agreement prior to putting an untested vision out there for others to react to.

Most often, an organizational vision is derived from many voices from within the organization as people speak from their hearts about a future that excites them as it relates to the mission of the nonprofit. Sometimes this process takes only a few hours, perhaps as part of a strategic planning retreat. Other times, the Executive Director and key internal stakeholders will spend many weeks and months discussing the vision for their organization. One key role of the Executive Director in any group visioning process is to provide reality checks. Make sure the vision being shaped is guided by the organization's mission and values and is responsive to the needs in the community.

Many visioning exercises can be used with a group. The simplest approach is to ask each participant to describe the community you serve once your organization is successful. Ask yourselves, if we are successful, what is different in the community from today? Why is this important? Answer these questions in the present tense—for instance, an animal welfare organization might respond to these questions by saying: if we are successful, all our community's companion animals are loved, respected, and in homes. A movement arts organization might respond by saying: if we are successful, our community is filled with vibrant, innovative dance works that are valued by all. Speaking about the vision as if it was happening now generates excitement and a creative process that can lead to a powerful vision statement and can inspire people to a great new future.

Usually, the Executive Director and a few of the participants will take all the ideas gathered and draft a vision statement for review and final approval by the larger group. This is another place for the Executive Director to make sure that the vision statement is truly in touch with the community and the organization's mission. It may take several drafts and several months before a vision statement is accepted. Take the time needed for acceptance because it is important for the people inside the organization to own the vision statement. If they are not inspired and excited by it, then external stakeholders will not support it. A shared vision is an opportunity to attract donors and gain important allies or stakeholders for your mission.

Developing the organization's vision statement is the first step. Making this statement known and remembered internally and externally is equally important. It should be visible on your Web site, posted in a public space in your organization, highlighted in your newsletter and other written materials. If your organization has MySpace or Facebook pages, make sure the vision statement is there too. Every time there is an opportunity for public speaking or contact with the media, the organization's representative should talk about the vision and why it is important to the whole community. Making sure the vision statement is highly visible is an important role of the Executive Director. There may be staff or volunteers who manage the Internet locations for your organization and communicate with external stakeholders, but it is the Executive Director who makes sure this happens and is always looking for new opportunities to make the vision known in the community.

Creating a vision statement is often part of a bigger strategic planning process that is also led by the ED. However, goals and priorities shift in organizations much more often than the vision. It should provide the future perspective for the organization with all short- and long-term plans tied to someday realizing this vision. The response to the next question shows how vision and planning are closely linked together.

WHY IS PLANNING IMPORTANT TO AN ORGANIZATION'S VISION, AND WHAT IS THE EXECUTIVE DIRECTOR'S ROLE IN THIS PROCESS?

The mission and vision statements describe the biggest picture of your nonprofit. A plan is your road map to realizing your mission and achieving your vision. Organization-wide plans that provide goals, objectives, budgets, and fundraising tasks to support the plan are often referred to as *strategic plans*. They are generally developed for three or five years, or longer. But because we live in a rapidly changing society, it is becoming increasingly difficult to think and plan for more than several months. Too many factors, such as economic downturns, staff turnover, unexpected surges or downward slides in demand for services—all these and more can make a strategic plan quickly obsolete. As a result, even the best strategic plans end up on a shelf and are forgotten.

This is not to say that organizational planning is not important. It is critical to success, and the Executive Director is often the person in the organization who provides the leadership in this process. But strategic plans today should be fluid enough to allow staff and Board to respond quickly to any unforeseen changes. Rather than having a strategic plan that sets out program and administrative goals, objectives, and activities for the next three to five years, we recommend the type of plan outlined in Exhibit 6.1. In this plan, the three-to-five-year goals, objectives, and activities are replaced with strategic directions and measurable one-year goals and objectives. Strategic directions are sometimes called priorities. They give focus to an organization's plan while also allowing flexibility. Strategic directions might include expanding one or more programs in response to a greater need or reducing services because a need is no longer there. They could also indicate an organization's priority to balance the budget, especially in uncertain economic times. Just remember that these strategic directions or priorities should stem from the analysis of strengths, weaknesses, opportunities, and threats rather than being created in a vacuum.

Having a strategic plan with big-picture mission and vision statements, broad strategic directions, and a one-year plan to move you toward the first three items gives a strong focus to an organization while allowing for flexibility when the environment changes. It is always good to start your strategic planning process with a clear understanding of the current environment. An assessment tells you how things are now in your organization and the community, and this can also be a guide for what is changing.

Exhibit 6.1
Strategic Plan Contents

A. Mission statement

B. Vision statement

C. Values statement

D. Environmental assessment of strengths, weaknesses, opportunities, and threats (SWOT analysis)

E. Strategic directions that respond to the SWOT analysis and further the mission and vision

F. One-year program and administrative goals and objectives that are tied to the strategic directions

G. Support documents, including the budget, fundraising plan, and dashboard measurements for success for the objectives

---

Sometimes the most difficult thing to do is decide it is time to do some strategic planning. In most cases, it is the Executive Director who starts the ball rolling with the planning process for one or more of the following reasons:

- The direction of the organization is no longer in line with the vision.
- The organization seems to be losing focus in its programs and services.
- Staff, Board members, or volunteers don't see themselves as part of the whole organization.
- Programs are decreasing in size with no understanding why this is happening.
- There is little interest in the community regarding the activities of the organization, and support is dwindling.

These are indicators that a nonprofit is losing touch with the community and its focus. Because Executive Directors are looking inward and outward for their organizations, they generally see these warning signs first.

Every organization approaches the strategic planning process differently. There is no gold standard for strategic planning, nor is there a one-size-fits-all approach. The following story from the field is one illustration of how an

Creating a Vision and Plan   **83**

Executive Director moved her nonprofit into planning mode and the leadership role she took to complete the process.

STORY FROM THE FIELD

Cathy, a recently hired Executive Director, was experiencing major disconnects with her Board and staff regarding the size and direction of the organization's core programs. It was somewhat unclear what the core programs were and how they made an impact in the community. This was a human services organization with a mission of providing food and nutrition counseling to low-income families in its community of 350,000 people. The organization had no vision statement, although Cathy did perceive a shared vision of every family in their community having access to nutritious food and a healthy lifestyle. Beyond this, there seemed to be little focus and lots of bickering.

Cathy met first with her Board and then with her management team to discuss the issues she saw and the benefits of strategic planning to understand the community and to focus programs to meet needs related to their mission. With everyone's blessing, she sought pro bono consulting help from a local university with a strong business school whose graduate students enjoyed helping nonprofits conduct environmental assessments. A small planning committee was formed consisting of two influential Board members and two managers, plus Cathy. Their role was to manage the pro bono consultants, provide leadership to the planning process, and ensure a healthy and transparent flow of communication throughout the organization.

The environmental assessment work lasted a few months and involved many stakeholders inside and outside the organization who shared their ideas and concerns about the work of this nonprofit. The consultants also reviewed many internal documents, including financial statements, program goals, organizational charts, development and marketing materials, and Board action plans.

The consultants ended their work with the nonprofit with a day-long retreat with the Board and managers to discuss their findings and make some recommendations. Their findings were difficult to hear because the organization's programs were not in step with what the community needed. The external environment had changed dramatically; more low-income families needed help with food, counseling, and support, but were not receiving quality and timely services from this nonprofit. Also, the community people interviewed by the consultants knew about this organization, but were not clear about what it did or why that was important. Additionally, the consultants pointed out that the organization was nearing a financial crisis due to deficits that were growing each year. Finally, they told everyone that the Board of Directors needed to develop itself to provide the oversight and direction required of it. Board members relied too heavily on the Executive Director position for leadership and needed to forge a better partnership with her. The consultants made several recommendations that were shaped into strategic priorities during the day-long meeting:

1. Ensure programs are following industry best practices and reaching the people needing assistance with food, nutrition counseling, and other support services.

2. Balance the budget and keep programs and services within their budget limits.

3. Build excitement in the community for the organization's vision, programs, and accomplishments.

4. Develop the Board of Directors to provide needed oversight and direction, as well as support to the Executive Director.

Bringing the managers and Board together to discuss the consultants' findings and to develop strategic priorities was beneficial to everyone. The immediate result was a greater sense of working together for shared priorities. The planning committee held several meetings with Board, staff, and volunteers to hear their vision of how the community would be different if their organization successfully met the needs of low-income people needing food and nutrition counseling. At the same time, Cathy assigned a manager to research best practices in other nonprofits offering similar services in the same and other communities. She chose a manager with the most knowledge of program operations and a curiosity to learn best practices, and gave others in his department more responsibility to develop their own management skills as they temporarily filled in for him.

Another few months passed by but an exciting vision statement and clear understanding of best practices were the result of the hard work of many people, and the guidance of Cathy. At this point, she was able to set annual goals with her managers that included indicators for success in working toward the strategic priorities.

The process Cathy and her people employed may sound lengthy and time-consuming. When an organization does strategic planning for the first time, it can take longer than expected and require more time than desired. But the results of the process can create a more effective and efficient organization that will need fewer hours in future years. Reviewing the environmental scan to check for new trends or changes should be an ongoing part of the ED's job. Setting annual goals and success indicators takes less time as managers become used to the process. Making sure those goals align with the vision, mission, and strategic priorities is an important activity for the Board and Executive Director. Quite often, this can be done in a specially scheduled Board meeting or as part of a retreat.

IF YOU'RE ALWAYS IN CRISIS OR CATCH-UP MODE AS AN EXECUTIVE DIRECTOR, HOW DO YOU FIND TIME TO PLAN?

The first thing to do is step back and understand what is causing the feelings of crisis or catch-up. Is this a temporary situation for the organization, as when a funding cut demands immediate attention? Or is this an ongoing, chronic condition? Sometimes some immediate priority really must be addressed before engaging in planning, but more often the perception that there is no time to plan means that the organization is in an almost constant crisis mode.

In reality, the absence of planning is often what causes the crisis or apparent need to catch up. When feelings of panic or stress kick in during difficult times, it is hard to imagine sitting down to come up with a plan. Yet this may well be the most essential step to moving beyond the current situation. Taking a few hours to do some short-term strategizing can save an Executive Director countless hours of stress and worry down the road.

Also, remember that the Executive Director does not have to do all the planning personally. As the leader, the ED is expected to make sure planning happens. In very small organizations where the Executive Director is the whole staff, the Board of Directors should be heavily engaged in mission and vision discussions, in setting direction and priorities, and determining its own role in achieving them. In larger organizations, the staff and volunteers are there to actively participate in setting annual goals and implementation strategies. They also are essential to getting the goals met for the year.

When an Executive Director sees the organization in crisis, ongoing planning processes may need to be temporarily suspended while crisis planning takes the forefront. But ongoing planning processes should not be forgotten. If the perception is that the nonprofit is always catching up, then the plans that have been set may be too ambitious. The Executive Director's leadership is needed to communicate with everyone in the organization that planning is needed to reset priorities and make work more doable. Plans are not set in stone, and the Executive Director's leadership helps allow for the flexibility needed to keep the organization moving forward at a realistic pace.

TIPS FOR SUCCESS

- Having a written vision statement gives everyone inside and outside your nonprofit a sense of excitement about the organization as well as focus and direction.

- Vision statements are developed with the passion, creativity, and inspiration of those who care about your organization. Make sure lots of input flows into the development.

- Leading your organization into a strategic planning process will help keep everyone moving toward the vision. Take time for this important process; it saves time down the road.

- Make sure your organization is ready for strategic planning. If you are going through a major crisis, plan your way out of the crisis first before attempting longer-term thinking.

Determining Organizational Effectiveness

*Each mission must be thought through in terms of results. People
are no longer simply interested to know, is it a good cause?
Instead they want to see a demonstration of achievement
as a responsible and effective organization.*

—Peter Drucker

As Peter Drucker eloquently puts it, nonprofits are finding increasing scrutiny regarding their effectiveness. Stakeholders expect nonprofits to be in touch with their communities and to make decisions based on knowing what will work. Partners and collaborators expect organizations to follow industry best practices for nonprofits in general and for their specific cause. Funding from individuals, foundations, the government, and other sources is given based on results and accomplishments. For its Executive Director to be successful, an organization must demonstrate it is operating efficiently and making a real difference.

Determining nonprofit effectiveness goes beyond good intentions, numbers of people served, or the financial bottom line. It is more than evaluating a single program or set of activities, achievements, or outcomes. It is measured in terms of achieving the overall goals in the organization's strategic plan and fulfilling the organization's mission. A fundamental question that every Board of Directors and Executive Director should ask on a regular basis is "How well are we fulfilling our mission in the community we serve?"

This chapter looks at ways Executive Directors can encourage and evaluate the effectiveness of an organization, and how that success ties to their own. It addresses these questions:

- What does an effective nonprofit organization look like?
- How soon after starting should the Executive Director begin to examine the organization's effectiveness?
- How does an Executive Director tie personal performance and effectiveness to that of the organization?
- What happens if the Board and Executive Director determine the organization is no longer effective?

WHAT DOES AN EFFECTIVE NONPROFIT ORGANIZATION LOOK LIKE?

The question of recognizing effectiveness goes to the heart of this book. The simple answer is that an effective organization is one that can demonstrate results toward fulfilling its mission and realizing its vision. This answer assumes that the mission and vision are still relevant and the results are measurable.

An effective organization will use the results of its measurements to change its behaviors as needed: it will quickly modify its methods of service provision until measurements improve, or it will reexamine its measurements to determine whether they are valid, or it will reexamine its program theory to see if the underlying assumptions are flawed. Effectiveness grows from these efforts to continually improve the services it delivers, based on the measurements it makes. That is where simplicity ends and the complex job of defining an effective non-profit organization begins.

Nonprofits can employ dozens of tools, methods, and types of evaluations to help evaluate organizational effectiveness. In recent years, new online tools have been developed that make the evaluation process even easier. A good example of an online survey can be found at www.centerpointforleaders.org/effectiveness .html. It is a relatively short survey that highlights all the key indicators of a successful nonprofit.

Nonprofit leaders can also create their own surveys through online Web sites such as Survey Monkey. It is possible to develop an online survey, e-mail stakeholders a link to your survey or have the link on your organization's blog or Web site, and have stakeholders respond to your questions quickly and easily online. One organization used Survey Monkey to ask stakeholders to help determine the effectiveness of its mission and programs. Instead of the usual 10 percent response rate, more than 25 percent of the organization's stakeholders gave their opinion. The information received was very helpful in the effort to make one core program much more effective in the community.

Surveys are only one way to evaluate your organization. We have assembled a list of resources for the chapter at the end of the book to guide and inform your process. Exhibit 7.1 summarizes some of the more common methods.

By using the methods listed in the exhibit, an organization can conduct needs assessments to make sure its mission, vision, and programs are still relevant, determine new trends in or affecting it and its environment, monitor organizational effectiveness, and conduct feasibility studies for possible new programs or partnerships.

Many Boards of Directors and EDs believe that understanding their organizations' effectiveness requires highly complex processes, almost always involving the employment of outside experts at significant expense. Others are sure they simply know what's best and define effectiveness based on personal perceptions. As a result, processes for measuring and defining organizational effectiveness range from highly personal and overly simplistic to extremely complex and theoretical assessments where the outcome can be lost in the process. But the truth is that evaluating effectiveness doesn't need to be complex, costly, or externally managed. What it does require is an organization-wide culture that openly embraces the following characteristics in both the organization and the Executive Director:

- Awareness of the emerging trends that affect the organization, its mission, and its clients, coupled with the agility to create responsive programs and systems.

- Insightfulness to look deep into the nonprofit's underlying culture and articulate it, along with the strength to change it if necessary.

- Ability to form and nurture positive relationships with Board members, paid and unpaid staff, and external stakeholders that allow the organization to pursue mutually agreed-upon goals effectively.

- Initiative to explore and form partnerships and strategic alliances that build on shared strengths to develop the nonprofit's capacity to serve its community.

- Vision for the organization and an ability to articulate it in a way that inspires others.

- Resourcefulness to attract adequate time, talent, and funding to keep the organization thriving, and to ensure these assets are wisely invested.

- Openness to feedback and an environment of continuous learning that monitors individual and organizational effectiveness.

- Courage to improve upon or change what isn't working well.

Every nonprofit displays these characteristics differently, but they are an essential foundation for an effective organization to build programs and services. Without this foundation, the best evaluation processes and tools will encounter resistance or inaction.

Boards of Directors have a fiduciary duty to their community to monitor the success of their organizations. As part of any strategic planning process, the Board and Executive Director should develop outcomes that measure organizational effectiveness. Outcomes should be program focused to make sure programs are progressing toward the organization's mission and vision. For instance, an organization serving low-income seniors developed a new strategic plan with several key priorities based on its mission of providing a safety net of services to keep seniors in their homes as long as possible. One priority was to prevent elder financial abuse. Several unsuspecting low-income seniors in the community had lost their homes to a scam artist, and this organization was determined to prevent such losses in the future. A new elder financial abuse prevention program was developed with several program outcome measures to make sure the priority was met:

- Number of low-income seniors educated about elder financial abuse

- Percentage increase in knowledge of preventing financial abuse among these seniors

- Success rate among these seniors in avoiding financial abuse

Numeric targets were established for the first year, and evaluated quarterly at Board meetings. Of course, staff evaluated the program much more frequently with the Executive Director. Staff observed during the first evaluation that the training sessions on preventing financial abuse were not getting the desired results, so they modified the training to improve it. This was a good lesson for everyone that continuous measuring and adjustments will increase effectiveness.

Determining whether your organization is effective is crucial to its sustainability. If measuring effectiveness has not been part of your standard operating procedures, we recommend beginning a program-by-program review so it is not an overwhelming process. Although it might take some time, knowing that your mission and vision are still relevant—and that your programs are really helping your organization fulfill its mission—makes the review well worth the time and effort.

HOW SOON AFTER STARTING SHOULD THE EXECUTIVE DIRECTOR BEGIN TO EXAMINE THE ORGANIZATION'S EFFECTIVENESS?

The short answer to the question of timing is *right away!* An Executive Director new to the organization needs to understand the current environment—what is working and what is not, what is in place and what isn't. Many nonprofits will undertake an assessment or audit as a prelude to their search process to help them define the skills and experience they need in their new ED. If this hasn't been done, newly hired Executive Directors need to initiate a review of finances, management, programs, systems, the Board, community relations, fundraising, and staff within the first few weeks. The information gathered will help drive the ED's priorities and negotiate performance expectations with the Board. In addition, a good way to begin conversations with staff and volunteers, Board members, and occasional key external stakeholders about the effectiveness of the organization is to ask each person these five simple but insightful sets of questions:

- What do you think this organization is very good at doing? What have its greatest accomplishments been?
- What are barriers facing the organization? Facing the Board? Facing the staff or volunteers? Of those barriers, which ones are the highest priority to address?
- What is the mission of this organization? Is it still relevant?
- What is it we are trying to accomplish with our programs? How do we measure if we are successful?
- If this organization were operating at its peak, what would that look like? What would the organization be doing differently?

Gathering this information from internal as well as external sources gives an Executive Director a broadly interpreted picture of the organization's strengths and the challenges it faces and helps define and prioritize the issues to resolve. The information also gives the ED an understanding of what individuals think the organization's mission is, what it is successful at doing, what it needs to do better, and what success would look like if the organization were functioning at its optimum.

Quite often, an Executive Director will be satisfied with the results, and be happy that the organization is serving the community effectively. There are times, though, that the newly hired ED will believe some tweaking should be done or even outright changes need to occur to increase effectiveness. Sometimes newly hired Executive Directors are so eager to please during these initial conversations that they make promises of "fixing the organization" that simply can't be kept. Feelings of being overwhelmed and stretched too far often result from unrealistic promises or expectations set in the first few months on the job. To avoid this, it is important to make it clear that the purpose of the evaluation is to gather information about the current state of the organization, meet everyone, and establish jointly developed priorities for the future.

Another common thought held by Executive Directors is that once all the information is gathered and a good picture of the organization has emerged, then it becomes the ED's job to do it all—to personally provide everything the organization needs. That's a noble intention, but generally impossible to fulfill—especially if the organization is not operating effectively.

A better practice is to make sure that key internal stakeholders in the organization (typically the Board and management staff) agree with your insights and your solutions. It is a shared responsibility of Board and staff to work with the Executive Director to break down any barriers and set realistic next steps.

The Executive Director's job is to lead the process, not just fix the problems. The ED can lead the process by

- Identifying strengths and challenges and communicating them to the staff and Board of Directors
- Building a new vision of success that energizes and inspires everyone in the organization
- Seeking solutions and motivating others to carry them out

HOW DOES AN EXECUTIVE DIRECTOR TIE PERSONAL PERFORMANCE AND EFFECTIVENESS TO THAT OF THE ORGANIZATION?

Just as organizations need some level of self-assessment to evaluate their effectiveness, Executive Directors need feedback from their organizations on their own effectiveness. The first challenge is making time for the process. The second challenge is determining appropriate indicators that tie the effectiveness of the individual to that of the nonprofit.

Even though the hiring and evaluation of the Executive Director is one of the few specific governance roles spelled out as part of a nonprofit's incorporation papers, many Boards are delinquent in these duties, leaving the Executive Director in the awkward role of requesting feedback and designing the process. Rather than postpone the discussion to a formal annual event, invite casual ongoing feedback and opportunities to discuss midcourse corrections.

Newer EDs will often ask the Board Chair or Executive Committee for verbal feedback during the organizational review, after it is completed (when priorities are set for strengthening it), and after some time has elapsed to work toward those priorities. Ideally, a check-in will occur every quarter as the new ED settles into the position. Seasoned EDs who find themselves caught up in a challenge or crisis often seek feedback on how they are doing and ways that they might improve or learn from any mistakes.

It is extremely important that verbal feedback sessions between the Board and Executive Director be well structured with agreed-upon expectations. Appropriate indicators or measurements are important. Without specific goals or indicators, some evaluations turn into venting sessions that don't get to the heart of the ED's effectiveness at leading the organization or accomplishments against specific goals.

There should be a formal written Executive Director performance review at least annually. The review should be based on performance indicators agreed upon in advance by the Executive Director and the Board. Useful indicators may be narrow or broad, but they need to be defined for the specific priorities of the organization.

For instance, say your organization serves homeless children and families. A Board indicator of success could be the number of families who left the streets and moved into their own apartments by a specific date. While the Executive Director may not be directly involved in getting individual families off the streets, the leadership the ED provides the organization is responsible for its effectiveness in this area.

Another key indicator of success is the tenure and effectiveness of staff. If the average tenure is long, then this probably means that the work environment empowers people to do their best. Again, it is the Executive Director's leadership that is responsible. If the Executive Director does not build and maintain good working relationships with everyone inside the organization, and is not motivating, inspiring, and encouraging each person to learn and grow on the job, then the organization is not being as successful as it could be.

For many Executive Directors, the indicators will already be established as part of a strategic plan and of the annual work plans for staff. For EDs leading a local affiliate of a national or regional organization, indicators may be mandated by charter.

The task of defining and prioritizing five to ten indicators that realistically define effectiveness for the organization can lead to a healthy discussion among the Executive Director, Board, and staff. When the indicators are agreed upon, then they become the foundation of the ED evaluation process.

But what do you do if the organization has no strategic plan, no national mandate, no work plans? Perhaps the nonprofit is in formation, or it has just emerged from a transition with plans not yet in place, or people have not made planning a priority. You don't need to hold off until a comprehensive strategic plan is in place to decide what makes your organization successful and design measures for the ED's performance. Exhibit 7.2 outlines a process you can use if no indicators have been developed yet. You may also find it useful to refer to Chapter Three, where we discuss developing a work plan with your Board.

The creation of criteria that measure effectiveness in the nonprofit and in ED performance may also be a first step to beginning the longer-term planning process that has eluded the organization.

The following story from the field demonstrates how one nonprofit's Board and Executive Director conducted a performance review. The Executive Director had been with the organization for some time, although just recently hired as the ED. In his previous role as a program manager, he had excelled in connecting with the community and developing programs that met their needs. However, the organization had no strategic plan and no clear indicators that measured the overall success of the nonprofit.

Exhibit 7.2
Defining Performance Measures

As Executive Director, you will probably have to identify some, if not all, of the indicators that measure the organization's short-term success and can be tied to your own performance. Working in partnership with your full Board or a smaller committee, you can do the following:

1. Identify the critical issues or barriers facing the organization based upon some process of assessment or reflection.

2. Determine three to five priorities that are critical to addressing these issues or barriers, or to achieving the organization's vision or achieving organizational effectiveness.

3. Decide on a few measurable success criteria to use for monitoring progress toward achieving the priorities.

4. Incorporate the priorities and criteria into the annual ED evaluation process and make sure they are communicated to and adopted by the Board and staff.

5. Establish opportunities for regular feedback to the ED and a process for renegotiating these factors as necessary in response to internal or external shifts.

STORY FROM THE FIELD

The Board of Directors of a nonprofit serving migrant worker families asked Jorge, one of the organization's program managers, to step into the Executive Director position when it became available. He readily agreed, and at the time of this story, he had been serving as ED for approximately one year. He had received little feedback from the Board, although he frequently requested their input on how well they thought the organization was doing and how well he was doing as a leader. The responses Jorge received were vague but positive. Finally, he requested a written evaluation of his progress and gave the Board sample evaluation forms to use for the process. A Board committee was formed to conduct the evaluation via surveys with key staff managers and the entire Board of Directors. However, the committee quickly realized they could not tie Jorge's performance to anything specific except his job description, which had not been updated since he took the position. When this dilemma was presented to the Board and to Jorge, they decided the first step in the evaluation process was to establish performance benchmarks that they could agree on for the past year, but could also be used for future reviews. This was not an easy task since Jorge and Board members did not agree on the organizational priorities. Ultimately, they used the mission statement as the key focal point of the performance review since they all agreed it gave the organization direction and purpose.

After a few weeks of struggling over the criteria to use, it was finally agreed that the first year's evaluation would be based on three areas: external relations with community partners, program growth, and staff leadership. These three areas were chosen because Jorge's success in these areas directly contributed to the organization's effectiveness with the migrant family community served, and thus had a direct impact on the organization's ability to fulfill its mission. It was also agreed that the Board and Jorge would complete this performance review process with a clear ED work plan that would guide future evaluations.

Using examples from other organizations and online resources, the Board and Jorge developed questions that focused on ED leadership, as well as questions for a few key community partners that focused on collaboration and leadership. They also conducted a mini-program review that looked at statistical growth in the time that Jorge had been in the position. The Board members proceeded to ask their questions to the list of staff and partners that they and Jorge had agreed upon.

The results of the interviews and analysis gave Jorge important feedback. He learned that he was viewed inside and outside the organization as a respected leader, but that he also needed to give his staff more opportunities to build their management and leadership skills. He also learned that the Board of Directors needed more information from him, particularly financial data, to help them understand the financial condition of the organization. And Jorge learned that one program he thought was growing successfully was, in fact, lagging. There was concern about the organization's effectiveness in meeting the needs of the migrant workers served in this program.

Equally important to the specific feedback was the design of a work plan with specific ED goals and priorities for the coming year and clear indicators of how Jorge's success would be measured. Although the first year's performance review was sometimes awkward and tense due to the necessity of agreeing upon what was going to be measured, it resulted in a healthy process with good feedback for Jorge and a plan for the next year.

WHAT HAPPENS IF THE BOARD AND EXECUTIVE DIRECTOR DETERMINE THE ORGANIZATION IS NO LONGER EFFECTIVE?

This question starts from the assumption that the Board and Executive Director have identified what effectiveness looks like for their nonprofit. They may have used an online effectiveness survey and rated the organization as ineffective. Or there may be external criteria unique to that organization that are no longer being met, which could result in a loss of funding, regulatory approval, or community confidence. In rare instances, an organization may have actually fulfilled its mission in the community, leaving nothing to accomplish on that score, and the Board and staff have not yet taken the step of determining a new purpose and vision. Whatever the reasons, this is a time for some long soul-searching discussions.

The truth is that some nonprofits become obsolete because their programs have been so successful that the problem has been eradicated. Others lose touch with shifting trends and community priorities, or with their clients' needs. In many situations, the organization's programs are still needed, but the infrastructure (staffing, systems, leadership, technology, finances) is not there to support them. An organization may suffer a major loss of talent or resources, or experience monumental internal struggles that make it impossible to maintain effectiveness.

The process for deciding to close or restructure often takes a long time unless a major financial downturn forces everyone to be laid off. It is not an easy process because many options need to be reviewed, legal issues need to be handled correctly, and the community impact needs to be addressed. One example is a small organization providing educational and emotional support to medical professionals addressing issues of death and dying in highly multicultural communities. This organization had one program, and it was staffed by one part-time ED and forty volunteer trainers who presented the program to hundreds of medical providers. In spite of three years of hard effort to expand the organization to meet the demand, there was still not enough funding, and one consistent foundation funder had just announced it was withdrawing its support. There was no infrastructure to support this popular and much-needed service, and the Board of directors chose to close the organization and give the program to a larger nonprofit that could make it thrive. It took more than a year of difficult and emotional discussions to reach the decision to close and another year to move through the legal challenges of transferring the program and closing the organization, even though this was a tiny organization with only one program. The shutdown process becomes even more difficult with a larger nonprofit that has multiple programs serving a broader community. What made this closure successful was the desire of everyone inside and outside the organization to make sure the program survived even if the organization could not.

Everyone in the organization needs to be creative about the future. It is important for the Executive Director to be fair-minded and encourage these other ideas to be stated and incorporated into decisions being made about the nonprofit. Remember that an Executive Director does not have to be the only leader in the organization. Others will step forward, especially when tough decisions are being made, and the Executive Director needs to stay open to possibilities that may seem startling or even unimaginable at first glance.

Restructuring or closing a nonprofit organization is often emotional for those involved. You are not alone. Every year, nonprofit organizations cease operations. Usually, nonprofits consider three main options: merger, shutdown, and strategic reorganization. Within these options are an infinite number of possibilities depending on the vision and creativity of the organization. (See Chapter Ten on leading organizational change and Chapter Sixteen on partnerships and mergers for more help in making this difficult decision.)

When an organization is no longer effective, the Executive Director needs to be a very strong leader. People in any organization tend to blame or find fault when it is struggling; they often point the finger directly but wrongly at the ED. Change can be difficult, but organizational restructuring or closure is traumatic, especially if it is seen only in negative terms.

The ED's parting leadership challenge is to create a positive ending and acknowledge past accomplishments as well as challenges. Organizations whose people can buy into the decision (no matter how difficult), speak with one voice, and move forward are recognized for finding solutions that can best meet client needs and fulfill their mission. Keeping focused on the mission and what is best for those served is of paramount importance in creating a positive ending.

TIPS FOR SUCCESS

- It is not necessary to embark on an expensive, time-consuming evaluation process to determine organizational effectiveness. Find a process that works for your organization's needs and situation.

- For the results of an organization's effectiveness analysis to be heard and accepted, there must be buy-in to the importance of doing the analysis. Make sure the Board and key staff are involved in the process.

- If everyone determines the organization could be more effective, provide the leadership needed for the changes, but make sure others are doing the work with you.

- Your own effectiveness is tied to the success of your organization. Make sure there are clear and acceptable measures for your own success as well as your organization's.

- If, for whatever reasons, your organization has lost its effectiveness and is closing, focus on its past successes and make sure needed programs and services are moved to an organization that will continue them.

PART THREE

Executive Director as Change Agent

They always say time changes things, but you actually have to change them yourself.

—Andy Warhol,
The Philosophy of Andy Warhol

Nonprofit organizations are facing an extraordinary time of change as consumer needs become more complex, technology alters the way we communicate, donors increase their demands for accountability and measurable outcomes, and organizations recognize the need to monitor the evolving marketplace. Staying ahead of the curve becomes critical as Executive Directors try to keep their organizations strong and relevant. The information on visioning and planning in Part Two of this book will help an organization stay grounded as it moves through the inevitable changes it faces from the outside.

While viewing the evolving world outside the nonprofit, Executive Directors must also look internally because an evolutionary process is working there as well. Nonprofits move through a life cycle that represents numerous changes for the organization, requiring the ED to understand and provide leadership while managing and supporting the change processes.

Leading internal change doesn't always come easily. Many healthy nonprofits have foundered as their Executive Directors tried valiantly to help them embrace the need to change to meet a crisis or seize an opportunity. Staff members are understandably resistant to change that may affect their personal turf. Boards can be skeptical of the benefits of new ways of doing things, and the consumers may be able to focus only on the short-term impact on themselves instead of on the long-term benefits to the community. When an organizational shift is needed, it is often the Executive Director who senses it first—only to find how difficult it can be to persuade others in the nonprofit that change must happen.

Chapter Eight explores the changing nonprofit sector and new trends that are emerging in the twenty-first century. We also focus attention inward, in Chapter Nine, explaining organizational life cycles and how Executive Directors need to grow and change along with their nonprofits. Finally, we talk specifically about ways to manage change and lead a healthy change process in Chapter Ten.

By looking both externally and internally, an Executive Director can be a successful change agent in the organization. At the heart of all this change lies the mission of the nonprofit and the need to ensure a healthy and stable organization that can continue to move toward a powerful vision.

Embracing a Changing Nonprofit Environment

*Contrary to the common belief that the nonprofit sector should operate
more like a business, we should instead be remodeling
business to look more like nonprofits.*

—Paul Light, New York University

The nonprofit sector is one of the most exciting, complex, and rapidly changing parts of the modern economy. As an Executive Director, you face incredible opportunities, shifting revenue sources, changing societal needs, evolving government and business values, new technologies, emerging competition, and ever-increasing public scrutiny. The next decade will challenge you and the entire sector to respond with new thinking, new systems, expanded capacity to learn and adapt, greater resilience, and an increased capacity to integrate change into every aspect of your organization.

By your very purpose, you, as Executive Director, are a champion of change in your community.

As you embrace the opportunities of this fast-moving sector it can be useful to consider the following thought-provoking questions about how it is evolving:

- Why is change synonymous with the identity of the nonprofit sector?
- What role does the Executive Director have in making change happen outside the organization?
- How are the lines that have traditionally defined the business and nonprofit sectors changing?
- What can the Executive Director do to influence funders' efforts to shape the nonprofit sector?
- How does the Executive Director manage effectively through boom-and-bust economic cycles?
- What are some of the new demands for accountability and measurable outcomes in nonprofits?
- How are rapid changes in technology impacting the nonprofit workplace?

WHY IS CHANGE SYNONYMOUS WITH THE IDENTITY OF THE NONPROFIT SECTOR?

Over time, the term *nonprofit* has been defined in myriad ways, from "a reflection of the collective consciousness of society" to "a legal tax advantage in exchange for doing good." In addition, the sector has been branded with a broad range of labels, most of which have clouded rather than clarified an understanding of exactly what a nonprofit is. Labels such as nongovernmental organizations (NGOs), social entrepreneurs, public benefit corporations, or the Third Sector have painted a better picture of what its members are not than of what they are. Attempts to define, classify, and explain the sector in theoretical and economic terms have also failed to establish agreement on a definition.

One definition, however, has survived the test of time; it seems as valid today in the twenty-first century as it was throughout the twentieth century. Nonprofit organizations are consistently seen as the conduit through which individuals channel their ideals, passions, and resources and initiate change that is intended to improve the lives of the people they serve and the communities in which they live.

In contrast to the mission of business to generate profits, or that of government to control and administer, the mission of the nonprofit sector is to create a better world. The "three-legged stool" is a great analogy for how businesses, the government, and nonprofits balance and work together. If one sector is weak or missing, the entire stool is wobbly and weak. Thus, the nonprofit sector is as important as the other two, and one of the ways it demonstrates its importance is by making change happen. Nonprofits have historically taken on services and causes considered to be unprofitable by business or politically risky by government. In exchange, they have relied upon government and corporate support to fund their work. Corporations donate to nonprofits and invest in them to promote the development of responsive programs to help strengthen the communities in which their employees and stakeholders live.

The nonprofit sector has served as an incubator for some of the most significant social, ecological, political, and technological ideas of the past century. From neighborhood development to term limits for elected officials, from child care to higher education, nonprofits continue to touch nearly every facet of life. To continue implementing constructive change and transform communities, the nonprofit sector must maintain its own internal vigilance as to what changes it needs to make, including how its own identity affects the way it is perceived and what it can ultimately accomplish.

WHAT ROLE DOES THE EXECUTIVE DIRECTOR HAVE IN MAKING CHANGE HAPPEN OUTSIDE THE ORGANIZATION?

Executive Directors can carry a lot of clout in their communities because of their leadership role in their organizations. Both the business and government sectors look to nonprofit EDs to help them understand societal needs, and community leaders confer with them in their areas of expertise to help make their communities a better place to live. Executive Directors are often the "conscience of the community" as they inspire others toward their highest aspirations. They mobilize people and entire communities to make necessary changes, and often work within complicated collaborations of business, private, and nonprofit sector organizations to achieve a desired community-wide change.

Connecting with your community by joining local Chambers of Commerce and other associations and having representatives from your nonprofit speak to service clubs, business groups, and civic associations helps business groups learn about changes your nonprofit is undertaking, and it helps you and others in your organization learn from the business sector. Support from these groups and the broader community is essential for the success of a nonprofit's attempt to fulfill its mission.

Executive Directors and others in their organizations also have a role of educating government on a local level and more globally. In the past few years, we have seen extraordinary changes happening due to the worst economic downturn since the Great Depression era of the 1930s. Government safety-net programs for all disenfranchised populations have been cut to the bone, and sometimes through it. Executive Directors have an important role in working with government officials to cobble together enough support to cover the basic needs of everyone adversely impacted by the government cuts. There should never be the expectation that nonprofits can step in and take over what governments can no longer support. But Executive Directors and others can help governments make tough decisions and work side-by-side to ensure societal needs have adequate support.

When Executive Directors band together around a particular cause, even greater change can happen. For instance, after the loss and death of thousands of pets during Hurricane Katrina in 2006, animal welfare group Executive Directors in the San Francisco Bay Area came together to determine a regional plan in the Bay Area to rescue pets when a major earthquake or other disaster strikes. The result, after years of planning, was a series of municipal, county, and regional plans, community education initiatives, and mutual aid agreements that will save the lives of companion animals as well as give comfort to their owners who may have to be separated from them in a disaster. Businesses and local governments were also involved in the planning, making it a cross-sector accomplishment. The work done by this group of Executive Directors helped build new opportunities for additional ways to work together to effect changes in the broader Bay Area community.

HOW ARE THE LINES THAT HAVE TRADITIONALLY DEFINED THE BUSINESS AND NONPROFIT SECTORS CHANGING?

Growth of the nonprofit sector and its shifting revenues have resulted in a new and very different operating environment. Increased competition for fewer resources, more complex social needs in a global society linked through technology, and greater emphasis on accountability are moving the more effective nonprofits into business models that mirror the for-profit sector. Additionally, more nonprofits are either adding a mission-related business component or building programs with a social entrepreneurial focus. Nonprofits founded by social entrepreneurs have been in existence for many years. However, they have gained in popularity due to their unique blend of creating and sustaining an enterprising business model that makes transformational changes in disadvantaged populations. The examples in the world today are numerous. Social entrepreneurs have founded nonprofits to

- Help impoverished women sell their crafts worldwide to raise themselves and their children from poverty.
- Provide education and health programs in communities that have none—to train teachers and health professionals, create community leaders, and create opportunities for the world's poorest children to succeed academically and break the cycle of poverty.
- Train disadvantaged communities to use technology to build more sustainable communities and improve their citizens' lives.

It would be easy to find many other wonderful examples of this growing field within the nonprofit sector.

Another aspect of social entrepreneurism can be seen with businesses and nonprofits aligning in new ways to reach beyond traditional support. As nonprofit organizations work to diversify and strengthen their funding streams, they are embracing new business opportunities that blend philanthropy and venture funding into venture philanthropy relationships with long-term investors. For example, organizations serving the homeless are partnering with businesses and investors to create enterprises that hire homeless individuals and train them in skills that can be used in other employment.

As nonprofit organizations are learning new ways to be more businesslike and accountable, some of the business sector is shifting values to mirror those in nonprofits. For example, a significant factor in Ben and Jerry's highly acclaimed brand of ice cream is the company's ability to tie social activism to the marketing of products such as "Peace Pops" and "One Sweet Whirled."

Many nonprofits are able to maneuver among these blurring sector lines successfully. Others find it difficult to be financially successful and still remain true to their mission. The challenge to Executive Directors and others in nonprofit leadership positions is to balance faithfulness to the mission with a sustainable business model for funding the organization. In all your management practices, you must work hard to maintain room for the cause while you keep your eyes on the change you are trying to implement in your community.

If you are interested in learning more about social entrepreneurship, visit the Skoll Foundation Web site at skollfoundation.org or follow some of the interesting links that Wikipedia provides. Other resources for this chapter are mentioned in the Resource Section at the end of the book.

WHAT CAN THE EXECUTIVE DIRECTOR DO TO INFLUENCE FUNDERS' EFFORTS TO SHAPE THE NONPROFIT SECTOR?

The nonprofit sector is fortunate to have numerous revenue sources to tap into for programs and operations. This is a different phenomenon from both the business and government sectors. Businesses raise funds through investors and profitable sales. The government sector raises funds through taxes, bond measures, and other sources. Nonprofits, on the other hand, can raise funds through donations, fees for services, social enterprises, grants, events, and bequests and other planned giving activities. For more about the variety of revenue sources available, see Chapters Seventeen and Eighteen, which discuss finance and fundraising.

One of the key funding sources for many nonprofits is revenue from foundations, corporations, and the government (local, state, federal). These funders give to the nonprofit sector, and they each expect something in return for their investment. For instance, foundations have specific initiatives they fund. These change regularly based on current trends in society and the interests of the foundation trustees. Receiving a grant from a foundation is wonderful, but such a grant often has strings attached, and the funding stream lasts only as long as the foundation maintains an interest in the nonprofit's mission.

Executive Directors find themselves seeking ways to position their nonprofits to fit into the frequently changing interests of government, corporate, and foundation funders. As long as the positioning does not stretch the nonprofit beyond its capacity, move it away from providing much-needed support, or take it beyond its mission, this is not a bad thing to do. However, Executive Directors can also provide leadership to help shape current and prospective funder priorities so they remain focused on the greatest community needs. Just as with the education of community leaders, the ED is often the best person to educate funders regarding changes that need support to make communities better places to live. Building relationships with funders is an important part of every Executive Director's job. If you put yourself into a position where you are called upon by funders when they are setting their priorities, you can work to ensure that revenue you depend on from foundations, corporations, and the government is having the greatest possible impact to improve your community. This is also an opportunity for Executive Directors working for a similar cause to collaborate on educating funders. Although you may be competing for these funders' revenues, working together will likely provide the most funding for your collective cause.

HOW DOES THE EXECUTIVE DIRECTOR MANAGE EFFECTIVELY THROUGH BOOM-AND-BUST ECONOMIC CYCLES?

Executive Directors often wish for a crystal ball to help forecast when the economy will be robust and generate ample donations and other funding, and when the economy will be extremely weak, with less donations and other income coming in to the nonprofit. It is impossible to really know when a boom cycle is starting or ending. The same is true for the bust cycle, so planning is necessary to keep organizational finances steady during whatever cycle the economy is in.

One important strategy is to maintain at least three months' operating capital in a reserve fund. Six months' to a year's worth is better but it is more difficult to do this. During the recession in 2008, 60 percent of small to medium-sized nonprofits had less than six months of operating reserves. Many nonprofits, especially the smaller ones, went out of business or cut programs during this recession, which was devastating to the populations they were serving. When the economy is weak, more services are needed for those in need. When organizations are forced to cut back or close due to lack of finances, the whole community suffers. It should be part of every Executive Director's financial management strategy to build up the reserves when the economy is booming so that money is there when the boom is over.

In addition to maintaining an operating reserve, organizations should have a diverse funding portfolio. Many Executive Directors who relied on government funding in the 1980s and 1990s learned a valuable lesson that the government cannot be depended on for full support. This is true for all funders and all donors, especially in a weak economy. The most stable and reliable donors are individuals, but when the stock market crashed in 2008 and wiped out billions of dollars from individuals' retirement funds and savings, those organizations dependent on individual donations had to severely cut back their programs. The stock market crash also affected the portfolios of foundations. These organizations can sometimes maintain a steady level of giving for several months after an economic downturn, but their grants can decline significantly in a bust cycle that lasts longer than a year. Executive Directors are wise to plan for this lag in foundation giving and think of other resources that can keep a heavily foundation-supported program stable.

The following story from the field illustrates the value of building a diverse revenue portfolio.

STORY FROM THE FIELD

A small visual arts organization with a mission of introducing arts in public elementary schools depended each year on funding from the National Endowment from the Arts and from local school districts. Its Executive Director, Gina, was surprised one year to learn that both these funding sources were making major cuts due to a national economic recession. Suddenly this organization's projected income for the next year went from $500,000 to $300,000—with the new fiscal year starting in three months and no plan for alternate revenue sources.

Gina brought together her Board and staff to discuss what they needed to do to survive this catastrophic cutback. They knew they would have to scale back and possibly eliminate programs, but they also decided to mount a fundraising campaign to try to bring in some of the lost revenue. One Board member talked to a friend with direct mail experience and they created a plan and budget for a letter-writing campaign. Another Board member began researching private foundations that focused on visual arts and education. Two other Board members planned a house party and invited everyone they knew to come hear about this organization, meet some of the visual artists, and make donations.

With everyone working desperately to raise some needed funding, Gina began to worry about the absence of any concrete plan and strategy. She and her Board president drafted a short-term (ninety-day) development plan that incorporated all the work the Board members were doing, set some goals, and also outlined a vision of a diversified revenue portfolio for the organization. Gina and the Board president, Mark, introduced the draft plan at the next Board meeting and it was enthusiastically accepted.

One of the tasks in the ninety-day development plan was to create an annual fundraising plan for the entire fiscal year. Gina was charged with this task and she sought help from ED colleagues who raised funds from numerous sources. She wanted to put together a realistic plan so her Board and her organization were not set up to fail. As she spoke to her colleagues she began to realize the magnitude of the job it would take to raise the $200,000 they had lost from their two traditional funders as well as bring in additional income in the years ahead.

Based on everything Gina learned from her colleagues, her own assessment of the poor economy, and the feedback she was getting from Board members who are actively seeking funds, she created a one-year development plan that raised $100,000 from foundations, individuals, service clubs, and the local business community. Although there would be a $100,000 shortfall for the year, Gina felt it would be impossible to raise the full $200,000 in one year.

The Board, Gina, and some volunteers did manage to reach their fundraising goals for the year in spite of the worsening economy. They attributed much of their success to their tenacity, but also to the fact they had never asked anyone before for money. Over the next few years, the organization was able to build and maintain a diversified revenue portfolio that would ensure it never got caught again with only two funders and no plan to sustain programs.

A revenue portfolio should consist of donations from individuals. It should also have grants from foundations and corporations, and if appropriate, government contracts. Most nonprofits should also have income from service fees and product sales. The Internet has made product sales a reality for even the smallest grassroots organizations who can sell T-shirts through online stores such as Café Press or unique products on their Web sites. When the economy is weak, the income from the assets in the reserve fund can be used. As necessary, the principal can be tapped but this should only be done as a last resort to save a critical program.

Every nonprofit will have a different portfolio depending on the services it provides, its size, and its location. The important point is to make it as diverse as possible. When the economy is booming, major individual gifts and grants may dominate in the portfolio, but this happy state cannot be counted upon indefinitely. When Boards and Executive Directors are creating their annual development plan, careful thought should be given to what economic cycle is occurring and what is predicted for the coming year. The plan should give more weight to those revenue sources that can bring in the most income during that particular economic cycle.

Some Executive Directors have said they cannot maintain an operating reserve or bring in excess income through a diversified revenue portfolio because funders will not donate if they see a surplus of revenue on the profit-and-loss statement or Form 990. There are indeed funders, usually foundations, who have denied grants to organizations that show a profit during a year. Most donors and funders, though, would prefer to see an organization ending the fiscal year with a profit rather than a loss. There is usually some clarification needed to help all current and potential donors and funders to understand the reasons for having a reserve fund or having a profitable year. As one Executive Director colleague likes to say, "Just because we are a nonprofit, that doesn't mean we can't make a profit!" She is right.

WHAT ARE SOME OF THE NEW DEMANDS FOR ACCOUNTABILITY AND MEASURABLE OUTCOMES IN NONPROFITS?

The demand for accountability is not just a derivative of bull and bear markets on Wall Street or the financial scandals in corporations such as Enron, or the outcome of the political scandals that enmesh elected government leaders. Nonprofit organizations, in exchange for their tax-exempt status, are charged with the legal responsibility to uphold the public trust.

Once upon a time, nonprofits upheld the public trust by first doing good work and then telling heartfelt stories of client transformation to verify their organization's effectiveness in meeting needs. Public and private donor scrutiny has moved the focus of measuring success to documentation of numbers and types of initiatives or services. The focus has further shifted in the past few years toward balancing overall fiscal accountability with individual program effectiveness. Nonprofits are now often asked to objectively demonstrate how each program or activity measurably affects the client, the core problem, and the needs, values, or causes that define the mission. A balanced budget and reasonable operating reserve level are no longer sufficient as measures of an effective organization. Interested donors and funders now want to know how much of their donation is actually being used for programs. Watchdog Web sites like Charity Navigator measure this, and much more, to provide anyone interested in a particular nonprofit with information.

In addition to the watchdog Web sites, the Sarbanes-Oxley Act of 2002 requires increased accountability from nonprofits. The Act was created and passed by Congress in response to corporate financial misdeeds. The law requires all Boards of Directors of publicly held companies to take much more responsibility in overseeing finances. Although the focus is on the corporate sector, nonprofit Executive Directors and their Boards should use the Sarbanes-Oxley Act as a guide to ensure their organizations can pass any form of public scrutiny. In particular, EDs should follow the Sarbanes-Oxley Act regarding the following:

- The Board of Directors should always have an independent audit committee made up of Board members.
- Financial statements should be accurate and the CFO, ED, and Board of Directors should read them, understand them, and agree they fairly represent the organization's finances.
- Board and staff members should not be given loans from the organization.
- The organization should have a conflict of interest policy that covers Board members.

Following these best practices will help create the public trust that nonprofits need to gain community support.

Another demand for accountability facing nonprofits is that of stakeholders. The diversification of the nonprofit sector has led to the increased involvement of a greater variety of stakeholders. As a result, communication of your accomplishments must be in terms and language that resonate with your specific populations of stakeholders. Some will measure your success in terms of the fulfillment of your promise to their community. Others may want you to define your outcomes in terms of return on investment.

While nonprofits have long been perceived as holding themselves to a higher standard of conduct than organizations in the corporate or government environments, the sector has unfortunately been rocked by its own scandals and misguided efforts. As a nonprofit leader, you must constantly encourage yourself, your organization, and your Board to embrace your collective due diligence roles. You cannot hesitate to ask the obvious and often difficult questions, because your external stakeholders are asking them. As more information about charities becomes readily available on the Internet, stakeholders can easily educate themselves about reasonable expectations of organizational effectiveness and efficiency, and about whether your charity fits their criteria. Boards of Directors and Executive Directors who try to keep financial and program information from the public find it increasingly difficult to do so as society becomes more transparent. It is a much better strategy to have your Form 990 readily available on your Web site as well as on the various watchdog Web sites like Guidestar and Charity Navigator. Have your program statistics readily available on your Web site as well.

HOW ARE RAPID CHANGES IN TECHNOLOGY IMPACTING THE NONPROFIT WORKPLACE?

Most nonprofits, regardless of budget, are "plugged in" with technology these days. While many are not capable of state-of-the-art technology, it is still wise for Executive Directors and their managers to know about emerging technologies and to determine ways to integrate those that increase efficiency in their organizations.

The biggest change occurring in nonprofits because of technology is that everything and everyone is more accessible. You can learn about current or prospective donor interests by reading about them on the Internet. While this has its advantages, many major donors still prefer personal information sharing rather than files being developed about them from the Internet. Executive Directors and development staff may be able to learn more quickly about current and prospective donors, but balancing online research with personal connections is a challenge.

Telecommuting has become more common, with fewer staff needing to be in the office full time. Technology allows staff to connect to their office computers from home, to share files with each other remotely, and to be in constant communication. Executive Directors sometimes feel that technology impedes their ability to manage staff because people are less present. However, it is possible to use technology to increase staff efficiency, and understanding what is helpful and what isn't will make a nonprofit more competitive. For instance, Executive Directors and managers can often get much more work done at home, particularly work that requires planning and thought, because there are fewer distractions.

The community you serve is also increasingly technology-savvy and expects nonprofits to perform at increasingly high standards with technology. Compelling Web sites with helpful information are an absolute given for any nonprofit. Instant and accurate client information is also a must. Blogs, Facebook, Twitter, and other social networking technology should be part of every nonprofit's communication strategy these days, and these require frequent monitoring and updating.

Community members are also quick to share their positive and negative opinions about your organization on the increasing number of Web sites that rate your services. It is fair to say that most people in your community use these Web sites to learn more about your organization and form their own opinions by what they read. It is a good idea to pay attention to these Web sites and to have a strategy for what to do if ever there is a flurry of negative reviews.

One of the downsides to becoming a technology-driven and technology-dependent society is the urgent need to protect communication and information systems from worms, bugs, and viruses. Nonprofits that lose their technology systems due to external or internal sabotage can take months to recover from the loss of information. It can also be very expensive to repair or replace everything to bring a damaged system to its former condition.

We believe the upsides far outweigh the downsides to becoming a society that is dependent on increasingly sophisticated technology. Nonprofits can do more efficient work in less time in a broader community, sometimes for less money. Understanding technology and thinking strategically how it can work for your nonprofit is an important skill for Executive Directors.

With the many internal and external priorities that Executive Directors face, it is sometimes easy to set aside the need for reviewing the trends that are changing the nonprofit sector. Executive Directors need to be vigilant of issues and trends in order to keep their organizations responsive, innovative, and resilient.

TIPS FOR SUCCESS

- Stay abreast of the changes and trends that can affect your nonprofit and your own success as Executive Director.

- Be open and observant to best business practices in the private sector. The boundaries that once divided the nonprofit and private sectors are blurring.

- Prepare for bad economic times during good ones. This will keep your organization financially sustainable and your clients well served.

- Translate your organization's success into tangible outcomes that are shared with the community. The more accountable you are to the public, the more your organization will be trusted and respected.

Understanding Changing Life Cycle Stages in Nonprofits

In addition to adapting to external factors such as funding cutbacks, organizations must also make periodic adjustments in response to their own internal evolution.

—Nancy Franco, Susan Gross, and Karl Mathiasen III,
The Management Assistance Group

Nonprofit organizations evolve just as the whole nonprofit sector does. In addition to being responsive to the changing external environment, Executive Directors must watch for the internal changes that are natural to their nonprofit's life cycle. Most nonprofits move through life cycles much as human beings do, and it can be useful to view them as dynamic, living systems with clear

119

stages that roughly look like ours—birth, adolescence, maturity, and decline—with the added chance for rebirth rather than dissolution following decline.

One important point to remember about organizational life cycles, though, is that not all nonprofits move through all the typical stages. There is no time frame or rule that states that an organization must move into another stage of its life cycle after a period of years. A nonprofit may start up and move into the first stage of the life cycle and remain there for the rest of its existence. Or an organization may move through several stages and then find itself backtracking into an earlier stage. The process of life cycle development in nonprofits is nonlinear.

There are also different phases that nonprofits go through within life cycles. An organization in its start-up life cycle phase may enter a period of increased conflict among passionate volunteers about the direction to take the programs. Rather than seeing this conflict as a problem for the nonprofit, the Executive Director should look at it as a certain phase in the start-up life cycle that needs attention and may ultimately move the organization into the next life cycle stage, where more planning is done. Similarly, Board and staff in an organization in the mature life cycle stage may find they have lost their focus on what is important and programs no longer seem connected to each other. This phase should trigger discussion and reflection on mission, vision, and purpose, which may bring a sense of renewal or rebirth to everyone in the nonprofit as they gain a new sense of focus and direction.

Executive Directors are wise to assess the stage of life their nonprofits currently occupy and to determine if areas of the organization are progressing faster than others. Different challenges and strengths characterize each stage in the life cycle of an organization. Each stage also may include shifts in organizational culture on what is valued and assumed, as well as differing policies and practices. Likewise, management and leadership priorities and skills must change to take advantage of the strengths and overcome the challenges.

This chapter helps you determine the life cycle stage your organization is in and provides you with helpful information on determining your role as Executive Director in each stage. It addresses these questions:

- What life cycle stage is my organization in?
- What skills does an Executive Director need in each stage?

WHAT LIFE CYCLE STAGE IS MY ORGANIZATION IN?

There are many theories on organization life cycles. Most agree they follow the pattern of start-up, development, expansion, maturity, and crisis, followed by restructuring or decline. The chart in Exhibit 9.1 gives a description of each nonprofit life cycle stage and the strengths and challenges associated with it.

As you read through the chart, you may be thinking, "Well, we're a little bit of this stage and a little bit of that one." That means you are in a transition between stages. Or it may mean your nonprofit has actually stretched itself into a couple of different stages. It is also possible for organizations to have one area in a more advanced life cycle stage than others. For instance, it is not uncommon for a nonprofit's programs to have developed into a mature life cycle stage, while the marketing effort is in an earlier stage of development. Organizations that seem out of balance are often this way because some areas are moving through the life cycle stages faster than others. When this happens, organizations are between one stage and another. If you think this is the case for you, focus on the stage that has the most characteristics that match your organization. This is where your nonprofit is most grounded at the moment.

It's important to talk to others in your nonprofit to help answer this question. People have differing views on where their organization is depending on their position in the structure. Sharing these different perceptions among Board and staff members can lead to a rich discussion that is often educational for the Board—and sometimes eye-opening for staff as they hear the viewpoints of Board members!

Having these discussions with Board and staff may also help them understand the need for change in the nonprofit, or at least for doing some things in a different way. If you are in the middle of a change process in your organization, it's also helpful to reflect on where your nonprofit has been and what life cycle stage it is moving into.

Here is a process you can use with others to help determine what stage or transition period your nonprofit is currently in:

1. Have everyone reflect on your organization's history, any changes that it has seen, and its past accomplishments. List the significant accomplishments and periods of change in your history.

2. Ask people to identify the nonprofit's current strengths and the challenges they think it is facing. List the significant strengths and challenges.

Exhibit 9.1
Organization Life Cycle

Organization Stage	Organization Description
• Organization start-up	• Generally no paid staff; volunteers do all the work; Founder establishes the culture; heavy focus on getting programs started; lots of energy and creativity.
• Development	• First staff hired (generally the ED), beginning of formalization with policies, job descriptions, structures; sometimes struggles over priorities and direction. Role of Founder diminishes or ends unless Founder becomes ED. Leadership is negotiated between Board and ED. Beginning of a new culture.
• Expansion and growth	• More staff hired; growth in programs and funding; early systems are outgrown and need replacing with formal ones; strategic planning and focus is a priority; roles and authority of paid staff and volunteers set; work plans and accountability measures established; Board expands and fully takes on governance role and ED has greater autonomy and authority. Culture shifts and settles into new mode.
• Maturity	• Growth levels off; formalized procedures are the norm; increased accountability and good relationships with funders; good financial management; sufficient funds. Viewed publicly as strong and stable organization.
• Crisis and restructuring	• Major change or crisis (internal or external) necessitates a retooling or merger. Frequent staff and Board turnover lead to crisis-oriented planning; systems, structures, and programs are reevaluated and changed using new success criteria. New leaders bring change in style and sometimes in vision; lots of new creative energy. If successful, this stage leads to a new expansion and growth cycle; if unsuccessful, to decline and closing.
• Decline and closing	• The changes needed to continue to operate cannot be made. Focus is inward; personnel and Board members depart; loss of funding and loss of public trust; programs cease or merger occurs.

3. Now show everyone the life cycle chart. Ask them to review the lists of historic changes and accomplishments and the strengths and challenges. Then have everyone individually choose a stage on the life cycle chart that they think most closely matches the data on the lists. There will probably be a variety of choices.

4. Allow a full discussion to occur with each person's choice of position in the life cycle.

5. Narrow the possible stages to the one that is favored by the majority of the people participating in this exercise. This is most likely where your organization is in its life cycle.

6. If no clear majority opinion emerges, then you may truly be in more than one stage. If this is the case, discuss which areas of the organization are in one stage and which are in another. This discussion should help participants understand why your nonprofit is in more than one stage.

WHAT SKILLS DOES AN EXECUTIVE DIRECTOR NEED IN EACH STAGE?

The ideal skill mix is a very important question for Executive Directors and for Boards who hire them. Too often Executive Directors find themselves with management or leadership skills that have become less valuable or less effective in the organization because it has shifted into a new life cycle stage. Understanding what new skills are most needed helps an Executive Director keep up with the organization. The following story illustrates this point.

STORY FROM THE FIELD

Peter was Executive Director of the youth services organization he'd grown up with. He had started as one of the youth served there, spent fifteen years in a variety of positions, and then twelve years as ED. At the time of this story, the organization had gone through a major growth period and was feeling fragmented, so Peter and his Board of Directors decided to start a strategic planning process.

A consultant was hired to conduct an environmental assessment as a first step in the strategic planning process. In her discussions with Board and staff about the strengths and weaknesses of the organization and its priorities for the future, it quickly became evident that Peter was a major weakness in the nonprofit. Everyone felt terrible saying that he was a weak link in the organization because he had brought the nonprofit to its current position of strength. Unfortunately, people were worried that Peter was holding them back because of a limited set of leadership skills. The Board had a major concern about whether he could really provide the skills needed for the nonprofit.

To address these concerns, the consultant worked with the Board and staff to develop an understanding of what life cycle stage this organization was in, using the process described earlier in this chapter, as well as identifying the skills Peter lacked that were currently needed. Everyone also looked at what stage the organization might move to with their strategic plan and what skills Peter would need in the future. Fortunately, he was very open to developing new skills and went to work finding classes and books to retool himself for his nonprofit. Three years later the organization is thriving and Peter is still there.

Clearly, it helps Executive Directors and nonprofits to know what stage their organization is in. Those EDs that successfully change themselves as the organization changes are the ones who ensure steady and strong leadership over a long period of time.

The chart in Exhibit 9.2 lists the specific leadership and management skills needed by Executive Directors for each stage in the life cycle. The five primary responsibilities (visionary, relationship builder, capacity creator, resource wizard, and change agent) are inherent in each stage. Obviously the complexity of applying these responsibilities increases as more staff, volunteers, and programs are added to an organization.

As you review the chart in the exhibit, reflect on what your organization decided its life cycle stage to be. Think about your own roles, responsibilities, and leadership focus or strengths as they relate to that stage. If you haven't taken the skills self-assessment described in Chapter Two, this would be a good exercise to do now. You can then compare your skills with those listed in Exhibit 9.2. How do you match up with the requirements listed in the chart? The truth is that all skills are needed for each life cycle stage. However, in each stage some skills are most important to have. You may find that you need to develop new

Exhibit 9.2
Executive Director Skills for Each Life Cycle Stage

Life Cycle Stage	Skills Needed
Start-up (Founder is generally the unpaid ED)	→ Program design → Visioning → Risk taking → Entrepreneurship
Development (First paid ED; sometimes no other staff)	→ Systems development → Financial management → Program implementation → Board development → Internal focus
Expansion and growth	→ Communication → Planning and visioning → Strategic thinking → Staff management, especially outcomes and evaluation → Fundraising → Partnership building → Change management → External focus
Maturity	→ Delegation → Integration → Stabilization → Staff and Board management → Partnerships and collaboration
Crisis and restructuring Decline and closure	(Same as expansion) → Communication → Planning → Financial management → Partnership and merger

strengths or add to your skill sets if the organization is to thrive in its particular stage—or at any rate, you need to make sure the organization has these strengths and skills available. This can be done by your own professional development, through the addition of new staff, or bringing in new Board member expertise.

Exhibit 9.2 is also a useful resource for Board members seeking an Executive Director. They should use the leadership skills identified with their nonprofit's life cycle stage as criteria for hiring an individual who best fits the organization's requirements. As the chart is reviewed, Board members should keep in mind not just what is needed now in their nonprofit but what will be needed in the years ahead. If an organization is moving from one stage to another, it may be wiser to hire a new Executive Director whose skills suit the incoming stage.

Understanding your organization's life cycle stage is crucial in order to develop healthy change processes, as described in the next chapter. These life cycle stages are also directly affected by the external environment and how the sector itself is evolving. Executive Directors who have a good sense of changes happening, both internally and externally, can be strategic and lead their nonprofits to success.

TIPS FOR SUCCESS

- Engage your Board and staff in an exercise to understand what life cycle stage your organization is in. This helps everyone understand more about your organization.

- Be open to changing and increasing your skills in certain areas if that is what is best for your organization's current life cycle stage.

- Every life cycle stage has challenges and opportunities for your non-profit. Work with others to determine what those are for your organization and make plans to overcome the challenges and take advantage of the opportunities.

- If you are taking on a new ED role, have your prospective Board of Directors explain the life cycle stage the organization is in, and decide for yourself if that will be a good fit for you.

- If you are moving out of a nonprofit, help the Board understand the life cycle stage your organization is in, and what skills the new ED will need to be successful.

Leading Organizational Change

*The most important things a leader can bring to a changing organization
are passion, conviction, and confidence in others. Too often, executives
announce a plan, launch a task force, and simply hope that people
find the answers—instead of offering a dream, stretching their
horizons, and encouraging people to do the same.*

—Rosabeth Moss Kanter, *The Enduring Skills of Change Leaders*

Usually the person who first realizes the need for change in an
organization is the Executive Director. It becomes the ED's job
to manage change by first understanding the inherent tensions among
those affected by any change taking place, and then by explaining its
importance and actually doing things in a different way.

Changes in an organization can be small (such as a shift of policy) or large (an organizational restructuring). Changes are needed because of positive influences (launching a new program) and negative pressures (any significant crisis). Regardless of the size or reason, the change process will have an impact on some or all the people in the organization, and should be thought through carefully before implementation begins. For larger changes, the ED should often do considerable research to determine the impact and the cost, and to help clearly articulate the end result. This is not to suggest that the Executive Director is totally responsible for making change happen in a nonprofit. Being entrusted with the organization, the Executive Director is expected to know when a change is needed and to provide leadership. However, all successful organizational change stems from the Board, staff, and volunteers working together with the ED to make it happen. Thus the Executive Director's role is to lead, manage, and support others (that is, to work through others) for a healthy and productive process.

Executive Directors often have doubts about the best way to move forward with a change process that affects the whole organization. This chapter addresses some of the key issues that Executive Directors have with organizational change and specifically answers the following questions:

- How can Executive Directors help their nonprofits embrace a healthy change process?

- What is the Executive Director's role and that of the Board, other staff, and volunteers in a change process?

- How soon after a new Executive Director is hired should a change process begin?

HOW CAN EXECUTIVE DIRECTORS HELP THEIR NONPROFITS EMBRACE A HEALTHY CHANGE PROCESS?

EDs are responsible for helping their nonprofits deal with organization-wide change, such as changing the focus of the mission, arranging a merger, making major programmatic changes that affect people and systems inside the organization as well as clients, restructuring the nonprofit, or transitioning to a new Executive Director.

Most theories of successful organization change processes suggest the desirability of the following elements:

- A trusted leader (the ED) with a bold vision that can lead change throughout the organization.
- Visible and committed Board and staff leadership that is present during all phases of the change process.
- Clear, consistent, and transparent communication at all levels and throughout the entire process to make sure everyone knows what is happening and why.
- Awareness that resistance is normal and should be handled constructively. People embrace change at different rates and with different responses.
- System-wide thinking, analysis, and communication that enables people to see that making a change in one part of the organization is going to affect other areas.
- A concrete plan of action for the change process with measures that allow everyone to see and celebrate success as it occurs.

If you are an Executive Director contemplating an organization-wide change, it is important to address the elements listed here before you start. If they are not in place, you may want to spend some time preparing the organization before moving forward. Having as many of these elements in place as possible becomes even more important if you must move your organization quickly through change because of some crisis in the organization.

Once a foundation for change is in place, you can begin to lead people through the series of steps in the change process illustrated in Exhibit 10.1. While these steps appear to be linear, understand they are not. People's response to change in any organization requires moving backward and forward throughout the process. To be successful, the Executive Director and other leaders in the process must stay aware of the concerns, emotions, and other resistance from those who are affected by the change. As you move through the process, be alert to the need to revisit steps to ensure buy-in and ultimate success.

The process outlined in Exhibit 10.1 will work if you and other leaders stay very visible and available to help people through the early days of the changed organization. It is also the Executive Director's responsibility to regularly communicate positive impacts that are occurring due to the change during and after implementation, as well as to acknowledge new challenges that emerge.

Exhibit 10.1
Change Process

Step One: Envision. Provide a compelling need for change and a picture of what can be. This often includes the potential risks of not changing as well as the benefits of changing. Create a compelling vision statement that depicts what the organization will look like if the change process is successful. Include Board members, key staff, and volunteers in this process of envisioning. To move to the next step, you need their commitment to both the need for change and the vision for the new state of the organization.

Step Two: Communicate. Share the case for change with all staff and volunteers and with the consumers who will be most affected by the changes taking place. Don't expect full commitment to the vision immediately, but you should see excitement and interest before moving on.

Step Three: Set Goals. Make the vision concrete with specific goals created by key leaders in your organization. For instance, if you are contemplating adding new programs and your vision is of an organization doubled in size, providing a continuum of comprehensive programs to a broader consumer group, then you could have goals along these lines:

1. In one year, technology and communication systems to support the organization's growth will be in place.
2. In two years, new programs will be fully integrated.
3. In three years, XX additional clients will be served.

Broad acceptance of the goals is essential before it's safe to move to the next step.

Step Four: Define Roles. Develop an action plan with Board and staff participation to achieve the goals. Lead your Board and staff in determining the roles to be played by the individuals in your organization. Share the action plan with everyone so that staff, Board, volunteers, and key consumers understand that the process of change is well planned, and that they have a role in making it happen. This understanding is crucial before actual implementation begins.

Step Five: Benchmark Progress. Set benchmarks in the plan that will enable you to measure progress, keep implementation focused, reevaluate processes, and celebrate success. For instance, with the goals listed in Step Three, you might have a benchmark for five months that states that a community needs assessment has been completed, identifying the new programs to be developed.

Step Six: Take Action. Put your organization's action plan into operation. It is important throughout this time to fully communicate how things are progressing with individuals in the organization. When resistance from individuals arises, handle it with compassion, remembering that change is difficult, but also with firmness and confidence that the vision you are working toward is best for the organization.

Step Seven: Establish Learning Opportunities. Concurrently with step six, create new learning opportunities for staff who find their jobs evolving as change takes place. Consider these questions:

- Do some staff need new skills to do their new jobs more effectively?

- Are communication patterns going to change and is there a need to provide some training to help staff work together more effectively?

- Is the Board's role going to expand and do the members need training to be able to provide new governance for the organization?

Step Eight: Celebrate. Although you have been celebrating successes throughout the change process, be sure to arrange a major celebration when the process is completed. This has been hard work and everyone needs a pat on the back for making it happen!

Step Nine: Emotional Check-Up. After the action plan is implemented, continue to monitor how well people are adjusting. Conduct a group debriefing to discover what worked during the change process and what should be different next time. Make sure the change is having the impact originally envisioned. And remember that resistance will reappear as people realize "the good old days" are really over.

The following story from the field outlines how one nonprofit used the change process in Exhibit 10.1 to restructure their entire organization.

One of the keys to success in the animal shelter example, and in any major restructuring, is to have a lot of patience for the resistance encountered. If the

An organization providing care and adoptions for homeless dogs and cats was at a crossroads. For years it had operated as an informal all-volunteer group and had been very successful in placing hundreds of abandoned animals in new homes. Recently, the Board of Directors had decided to raise enough funds to purchase land and build a shelter for abandoned animals rather than expecting volunteers to care for them in their own homes. They envisioned a resource center where families could adopt a new pet, and where there would be programs that brought people and animals together. This vision was met with resounding applause from everyone associated with the organization because of the pressing need for consistent standards of care and a place to showcase the animals to make the adoptions happen more quickly and efficiently.

Although the vision of a new shelter with community programs and the reasons for this change were very clear to volunteers and the broader community, the process to achieve the vision was not clear at all, and a lack of leadership bogged everyone down. After a year of floundering, consultants were asked to help the volunteers regain their momentum toward the vision, and a plan was developed with specific three-year goals with the new shelter construction breaking ground in year 3 and new programs starting before then. The work of the consultants helped the Board and other volunteers realize the need for strong leadership, and the tough decision was made to move from an all-volunteer organization to one with staff leadership. Most of the volunteer leadership felt someone full-time was needed to keep everyone focused and motivated, and to manage daily operations. Others thought a staff person would damage the informal culture of this nonprofit. It took much longer than anticipated to hire a paid Executive Director, and several volunteers left because they could not accept having paid staff working there.

One of the first steps Bruce, the newly hired Executive Director, took was to establish roles for the Board, the volunteers who cared for the animals and did other tasks, and for himself. Because there had not been this level of formality before, it took months of persuasion and discussion before clear roles were defined for everyone. Job descriptions were developed with volunteers who emerged as natural leaders taking on management tasks to help Bruce.

A special group with an interest in fundraising became the volunteers in charge of raising the money for the new shelter. Another group of volunteers was more interested in creating new programs and they became involved in this area.

By now, the organization was already two years into its three-year plan, and in a series of meetings the original plan was revised to be more realistic. Bruce and the Board were informed by consultants that it would take at least several more years to raise the needed funds for a shelter. An action plan for fundraising was developed, monetary benchmarks set, volunteer teams created, and earnest fundraising began. At the same time, Bruce and the volunteers began to make their organization a resource center for pet-lovers in their community, and new programs were launched that provided education to children, companionship for lonely elders, and other popular programs.

It took several years, and the process was not smooth, but the vision has held firm. This organization moved from a small group of volunteers caring for animals in their homes to a much larger group of staff and volunteers who provide essential services to their community and essential shelter for homeless animals.

---

leaders in a change process can hold the vision despite conflict and stay calmly confident that it is normal and will pass, chances that the vision will be achieved are good. Another key to success is to take small steps forward and allow more time than you think is needed for any major changes to occur. One organization that was trying to shift staff in a medical center to a customer-centered philosophy found that the only way to succeed was to provide a monthly training on a new set of tasks with time to assimilate them into the new routine. The leadership of this medical center also made the trainings fun and remained patient with those staff who had been working there a long time and had little interest in changing. It took a year for the new customer-centered philosophy to take hold. When they were beginning the process, the medical center leadership had estimated that six months would be the most that was needed.

Of course, if the required changes are being caused by a pressing crisis that does not allow for a lot of time to create a new vision, gain support, develop plans, and take action, then everything has to be accelerated to warp speed.

The most important element in a crisis-centered change is communication. Be clear, be consistent, be transparent, and communicate often about what is going on. As much as possible, make everyone part of the change rather than having the Board and ED huddling behind closed doors and making decisions that will impact people inside and outside the organization.

WHAT IS THE EXECUTIVE DIRECTOR'S ROLE AND THAT OF THE BOARD, OTHER STAFF, AND VOLUNTEERS IN A CHANGE PROCESS?

Your role as Executive Director is to be the change leader. You are the person who inspires, motivates, and leads change toward the vision you have articulated. If an organization is undertaking a major change in response to a fiscal crisis or other tough situation, the ED is the leader who articulates the problem, explains what has to be done to resolve it, and moves people toward that resolution in a steady, calm manner. You are also a key manager and work to ensure that communication processes are working, that goals are being met, and that change is happening. Finally, you provide support to others in the organization who are doing their part to lead or manage the process.

Your Board members are your partners in this change. They provide support with expert advice, strategic thinking, and planning. In a sense, it is the Board's job to keep the big-picture perspective—to be thinking about ways the change will affect the community being served and to be talking to the community about those changes. Board members should also be discussing among themselves how their roles may need to change as a result of the process.

However, one change process requires the Board to take the responsibility of change leader. That is the hiring of a new Executive Director. This is probably one of the most important responsibilities of the Board of Directors, and one that cannot be delegated to staff. Hiring an Executive Director generally has an impact on the whole organization, and often on the community as well. This is an exciting change for any nonprofit and one where Boards can show strong leadership. We discuss Executive Director transitions in greater detail in Chapters Nineteen and Twenty.

Among Board and staff, some will be leaders who, with the Executive Director, will be able to inspire others and communicate progress. When change involves the institution or dissolution of a program or implementation of new technology, all staff should also participate in making the change happen. In the end, staff members should be involved in planning any change that affects their work. They should also be kept informed of progress toward the new vision every step of the way.

HOW SOON AFTER A NEW EXECUTIVE DIRECTOR IS HIRED SHOULD A CHANGE PROCESS BEGIN?

The answer to this question is the classic "It depends." If an Executive Director new to the nonprofit discovers a dire situation, then change needs to happen immediately. An organization facing bankruptcy, lawsuits over employment practices, or threats of funder cutbacks unless it makes some programmatic or organizational change must do something right away, and so must one suffering from an unhealthy culture that has people stuck or in constant conflict. In situations where you must implement a change process within a few months after being hired, it becomes imperative to identify other leaders in the organization who can help you formulate, articulate, and lead the vision, and set the course for achieving it. Executive Directors new to an organization need strong allies, particularly during tough times. A change process can help you create these alliances and forge partnerships that will support and sustain you for years after the change is completed.

If no major crises are facing the organization when you arrive, we recommend waiting a minimum of six months before beginning discussions about any organization-wide change. Even relatively small changes such as redirecting a program focus or establishing a new position can take more time to launch and should be part of a bigger planning process. Remember that one key criterion to a successful change process is a compelling need, and your vision for what the change can do. It takes time to develop this vision. If you are a new Executive Director and see no need for any changes, or only minor ones, then consider yourself very lucky! It is much better to wait for a strategic planning process to make any changes based on community needs or external threats or opportunities your organization is facing. And remember, no change process should begin until you, the Board, and key staff have a very clear understanding of the need for change and the vision to bring it to life.

Also, this time period gives you, the new person in the organization, a chance to build trust with Board and staff members. You also have some time to take a hard look at what change might be needed and to gather information from key stakeholders.

TIPS FOR SUCCESS

- Envision the results of any change process, and get buy-in for it, before getting it under way.

- Make the change process as transparent as possible for people inside and outside the organization—this will help you avoid the resistance and rumors that can slow down or derail the process.

- Patience is needed for any change process, small or large. Expect your desired result to take much longer than you can possibly imagine.

- For all change processes, make sure you have allies working alongside you every step of the way.

PART FOUR

Executive Director as Relationship Builder

Relationships of trust depend on our willingness to look not only to our own interests, but also the interests of others.

—Peter Farquharson

One of the characteristics that separate the truly great Executive Directors from the simply good ones is the ability to build strong relationships that benefit the organization. To do this, you must be a powerful communicator, believe in the beauty of teamwork and collaboration, be genuinely curious about and engaging with everyone you meet, and carry the respect of your community.

137

Relationship building is not always an easy task for the busy Executive Director. New EDs who are used to doing the work in other jobs often struggle with the fact that the Executive Director often works through others to accomplish something. This is one of the most important concepts for an Executive Director to learn. The job is not about doing things, it is about leading, managing, and supporting others through relationships.

In this section of the book, Chapters Eleven and Twelve describe effective relationship-building strategies with Board members. Here is where Executive Directors often struggle the most in their positions, and a poor ED-Board relationship is cited as one of the most common reasons an ED chooses to move on—or a Board chooses to fire an ED. Having a good relationship with the Board as a whole and with key individual Board members is essential to your success as an ED and to overall organizational success. As with all relationships, it is a two-way street, so these chapters can also be useful to Board members who need to be building a relationship with their Executive Director.

Chapter Thirteen describes leading, managing, and supporting paid and unpaid staff. Skilled Executive Directors gain the respect of their staff and provide inspiration to them. The focus of this chapter and the two that precede it is on building internal relationships is to provide you with ideas and tools to find your own level of ease and satisfaction while motivating others to work together and be productive.

Chapter Fourteen focuses on working with Founders or following in their footsteps. There are special challenges associated with filling the shoes of the visionary who started the organization. It will make your life easier every step of the way if you can build a solid relationship with the Founder.

Nurturing a Relationship with the Board

If all nonprofit Boards focused on the mission, did not allow individual agendas and personalities to overwhelm the collective needs of the organization, and worked in partnership to define the organization's future, a great deal of dysfunction would disappear from the nonprofit sector.

—Deborah Linnell, Zora Radosevich, and Jonathan Spack,
Executive Director's Guide

We have found in our years of nonprofit work that the single most important factor in determining the success of a nonprofit is how well its Executive Director and its Board partner together. If the relationship is healthy, the organization thrives. If the relationship is unstable or poor, the organization suffers.

The second most important factor in nonprofit success is internal Board leadership. If there is strong, consistent leadership from the officers the nonprofit will thrive. If not, the Board will be ineffective and add little value to an organization.

In this chapter, we explore what makes a healthy relationship between a Board and its Executive Director, and what makes a strong Board, by answering the following questions:

- What are the attributes of an effective Board, and what does it take to create one?

- What does a healthy relationship between a Board and its Executive Director look like, and how is it established?

- How does one differentiate between Board and Executive Director responsibilities?

- What information does the Board need, and how often?

- Who makes what decisions in a nonprofit?

WHAT ARE THE ATTRIBUTES OF AN EFFECTIVE BOARD, AND WHAT DOES IT TAKE TO CREATE ONE?

A tremendous amount of research has been done on the question of Board effectiveness—libraries of books, articles, research papers, interviews, newsletters, and other materials in print and on line have been developed to help nonprofit Boards do their work better. Yet a great many Executive Directors wonder why they need a Board at all, because in their experience very little about the Board's role adds value to their organization.

The most important point in all the literature on Boards of Directors is that the effective Board is one with the following attributes:

- A commitment to forge a strong partnership with the Executive Director that relies on transparency, integrity, respect, and good communication.

- A focus on and passion for the organization's mission, coupled with a commitment to setting and achieving the vision, and to establishing and modeling the organization's core values. Decisions are made with the mission, vision, and values always in mind.

- An agenda focused on big-picture, strategic thinking that sets and evaluates the organizational priorities and steers the Board away from any possibility of micromanagement.

- An ability to realistically determine the financial resources needed to meet priorities and fulfill the mission, and a willingness to obtain and protect those resources.

- A results-oriented mentality that gauges organizational effectiveness in fulfilling its mission, providing oversight for program impacts and best practices.

- A desire to work together as a group, to listen to divergent viewpoints, and to build consensus based on what is best for the whole organization.

- An intolerance for personal agendas of Board members and an avoidance, at all times, of self-dealing.

- Board officers that provide the leadership necessary to keep the Board focused on its agenda and work plan, and ensure follow-through on commitments.

- A governance structure that is flexible and changes to fit the life cycle and circumstances of the organization.

- An understanding of and ability to help shape the organization's culture in a way that sustains the values and ensures best practices.

- An interest in being informed about the good, bad, and uncertain in the nonprofit, and a willingness to ensure organizational accountability and transparency to its community.

- A commitment to self-reflection and evaluation, with expectations clearly stated and each person accountable to meet them.

No one-size-fits-all formula can make every Board of Directors effective. Similarly, no one model will work equally well for all Boards. Creating an effective Board requires hard work by the Board members and the Executive Director, and it happens over a long time.

With that said, it is useful to know several different models of Board effectiveness and use them as a frame of reference for determining what might work for your own Board of Directors. Many groups mix and match between these and other models. A number of hybrids are extremely effective. Determining what works often requires a trial-and-error approach that evolves over time into your own unique model. The chart in Exhibit 11.1 describes some of the current popular models. All of them contain some wisdom, but your organization needs to choose or build one that best fits its culture and needs.

Exhibit 11.1
Board Roles and Responsibilities Models

Model Creator	Overview	Key Board Responsibilities
Cyril Houle	Boards make policy, staff implement it	• Create and monitor the mission • Develop policies • Develop long-range plans • Evaluate programs • Hire and work with the Executive Director • Arbitrate conflict among staff • Fulfill the legal responsibilities of the nonprofit • Secure adequate financing and manage it well • Make the organization visible in the community • Evaluate itself
John Carver	Policy governance	• Ends—determination of which needs are to be met, for whom, and at what cost (a Board role) • Executive Limitations—determination of the boundaries within which the Board and staff operate to establish methods and activities to reach the ends (a Board and ED role) • Board-Staff Linkage—determination of the authority delegated to the ED and how that person's performance will be evaluated (Board and ED role) • Board Governance—determination of the Boards' philosophy, accountability, and the specifics of its job (a Board role)
Karl Mathiasen	Board passages	Board life cycle stages:

Model Creator	Overview	Key Board Responsibilities
		Organizing: Boards of Directors are made up of volunteers who follow a founding leader, or who, as a group, run the organization.
		Governing: Boards of Directors move from doing all the work of the organization to performing only governance functions.
		Mature: Boards of Directors perform largely a fundraising role in a nonprofit, both in giving and asking.
Richard Chait	New work of the Board	This model looks at Board member impact and process. Specifically,
		1. Boards must add value to their nonprofit. This will look different in every organization.
		2. Board members should become involved in those issues that really matter to the nonprofit and take action right along side of staff.
		3. Boards need a flexible structure to change quickly as the organization does.
Robert Herman	Board-centered leadership	Executive Director is central focus of the nonprofit and leads the Board in the following areas:
		• Defining the direction of the organization
		• Ensuring the effectiveness of programs
		• Key decision making right along side of the Board
		• ED collaborates on most governance issues
		In addition, the ED is evaluated partially on the quality of leadership provided to the Board and organization.

(Continued)

Model Creator	Overview	Key Board Responsibilities
Diana Duca and Candace Widmer	All-volunteer organization	The Board is in the position of being more involved in the direct operations of the organization because it has no staff members. Boards with this model have the following characteristics: • Board members are service providers, program coordinators, fundraisers, and administrators. • Board members have a good understanding of the intricacies of the organization, determine policies, and carry them out. • Board members are deeply dedicated to the cause and often reflect a grassroots orientation to solving community problems.

Using the models in Exhibit 11.1 as a frame of reference, Executive Directors can work with Board leadership on a process to move the Board of Directors toward effectiveness. Generally speaking, it is not a good idea to travel this road alone as the Executive Director. You need commitment on the part of some of the Board leadership to change and become more effective, or no change will occur. Exhibit 11.2 provides a good example of how to move a Board toward greater effectiveness.

This process cannot be completed in a one-day retreat or as part of a few Board meetings. A retreat can serve as the starting point, but the Board should expect to have ongoing conversations over time with the transition taking a year or longer. Also, it is important to realize that the process outlined in the exhibit only partially leads to a more effective Board. Working well together as a group may result from the effort. However, we encourage ongoing work on team building, consensus decision making, and meeting management to strengthen the group.

The next story from the field describes how one nonprofit used the process described in Exhibit 11.2 to make its Board more effective.

The success of Katherine's organization resulted from the Board members' recognition that they could be more effective—and that they needed to be more

Exhibit 11.2
Building an Effective Board

Step One: Spend time as a Board of Directors discussing the organization's culture and where it is in its life cycle. (You can do this by using process examples given in Chapters Four and Nine, which address these topics.) This is a step that provides a grounding for moving forward.

Step Two: Make sure the Board members know and understand the mission and vision of the organization. If any of them do not, the Board needs education on these topics.

Step Three: Clarify the organization's priorities and critical issues. Discuss individual members' interest in meeting those priorities and resolving the issues.

Step Four: Create a list of mutually agreed-upon Board responsibilities and expectations for the coming year that reflect the life cycle stage, culture, and priorities of the organization.

Step Five: Prepare a commitment form for each Board member to sign that states their willingness to be accountable for meeting the responsibilities and expectations. Members who choose not to sign the commitment form should be excused from the Board and thanked for their service.

Step Six: Develop Board goals that will allow it to fulfill the responsibilities and help to meet the priorities.

Step Seven: Form committees, based on individual interest, that will complete the goals.

Step Eight: Establish a regular schedule to check on committee work (at every Board meeting or once a quarter) and a Board evaluation process for completing the goals. *Note:* While many packaged Board evaluation forms are on the market, it's best for the Board and Executive Director to develop and use a form tailored to the organization.

effective—for the organization to thrive. Their own passion for the mission and desire to be of value sustained them through a long process and some very long meetings.

All of the steps in Exhibit 11.2 are crucial, but the development and acceptance of a written commitment by Board members should be a high priority. This form establishes a Board's expectations for its own performance. It often

Katherine—new to her organization and to the profession of being an Executive Director—found herself with a staff of five and a Board of seven people who were primarily interested in helping the staff run their programs. Katherine was following on the heels of a very strong Founder who had used the Board primarily as adjunct program volunteers and had seen no need for it to take on a governance role.

The first thing Katherine did was have a candid conversation with her Board Chair about the importance of Board members providing governance rather than assisting staff. She shared materials about what Boards do and how they can add value. The Board Chair agreed that their governance tasks had been neglected. They both agreed that new Board membership was needed to build the Board, that training was needed for everyone, and that part of the training should include ways to be accountable to the organization and the community served. At the same time, both Katherine and the Board Chair wanted the experience for all members to be fun as well as educational.

At the next board meeting, Katherine and the Board Chair presented their vision of a Board with a governance role. One member argued that the program work she was doing was more important to the nonprofit than making policies, providing oversight, and ensuring fiscal success. Another Board member stated that if any changes were made, he would resign.

The Board Chair met privately with these two individuals after the meeting and found that both of them wanted Katherine fired because she was "ruining the organization." At the next Board meeting, the two members challenged everything the Board Chair and Katherine said and completely disrupted the meeting. Knowing that this behavior could not continue, the Board Chair met separately with the two members and persuaded them to resign.

A recruitment campaign was held to find a minimum of four new Board members who had skills not currently found in the existing membership, and some who had served on other nonprofit Boards. After a few months, the new members were voted in, and a day-long orientation was held.

With all five staff present, the Board members reviewed the mission statement, discussed the next year's program, fundraising, and administrative priorities (they had no strategic plan), and talked about their interests in serving on the Board as well as their skills. In the end, the Board talked about how they could individually and collectively add the greatest value to the organization as it entered a heavy growth stage in its life cycle. They also talked about how they wanted to work together as a group, and what they expected from each other.

Following the meeting, and over the next several months, the conversations at the retreat were shaped into a list of responsibilities and expectations and a work plan. This work was done by a subset of the Board along with Katherine. Committees were formed as the work plan was approved. It was agreed that each committee would establish its own tasks, and report on progress at each quarterly Board meeting.

Developing the Board's effectiveness continues to be a high priority for the Chair and Katherine. Meetings consist of exercises to create cohesiveness as well as ongoing education on the nonprofit's work in the community.

takes considerable time to develop—one Board we know took nine months to agree on the contents of it—but it still saves time and frustration down the road. This should not be an ED-driven task, although it frequently is the ED who provides samples and support to its development. Generally, one or two Board members will take the responsibility for creating the commitment form, getting acceptance from the rest of the Board, and making sure all the commitment forms are signed. Exhibit 11.3 gives one example of a Board commitment form for an organization that has had its ups and downs on the journey of creating an effective Board. The commitment form helped considerably in boosting the up phases and minimizing the downs of this process.

One lesson this organization learned after getting Board approval and signatures on the commitment form is that someone (a Board member) must be vigilant in making sure all the commitments are carried out. A process for holding Board members accountable needs to be developed along with the commitment form.

A good process is to review the commitment form once a year at a Board meeting and have everyone recommit to their responsibilities. If a Board member is not performing at the level expected, the Board President should meet with the person prior to the annual recommitment so that individual can choose to step up in performance or move off the Board.

The commitment form is also an important part of the Board recruitment process. As prospective members are learning about activities of the organization

Exhibit 11.3
Sample Board Commitment Form

I, _____, understand that as a member of the Board of Directors of the [nonprofit], I have a legal and moral responsibility to ensure that the organization does the best work possible in pursuit of its goals. I believe in the purpose and the mission of the organization, and I will act responsibly and prudently as its steward.

As part of my responsibilities as a Board member: I will

• Attend a minimum of 75 percent of Board meetings, including retreats, special meetings, and committee meetings. I will attend at least two [nonprofit] special events per year and will serve on at least one Board standing committee.

• Consider fundraising to be a key responsibility in support of the [non-profit's] short- and long-term development goals. I will be responsible for a minimum contribution of [insert agreed-upon amount] each calendar year to [nonprofit] and understand that a cash contribution of $[amount] must be given by each Board member. To meet the remainder of the minimum contribution requirement, I realize I have the following options:

• The remaining $[amount] minimum contribution may be a cash donation from me or be solicited by me for cash gifts or corporate matching gifts.

• A maximum of $[amount] may be given as an in-kind donation of materials or supplies requested by staff, or as ticket purchases.

• Regardless of the donation combination chosen, I realize there is no maximum to cash contributions given by me or solicited from others.

• Assist with creating and implementing a fundraising strategy.

• Participate in the Board development process and ensure the Board is self-perpetuating and efficient through identification of skills needed and recruitment; I will participate in a self-evaluation process regularly.

• Participate in the Executive Director evaluation process. I appreciate, understand, and am committed to the Board-Executive Director partnership and recognize its interdependence.

- Approve budgets and review regular financial reports and ensure proper internal controls and that no inappropriate liabilities occur. I will review the audit and management letter.

- Interpret the organization's work and values to the community and represent the organization in a positive manner. I will participate in discussions to define the community and understand their needs.

- Define and approve the [nonprofit] mission, vision, and values statements; develop, evaluate, and support the strategic plan. I will work in good faith with staff and other Board members as partners toward achievement of our goals.

- Speak with one voice when a Board decision is made and will maintain confidentiality on Board discussions.

- Act in the best interests of the organization, and excuse myself from discussions and votes where I have a conflict of interest.

- Stay informed about what's going on in the organization. I will participate in and take responsibility for making decisions on issues, policies, and other Board matters.

If I don't fulfill these commitments to the organization, I will expect the Board president to call me and discuss my responsibilities with me.

In turn, [nonprofit] will be responsible to me in several ways:

1. I will be given, without request, regular financial reports and an update of organizational activities that allow me to meet the "prudent person" section of the law.

2. Opportunities will be offered to me to discuss with the Executive Director and the Board President the organization's programs, goals, activities, and status; additionally, I can request such opportunities.

3. The organization will help me perform my duties by keeping me informed about issues in the industry and field in which we are working, and by offering me opportunities for professional development as a Board member.

(Continued)

4. Board members and the Executive Director will respond in a straightforward fashion to questions I have that I feel are necessary to carry out my fiscal and legal responsibilities to this organization.

5. [Nonprofit] will provide Directors and Officers Insurance.

If the organization does not fulfill its commitments to me, I can call on the Board President and Executive Director to discuss these responsibilities.

Signed:

_____ Date: _____

Member, Board of Directors

_____ Date: _____

President, Board of Directors

and the role of the Board of directors, they should be given a copy of the Board's commitment form to help them understand what will be expected of them if they accept an invitation to serve on the Board.

WHAT DOES A HEALTHY RELATIONSHIP BETWEEN A BOARD AND ITS EXECUTIVE DIRECTOR LOOK LIKE, AND HOW IS IT ESTABLISHED?

Imagine this. Your Board of Directors meets regularly with a planned agenda established by the Board Chair with your advice. Committees are active and doing important work. Discussion and decisions are based on the knowledge Board members have about their roles and responsibilities in the organization, and on the voiced expectations they have for each other. As you sit in the meeting with them, you see each person engaged in the decision-making process and everyone actively accepting responsibility for their work. Board members ask you, the Executive Director, what support you need from them, and you feel safe enough to honestly and directly answer this question and the others that they ask you. The whole tone of the meeting is one of mutual trust and respect for one another as well as a genuine desire to be in a solid partnership with you.

This is what a healthy Board-ED relationship looks like. And, like all relationships, it involves constant work, attention, honesty, and continuous nurturing to thrive.

Here are the qualities that form a healthy Board-ED relationship.

For the Board of Directors

- Board members know their responsibilities; they are neither micromanaging the organization nor absent from it.
- Board members express their expectations to one another regarding commitment, participation, and level of activity.
- Board members express their expectations to the Executive Director regarding communication, management style, leadership style, or other relevant behaviors. These expectations are realistic.
- Board members participate willingly and work actively in areas of their strengths.
- Board members have enough information to feel knowledgeable and engaged.
- Board members feel trusted, respected, and viewed as partners by the Executive Director. In turn, they value, trust, and respect the ED.

For the Executive Director

- The Executive Director is willing to share the good, the bad, and the uncertain with Board members without fear of reprisal or blame. Information is shared on an ongoing basis with the philosophy of no surprises.
- The Executive Director, with the Board, establishes clear lines of decision-making authority.
- The Executive Director is quick to ask for help when needed, and seeks advice or support from Board members knowing a request for aid will not be viewed as evidence of ineffectiveness in the position.
- The Executive Director sees the value of shared or collaborative leadership with the Board.
- The Executive Director expresses expectations to the Board in a positive, constructive way that is also realistic.
- The Executive Director provides support as needed and makes the work of the Board a priority.

These lists of qualities can be distilled into a list of the four essential ingredients for creating a healthy relationship between you and your Board: clear communication, clear decision-making authority, clear roles and responsibilities, and clear criteria for success. In other words, you and your Board must have agreement on these questions:

- Who does what?
- What information do the Board and the ED need?
- Who makes what decisions?
- What does success look like for the Board-ED relationship?

Every organization will answer these questions differently depending on the unique partnership that exists. For many, the answers will involve some blurred areas. In all cases, the healthy partnership is a dance that evolves over time—and toes sometimes get stepped on. When this happens, it is important to talk about what happened and mutually decide on a better way to work together.

HOW DOES ONE DIFFERENTIATE BETWEEN BOARD AND EXECUTIVE DIRECTOR RESPONSIBILITIES?

An example of how one Board and Executive Director sorted out their respective responsibilities is described in Exhibit 11.4. They decided they had some shared activities, and some where either the ED or the Board should take the lead. This is just an example. The chart may be used as a tool for starting discussion with your Board to bring clarity to who does what. By filling out this chart for your organization, you and your Board are defining your own model of Board-ED partnership. The chart can be extremely helpful to new Board members who are trying to understand the partnership, and to the Board President, who needs to make sure the Board members are upholding their responsibilities in this crucial relationship.

Exhibit 11.4 describes a division of labor that works best for a group with a paid Executive Director. Organizations in the start-up or development stage may not have someone with the designated title of ED, in which case all Board members share in all the activities needed for success. As an organization moves from having Board members handle many of the day-to-day program and administrative responsibilities to having them provide an oversight role, some tensions

Exhibit 11.4
Sample Board–Executive Director Partnership

Activity	Board of Directors	Executive Director	Both
Relationship Building			
• Build and sustain organization culture			Share
• Board team building	Lead	Support	
• Board meeting management	Lead	Support	
• Board recruitment and orientation	Lead	Support	
• Board development and assessment	Lead	Support	
• Hire, assess, and remove Executive Director	Lead	Support	
• Hire staff and volunteers	Support	Lead	
• Staff development and assessment	Support	Lead	
• Staff and volunteer team building	Support	Lead	
• Staff and volunteer recognition			Share
Community Building			
• Build community partnerships	Support	Lead	
• Raise organizational visibility			Share
• Ensure broad representation			Share
• Build a culturally competent organization			Share
Visioning and Planning			
• Ensure mission-based decisions	Lead	Support	
• Create organizational vision	Support	Lead	
• Establish organization priorities			Share
• Develop operations policies	Support	Lead	
• Monitor strategic plan's accomplishments	Lead	Support	
• Develop and assess programs	Support	Lead	

(Continued)

Activity	Board of Directors	Executive Director	Both
Resource Development			
• Create fundraising plans			Share
• Cultivate and ask major donors	Lead	Support	
• Develop and analyze annual fund	Support	Lead	
• Build funder relationships			Share
• Develop annual budgets	Support	Lead	
• Prepare financial reports	Support	Lead	
• Monitor budgets and finances	Lead	Support	
Change Agent			
• Develop and manage organization change processes	Support	Lead	
• Create and manage executive transition process	Lead	Support	

Note: Lead = Overall responsibility and accountability; makes sure the job gets done

Share = Agreed-upon leadership responsibilities and accountability for each

Support = Provide information, expertise, and assistance to get the job done

can arise. Board members who have been the doers may not like giving up that responsibility to become the trustees. We have seen this tension to be especially strong between Board Presidents who have functioned as a de facto ED in an all-volunteer organization that has just hired its first staff Executive Director. Usually staff are being hired because the organization is moving to a new life cycle stage and has grown to the level that Board members cannot both run the programs and provide the needed oversight. The move to having paid staff is what is best for the organization, and Board members as well as the newly hired staff should keep this in mind as they go through their transition.

Board members should not be expected to slip into their new responsibilities comfortably overnight, and the Executive Director will need to work with them to clarify their new role in the organization and identify the steps members should take to move into that role. The exhibit can be helpful at that point in providing a clear picture of who does what.

In addition to having a Board commitment form and clarify on who does what, it also helps to have a Board annual work plan. Just as it helps the ED work to have a plan, the Board needs one to establish goals to strive toward. Ideally, the ED and Board goals will be closely coordinated to clarify responsibilities, expectations, accountability, and areas where support is needed.

Exhibit 11.5 is a sample Board of Directors annual work plan. It was developed at a half-day meeting attended by the Board and ED. This particular nonprofit had been struggling to raise unrestricted funds and the Board had finally realized that one important goal for their plan was to educate themselves to fundraise, and to get started. However, the Board did not want to lose sight of their important responsibilities of governance and monitoring effectiveness. They chose to have specific goals for each of the four committees that covered their priorities of raising unrestricted dollars, measuring program effectiveness, balancing the budget, and recruiting new Board members.

Clear performance objectives and defined responsibilities help Board members monitor their success of adding value to the organization. Progress toward the Board's objectives should be reviewed at each Board meeting. This should be a written summary by each committee chair distributed to all Board members with a listing of accomplishments toward achieving objectives and where the committees are struggling. Board meetings should allow enough time for discussion of the summary report.

WHAT INFORMATION DOES THE BOARD NEED, AND HOW OFTEN?

We've been on Boards where we were just swamped with information, all of it good but probably not all necessary. We've also served on Boards where we had to drag the most basic information out of the Executive Director. Neither situation is desirable. So what is a good balance?

At the very least, here is what Board members should receive from their Executive Director on a monthly basis:

Exhibit 11.5
Sample Board of Directors Work Plan with
Performance Objectives

PLAN TIME FRAME _____

Development Committee

- Set the date for a Board fundraising training and hold it during the first quarter.

- Establish a Board fundraising goal at the training; develop a major donor plan to achieve it.

- With staff, identify the organization's major donors and develop profiles of them by June.

- Conduct a major donor fund drive during the third quarter.

- Measure success towards achieving the goal during the fourth quarter and plan for next year.

Finance Committee

- Develop a deficit reduction plan during the first quarter with a goal of $0 deficit by end of year.

- Monitor the ED's success monthly in carrying out the plan.

- Review and update the financial manual's section on internal controls during the second quarter.

Planning Committee

- Set date for a Board and Managers retreat during the second quarter to discuss community needs, review program effectiveness, and measure overall progress towards the organizational vision.

- Monitor program effectiveness monthly by reviewing program staff reports. Provide summaries to the Board at the quarterly meetings.

Governance Committee

- Identify skills gaps among Board members and discuss with the Board during the first quarter.

- Establish a Board member recruitment plan during the first quarter and train the full Board to implement it.

- Bring in four new Board members and provide orientation by the end of the year.

- *An update:* A two- or three-page paper that describes what is going on at the organization, including successes and challenges. If program metrics are established, the Board should receive these as part of the report.

- *Financials:* Reports that present monthly and year-to-date revenues and expenditures compared to budget, along with an explanation for any major discrepancies, and a balance sheet.

- *Fund development status:* A list of grant proposals mailed and grants received, major donor gifts received and recognition given, and any other important activity related to fundraising.

- *Community creation:* An update on efforts to build the visibility of the organization and its partnerships.

- *Background information needed for decisions:* Written summaries that communicate options with pros and cons for any decision a Board has to make.

If Board members have all this information well in advance of a meeting (at least five days prior) they generally have time to become informed. When Board members are well informed, they are apt to become more involved and to trust the Executive Director's leadership.

Communication between the Board and Executive Director is equally important when the organization is facing a crisis and when it has a major success. For example, a crisis might be when your nonprofit is unable to make payroll because of cash flow problems. Or an article is about to appear in the newspaper or online that presents a negative view of your organization. Or a former employee has filed a lawsuit. Whatever the crisis, you should inform the Board before it becomes public knowledge. This may necessitate a quick e-mail for a small crisis, a phone call to explain a more serious impending problem, or an emergency meeting under the direst of circumstances.

Executive Directors may feel anything from mild apprehension to full-blown terror when faced with informing a Board of a crisis situation. Regardless, those Executive Directors who are slow to communicate with their Boards often face larger problems when Board members find out from other sources. Wondering why you did not tell them what was happening, Board members are likely to put the worst spin on events, become suspicious, and lose trust in you. Rebuilding this trust can be very difficult and time-consuming.

When a major success has occurred such as launching a new program, or receiving special public recognition for someone in the organization, or reading a complementary story published about your organization—then the Board needs to know this too. Of course, it is much easier to talk about organizational successes with your Board! If there will be a staff celebration, always invite the Board to attend too so they may join in the recognition of a job well done.

Board members are partners with you in your capacity as Executive Director, and as partners they have much to contribute to finding the solution in crises and celebrating successes.

WHO MAKES WHAT DECISIONS IN A NONPROFIT?

A healthy Board-ED relationship also involves clear understanding of who makes what decisions. It's much more complicated than "Board decides this, ED decides that." It's also often not enough to say that the Executive Director makes all day-to-day decisions while the Board makes policy decisions. For most groups, the lines blur. A more efficient way of thinking about decision-making structure is to divide decision making into Board Executive Committee decisions, Board of Directors decisions, and Executive Director decisions.

For instance, you and your Board may conclude that the Board Executive Committee has the authority to decide on the following:

- Steps to take in an immediate crisis
- Any decision that must be made between Board meetings that does not involve changing the structure, by-laws, budget, or Executive Director

The full Board may have authority for the following decisions:

- Selection of new Board members

- Hiring and firing of the Executive Director
- Selecting the auditor
- Setting the mission and vision for the organization
- Defining policies on key areas such as overspending the budget, accepting controversial donations, making decisions on human resources, adopting new programs and abolishing established ones, and other choices likely to affect the direction or character of the organization
- Purchasing or selling a building or other capital asset

The Executive Director may have authority for these decisions:

- Hiring and firing staff and volunteers
- Developing program design and implementation strategies
- Developing fundraising strategy, including selection of prospects and of individuals to build connections with them
- Identifying best candidates for partnerships and strategic collaborations
- Preparing annual staff plans and performance criteria
- Making routine contracts and setting day-to-day policies for operations, financial management, and evaluation procedures

These lists are not exhaustive, nor should they be viewed as the only way to delineate decision-making authority. Having job descriptions, written expectations, and work plans for the ED helps in determining who makes what decisions.

Here's an example of how a group grappled with and resolved a decision-making issue:

A thirty-member Board of Directors was presented with an agenda item to approve a contract for a large planning grant, and the Board Chair and Executive Director asked for the approval without presenting any background information on the contract. Board members balked at giving approval and questions were raised about who should be making new contract decisions. The ED realistically said that if he had to get Board approval for every contract, it would take forever with this size Board. On the other hand, Board members wanted to know what they were getting the organization into—a wise perspective to take!

The Board asked the Executive Director to present a summary of the contract via e-mail. They decided that if e-mail discussion showed everyone to be in favor of the contract, they would go forward. If consensus could not be reached, the Board agreed to attend a special meeting for further discussion and decision making. They also agreed that the ED should decide on all contracts not affecting agency direction.

The situation in this example would have been easier to deal with had the Board and ED had a clear understanding of authority on signing contracts. This can be done through a contract approval policy that spells out the types of contracts an ED can sign and the financial limits.

It becomes crucial to take time to orient new Board members into the delicate decision-making structure you have established, so that they can quickly adjust to your organization's way of working together. Thus a Board orientation becomes much more than providing the history, program information, and financial data of your nonprofit. It's also about all the subjects of this chapter. Remaining attentive to the relationship between you and your Board up front and particularly as new members join the Board can save you many headaches and heartaches down the road.

TIPS FOR SUCCESS

- Taking the time and making the effort to build a strong partnership with your Board is well worthwhile. A healthy partnership is central to the sustainability and effectiveness of you and your organization.

- Help your Board develop a clear list of commitments and responsibilities and make sure a review of the list is on their agenda each year.

- If both you and your Board have work plans with measurable tasks, then evaluating progress and areas that need more support can be done readily and objectively.

- Find out from your Board what information members want, how often, and at what level of detail. When the situation is unclear, always err on the side of giving them too much information rather than too little—and don't purposefully withhold bad news from them.

Developing Relationships with Individual Board Members

> *A board-centered executive [director] is aware that there are multiple motivations board members may have for board service. . . . and that it is important to know what it is that attracts an individual board member to serve.*
>
> —Robert Herman and Richard Heimovics, *Executive Leadership in Nonprofit Organizations*

I t is important to distinguish between the full Board's work with an Executive Director and the best ways for certain key Board members to interact and partner with the ED to ensure strong leadership. One of the most critical partnerships is between the Executive Director and the Board President. But the ED interacts with each Board member in a variety of ways (answering questions, hearing praise and complaints about programs, giving and hearing advice, and supporting each in their responsibilities).

Sometimes, the ED is faced with Board members who are out of line. These are the renegade Board members—and any Board can have them. It is the Board Chair's responsibility to stop a renegade from taking inappropriate actions, but often it is the ED who must notify the Board Chair of the problems being created by such a person. Similarly, it is often the Executive Director who is aware of Board members who are not fulfilling their duties for whatever reason, but it is not the ED's responsibility to hold these Board members accountable.

To help Executive Directors navigate the relationship with individual Board members, this chapter answers the following questions:

- How important is the relationship between the Executive Director and the Board Chair?

- What do you do if problems arise between you and the Board Chair?

- What should an Executive Director do with a renegade Board member?

- If Board members are not fulfilling their responsibilities, what can an Executive Director do?

- How much influence should an Executive Director have when recruiting new Board members?

HOW IMPORTANT IS THE RELATIONSHIP BETWEEN THE EXECUTIVE DIRECTOR AND THE BOARD CHAIR?

We usually hear questions about the importance of the relationship from either a Board Chair (an alternate title for this position is President) or an Executive Director when the two are having trouble dealing with each other. The short answer is that there is no more important relationship in your nonprofit than the one between Executive Director and Board Chair. If these two leaders are not aligned, it often spells disaster. On the other hand, when they are working cohesively together, the whole organization usually enjoys harmony and progress.

It's very important for an Executive Director who is new to an organization to get off to a good start with the current Board Chair. One way to do this is to have a conversation about what the Chair expects from you, and vice versa.

This conversation should also include the development of a social contract, formal or informal, that indicates how frequently you will meet for sharing information, getting advice, and so on, and also gives details on how you and your Board Chair want to communicate with each other. Any time you have a new Board Chair, be sure to go through this process again. Never assume that what worked for one person is going to work for another.

In most situations, maintaining a harmonious relationship between you and the Board Chair is not that difficult. Here are some ideas that you might want to include in a social contract:

- *Regular meetings.* By phone or in person, it's useful for the two of you to discuss any current or emerging issues and consider how to mobilize Board and staff if needed. You can also update each other on the organization as you see it—and take some time to just have fun together, which is the best way to cement a working relationship.

- *No surprises.* Both the Chair and the Executive Director should lock into their brains the concept that anything one knows about something that is going to affect the organization needs to be communicated to the other.

The importance of regular communications and the prevention of surprises applies to things that happen that may impact the Board. Not every operational issue needs to be relayed to the Board Chair, but important events that challenge organizational survival (the loss of major funding support, for example) certainly do, as does news of a disgruntled employee who has decided to post negative comments on the Internet. It's generally best to be the first to let your Chair know about an issue—that way you'll have the Chair's support (or at least know how the Chair will react) when the inevitable complaint makes its way up the line. Sometimes it is hard to determine when to let the Chair know about an issue, and when it isn't necessary. Generally, the best idea is to err on the side of too much communication rather than not enough.

It's also helpful to have a clear job description for the Board Chair position. This list of responsibilities can make it clear what the Board Chair's role in the organization is, and what expectations there are for the position. Even more important, the job description helps the ED and Board Chair understand who does what regarding the Board of Directors. A sample Board Chair job description can be found in Exhibit 12.1.

> **Exhibit 12.1**
> **Sample Board Chair Job Description**
>
> ---
>
> The Board Chair of XYZ Nonprofit has the following duties:
>
> - Partners with the Executive Director to achieve the organization's mission
> - Chairs the Board meetings and prepares agendas for those meetings with the ED
> - Assigns Board members to standing and ad hoc Board committees
> - Works with the Executive Director to develop a Board commitment form, and to ensure it is signed by all Board members and reviewed annually
> - Initiates the process for Board goals and work plans, as well as the Board's self-evaluation
> - Keeps the Board at the governance level of thinking at meetings and in all discussions
> - Provides leadership to organizational fundraising with personal contributions as well as asking others
> - Ensures the Board is in compliance with the by-laws and any local, state, or federal laws governing Boards of Directors
> - Listens to and reflects concerns the ED and management have about the role of the Board, and reflects concerns the Board has about the organization to the ED
> - Leads the Executive Director evaluation and salary review process; communicates the results of the evaluation and salary review process to the ED
> - Serves as a spokesperson for the organization in conjunction with the ED and communications staff

As you can see, the Board Chair has many responsibilities for leading the Board of Directors and partnering with the ED. Together, the Board Chair and ED are the organizational leadership, and when these two individuals are working closely and positively together, they are a powerful team.

WHAT DO YOU DO IF PROBLEMS ARISE BETWEEN YOU AND THE BOARD CHAIR?

It is best for you to take the first step to proffer the olive branch to a difficult Board Chair. Remember that your Board Chair is a volunteer and needs to be recognized and valued for giving time and effort freely to your organization. Herc is one way you can take to establish or reestablish a good relationship. Ask for a meeting to clear the air. At that meeting, use the following approach:

- Reestablish the common ground of your mutual passion for the mission of your organization.

- Explain how the difficulties between the two of you are hurting what you both are passionate about.

- Use "I" statements to describe how you feel, how you see that you may have contributed to the situation at hand, and what you need from the Board Chair to have a more positive relationship.

- Ask the Board Chair for a similar description of feelings and needs relating to the current situation. In all of this, your goal is to negotiate a win-win outcome, where both of you are better off.

- Reaffirm or establish expectations you have of each other in the areas of communication, decision making, and supporting each other.

Most of the time, a good honest conversation will bring you closer together again. If you are not able to resolve a situation, then involve another Board member (you can be certain they all know you and the Board Chair aren't getting along, even if you're both sure you've been hiding the fact). Sometimes it may be necessary to involve an outside person who can listen objectively to the feelings and needs of both of you and possibly offer suggestions for mending the relationship.

It is best if the Executive Director does not vent frustrations about the Board Chair to staff in the organization. There is usually a natural tendency to do this because it is also obvious in small to medium-size organizations when the ED and Board Chair are at odds with one another. Getting support from a friend, coach, peer, or someone you trust outside the organization is a better way to vent frustrations and gain clarity on what should be done to resolve the situation.

Generally, the difficulties between a Board Chair and ED can be resolved through communication and the realization that a poor relationship hurts the nonprofit they both care deeply about. However, there are times when the relationship cannot be improved. In these cases, it may be best for the Board Chair to step aside or the ED leave the organization. New leadership in either position allows a better relationship to develop and brings more stability to the organization.

WHAT SHOULD AN EXECUTIVE DIRECTOR DO WITH A RENEGADE BOARD MEMBER?

Renegade Board members come in several varieties. There's the Board member who calls the Executive Director and gives direction on matters that are the purview of the whole Board, not just one member. Or the one who goes to staff, bypassing the Executive Director, and gives direction to them. Or the one who disagrees with the group on some issue and proceeds to follow a private course of action rather than the one chosen by the Board.

Every Executive Director has had run-ins with people like these. They are generally well intentioned and have no idea of the problems they cause for an organization. However, the unmanaged renegade Board member can become a real nightmare for the nonprofit and the Executive Director.

The first thing to remember is that the Executive Director is not responsible for renegade Board members. The Board holds that responsibility. When you believe that a Board member has been out of line, the best first step is to contact the Board Chair. If, by some unfortunate circumstance, the renegade is the Board Chair, then contact the Vice-Chair. Talk over the situation with your Board leader and let that person do something to stop whatever action the renegade member is engaging in. Most of the time, a quick phone call or meeting between the Board Chair and that member is all that is needed. More often than not, individuals don't know they are out of line and just need a reminder.

Occasionally, you may get some valuable feedback out of a conversation with a renegade Board member. The Board member may not have had enough information to understand that a course of action taken was inappropriate or could be problematic. Or perhaps the Board member went off on a tangent as a result of feeling out of the loop. Getting to the bottom of the renegade Board member's behavior is the best way to put an end to it.

Sometimes, though, when there is a weak Board of Directors, a renegade Board member can run amok and create difficulties for the ED and the entire organization. In situations like this, an Executive Director has to choose whether to challenge the renegade Board member or let the actions continue. The ED cannot possibly win in these situations unless there is Board support from the other members and these individuals will ultimately step up and stop the renegade's actions.

For example, a recently hired ED was working with her Board to overhaul a program that was seriously over budget and underperforming. Many of the Board members were also new and they generally deferred to a long-time Board member who was, at times, intimidating but also quite knowledgeable. This Board member had been instrumental in starting the program under discussion and had no interest in making the changes needed. When the issue first came up at a Board meeting, the ED was accused by the renegade Board member of lying about the program and mismanaging it. No other Board member came to the defense of the ED and the issue was finally tabled when the discussion became unbearable for all. After a year of ongoing allegations by this Board member about the ED, and a continuing loss of revenue from the program, a few Board members finally told the renegade to cease and desist, and the full Board agreed to the original overhaul plan recommended by the ED. During this long year, the ED provided documentation to the Board about the program's performance and about best practices in similar programs in other organizations. With this information, some of the Board felt empowered to step up and take control of this unfortunate situation.

If the renegade Board member is seriously undermining the ED or damaging the programs of the organization, and the Board refuses to stop this, sometimes the ED's only honorable choice is to leave. If this happens, the outgoing ED should be honest regarding the reasons for leaving while also walking the fine line of not burning bridges with the Board or other stakeholders. This is generally a lose-lose situation for an organization. A committed and dedicated Executive Director chooses to leave because one Board member has become unmanageable.

Situations extreme enough to drive out the ED fortunately do not happen regularly in nonprofits. A more common example is one where a Board of Directors is made up of consumers of the nonprofit's services. This heightens the possibility of someone taking action on a matter that might be personally important to them, as a consumer, without waiting for Board determination on the best course of action for the organization to follow.

In training sessions with Boards that have consumers among the members, we always talk about the "two-hat theory." This theory sets the boundaries by which a consumer knows when to act in a Board capacity (first hat), and when to act as a consumer (second hat). The following story provides an example of this situation.

STORY FROM THE FIELD

A youth organization had a Board where more than half of the members were parents of children who attended the camp run by the nonprofit. Like all other consumers of this camp, they wanted it to be an ideal experience for their children. Unfortunately, this often meant that a consumer Board member would go directly to counselors or the camp director and tell them what they were supposed to be doing. Staff members would be reminded that it was a Board member talking, and action needed to happen quickly! On one occasion, staff received totally opposite instructions from two Board members—and both sets of instructions differed from what Sandy, the Executive Director, was asking the staff to do, as well as from what they themselves thought was best for the children. They were caught in an impossible situation and were left feeling frustrated and unable to make good decisions.

A consultant was brought in to work with the Board and staff to clarify Board roles and help them establish a reasonable policy that all could follow. At a day-long meeting, the consultant listened to the consumer Board members' desires to have what was best for their children, and the staff's frustration over all the differing viewpoints of what they should do. The consultant spent considerable time explaining the two-hat theory to both Board and staff and explained how it needed to be used by this organization. The two-hat theory helped the parents see that when they were at camp, they were consumers and could ask staff to make changes, the same as any other consumer. They should expect staff to go to Sandy with their ideas, just as staff would do with any consumer idea. Any request needing Board action would be brought to the Board, where a decision would be made and all Board members were expected to abide by that decision. The staff heaved a visible sigh of relief with this new policy. And the Board members also accepted it because it helped them understand the problems of taking action individually rather than as a group.

In this example, some of the parent Board members had gone renegade. It took clear setting of boundaries and a better understanding of Board responsibilities to remind the group that they were to make decisions as a group and then live by those decisions. Board members also committed to be careful in their private conversations with staff, making it clear that though they are on the Board, they are not speaking for it. This reminds staff not to overreact to a Board member's comment or to assume that one member speaks for all.

IF BOARD MEMBERS ARE NOT FULFILLING THEIR RESPONSIBILITIES, WHAT CAN AN EXECUTIVE DIRECTOR DO?

To start to answer this question, it needs to be clear what an individual Board member's responsibilities are. If your organization has a Board commitment form or Board member job descriptions or both, then it becomes easier to discuss whether someone is or isn't fulfilling the responsibilities of being on the Board.

Assuming there is some written description of Board member duties, the Executive Director is often the person who sees that an individual is lagging behind. This might be evidenced by someone committing to a task that supports the ED in fundraising, but who never does that task (phone calls not made, visits not done, thank-you notes not sent). Or someone agrees to an assignment given by the Board Chair and then calls the ED to take it over because the Board member is just too busy to get it done. Or a Board member might never show up to committee meetings and never offer an explanation for the absence. In all these examples, the Board member probably has good reasons for not fulfilling responsibilities, but these individuals keep the Board from being successful, and they put an unfair burden on the ED to fill the gap. They are generally not renegades; they are simply missing in action.

The reality is that most Boards of Directors have one or more individuals who are underperforming. In some cases, a Board member will be very active and then will get extremely busy with other activities (work, family, or whatever) and will need to make Board work a lesser priority for a while. Other times, a Board member will never fulfill the responsibilities. In the first case, the Executive Director needs to exercise patience and work with the Board Chair to give an overwhelmed Board member some time off to deal with more pressing activities. In the second case, the Executive Director should give specific examples to the Board Chair of the responsibilities not being fulfilled by the Board member. It should be the Board Chair, working with the Executive Committee, who decides on the course of action to take with an underperforming Board member. Once the Executive Director has brought the matter to the attention of the Board Chair, it is in that individual's hands to resolve.

The Board Chair should talk with the Executive Committee about the best process to follow to discuss a Board member's underperformance. One good process is for the Board Chair and another Executive Committee member to invite the underperforming member to meet with them. They should have a copy of the Board job description or commitment form and use it as the basis for explaining how the underperforming member is not meeting expectations, and how that is harming the organization. Usually, this frank and honest conversation will work wonders. Board members who are underperforming know they are, and are sometimes stuck (and feeling guilty) about what to do because they cannot meet their commitments. The conversation allows these Board members to graciously (and gratefully) resign or to ask for a leave of absence if they know they will be able to step up to their commitments in the near future.

On rare occasions, a Board member will become angry when informed of underperformance and challenge the Board Chair. If the situation cannot be resolved, the full Board of Directors should be made aware of the action taken to discuss this person's underperformance, and an opportunity should be given to the angry Board member to explain the situation to everyone. If the Board member refuses to resign and refuses to meet the commitments that all other members have agreed to, then the person may have to be voted off the Board. Make sure your organization's by-laws allow this to happen. This is an extreme situation, fortunately. Having a clear commitment form and job description generally prevents it.

HOW MUCH INFLUENCE SHOULD AN EXECUTIVE DIRECTOR HAVE WHEN RECRUITING NEW BOARD MEMBERS?

The short answer is—a lot! We recommend that organizations have a healthy process in place for recruiting new Board members. Whether new Board members are elected by the organization's membership or by the current Board, the Executive Director is a key part of the recruitment process. Numerous publications and online resources describe the Board recruitment process. The one outlined in Exhibit 12.2 focuses on the Executive Director's role in recruitment.

The Board of Directors makes the decisions about who to meet with and who to select as new Board members (unless the membership must have the final say on selection). The Executive Director is instrumental in guiding the Board to

Exhibit 12.2
Executive Director's Role in Board
Recruitment Process

Step One: The Board and Executive Director identify gaps in skills, experience, and demographics needed to have a Board that adds maximum value to the organization.

- Executive Directors bring knowledge of organizational needs (fundraising, marketing, legal, HR, and so on) where new Board member expertise would add value.

- Executive Directors live the mission and vision on a daily basis and are best persons to help the Board identify gaps to fill so the organization can achieve its mission and vision.

Step Two: The Board and Executive Director identify individuals who offer the skills, experience, and demographics needed and inquire about their interest in serving on the Board of Directors.

- Executive Directors generally have a strong network of people they interact with regularly and can tap into for Board members. They are often most familiar with donors and volunteers who might fill the gaps on the Board.

- Executive Directors also need to think about the best personality fit for the Board and the organization. If there are certain personality characteristics in prospective individuals that might cause problems for the Board or the ED, those need to be brought up and discussed.

Step Three: Meet with prospective Board members to introduce the organization and Board requirements, and to answer questions from the prospects.

- Executive Directors should attend these meetings with at least one Board member and provide background information about the organization.

- Executive Directors should give feedback to the Board after the meetings about the qualifications and fit of the prospective Board members.

Step Four: Rank and decide who to invite to full Board interviews.

- Executive Directors and Board members who met with prospects decide together on those individuals who should be interviewed by the Board.

- Executive Directors attend the interviews and ask questions and provide information to the prospects.

Step Five: Board decision on new members and orientation of them.

- Executive Directors generally lead the orientation process, which includes a tour of the facility, introductions to key staff, and an explanation of all pertinent financial, legal, and organizational documents.

find new members who fit well within the organization and will give added value to the work of the Board and the success of the organization.

We have covered a lot of ground in these two chapters about the Board of Directors. The bottom line is the importance of having a healthy relationship between you and your Board of Directors, and especially between you and your Board Chair. If you take the time to make sure you have mutually understood responsibilities and expectations, good communication systems, a clear process for decision making, and an understanding of individual Board members' relationships to the group, then you have taken the essential steps toward a healthy and happy partnership.

TIPS FOR SUCCESS

- A clear job description for your Board Chair will help you have a healthy relationship with this individual. Having this healthy relationship is key to your overall relationship with the Board of directors.

- Let the Board Chair provide the leadership when dealing with renegade and underperforming Board members. You may need to let the Board Chair know about issues and concerns, but that individual has the responsibility for handling the situation.

- Take a proactive role in selecting new Board members. You can provide considerable assistance in determining the new skills needed and the best fit for the organization.

Establishing Productive Staff Relationships

Almost no one is going to have the luxury of working alone. All of us are going to be working in ways in which we're interdependent with other people. The only way we can do that effectively is to build competence in relationships.

—Max De Pree, *Leading Without Power*

A wise Executive Director views an organization as a community of people with diverse talents, ideas, beliefs, and interests. Within this community, the Executive Director wears many hats from moment to moment: manager, leader, mentor, coach, team player, or supporter. Understanding what hat is needed in interactions with paid and unpaid (volunteer) staff is an important skill to have and is crucial to building and maintaining good relationships.

Perhaps the most important function an Executive Director has with staff is that of communicator. In small organizations with few staff and volunteers, this is a relatively easy task. In larger organizations, the ED often has to communicate through program managers and others. Regardless of the size of the nonprofit, it often seems that the Executive Director is in constant communication mode with staff—dispelling rumors, keeping programs on track, and motivating everyone to work to achieve the mission and vision of the organization.

This chapter is not an HR primer for nonprofit leaders. Many resources can help you with hiring, firing, evaluations, establishing HR policies, and all the sticky issues that surround these topics. Instead, this chapter talks about communication, building relationships, and establishing trust. These are critical topics for all nonprofit leaders, especially Executive Directors. We provide answers to the following frequently asked questions about working with staff and volunteers:

- How does an Executive Director who is new to an organization build quick credibility with paid and unpaid staff?

- How does an Executive Director encourage positive relationships and establish a healthy culture among staff and volunteers?

- What are ways to build leadership and management skills among paid and unpaid staff?

- How does an Executive Director work across the generations to have staff work productively together?

- What are strategies for establishing strong lines of communication with staff?

- How can technology aid relationships and be used as an effective communication tool with staff?

- How does an Executive Director offer and receive support from staff and volunteers while keeping an arm's-length relationship?

HOW DOES AN EXECUTIVE DIRECTOR WHO IS NEW TO AN ORGANIZATION BUILD QUICK CREDIBILITY WITH PAID AND UNPAID STAFF?

When you are hired as Executive Director of a nonprofit you are usually received with great expectations for success. The first few months as ED are the formative ones, and one of your goals should be to create an atmosphere of mutual trust and respect with your paid and unpaid staff. This is also the time when Executive Directors make their leadership and management styles known and test them within the existing culture. Every ED brings a unique management and leadership style to the job. Being candid about this in the early days of working in the organization helps others develop understanding and trust for you.

There are many ways to get off to a good start with your staff and crystallize your personal style. However, we encourage all new Executive Directors to meet with each person who is a direct report within the first few weeks of beginning work to ask the following questions:

- Do you feel you are effective in your current position? If not, is there some way I can support you to become more effective?

- What are you expecting from me as the Executive Director?

- In what ways would you like to develop yourself in your job?

- What excites you about working here?

- What barriers to getting your job done do you experience?

- What is your preferred method of communication—e-mail, staff meetings, memos, phone calls, casual drop-ins?

- How do you prefer to receive feedback?

The second question provides a natural opening for you to describe your expectations of them as a staff member. If you've clearly heard what they expect from you, it will be natural for them to listen to you in return. The last question provides a similar opportunity to discuss your own preferences for receiving feedback—and to emphasize that you want and need feedback from your staff. At the conclusion of the conversation, talk frankly about your roles as leader, manager, and supporter, and how you work with staff in these roles. This helps staff see that you see yourself adapting to various situations, and that you intend to be flexible depending on the circumstances.

Of course, you should also make it clear to the staff you've met with that you cannot immediately fix all the concerns they may have laid out during your conversation with them. A staff person who perceives several barriers to working effectively, and who informs you of all those barriers, may expect you to get rid of those barriers quickly. It's important to let staff know you have heard their needs, and even make a list of them that is shared with the staff person, but it's equally important to let them know you may not be able to do a quick fix because of other priorities. For many staff members, feeling they have been listened to by a new ED is a very powerful experience, and it goes a long way to building trust.

Some organizations have a paid Executive Director with all other work being done by unpaid staff (generally called volunteers). Others have unpaid staff providing important support functions that assist those who are paid. Identifying who is key in these organizations is not just a matter of determining who has a position comparable to management, it requires finding out who the leaders are throughout the organization. Ask your staff who they go to when they want help, or need information, or just want to discuss something. The names that pop up repeatedly are people you should probably meet with, whether or not they are in supervisory positions.

Once you have met with your direct reports and the informal leaders, you should set up a group meeting with remaining staff and jointly address some of the questions listed for the individual staff meetings, particularly those on expectations, job satisfaction, and job frustration. As Executive Director, you'll find it useful to know what motivates and what challenges your staff, as well as what they expect of you and what they need from you to get their jobs done smoothly. By taking time for these initial conversations, you show you are interested in those who work there, which helps create an environment of partnership and establish a foundation of trust. As a side note, it's a good idea to have these all-staff meetings on a regular basis (quarterly at a minimum) to help staff stay connected with you, and vice versa.

There is no one way to learn more about those who work in the nonprofit. The crucial point is to take the time to do so. It is important to determine what is going to work best in your particular organizational culture.

These meetings are just the beginning of building credibility with staff. Periodic follow-up is essential. One way to build a healthy environment is to establish an "expectations statement" with staff—a document that spells out expectations of how people will work together in partnership. This serves as the foundation for your ongoing relationships with everyone. The list in Exhibit 13.1 offers some ideas on what you might want to have in this statement. We recommend reviewing it once a year with everyone to gain a recommitment to the values and tweak them if necessary.

If you can jointly develop an expectations statement with staff, then you more readily assure your credibility. When people in an organization trust and respect

> **Exhibit 13.1**
> **Key Elements of a Staff Expectations Statement**
>
> We will keep commitments we make. If we cannot keep a commitment, we will explain why.
>
> We will stay focused on priorities and be accountable for agreed-upon outcomes and deadlines.
>
> We will follow through on every assignment we accept. If we cannot meet a deadline for a task, we will give sufficient notice and explain why.
>
> We will give and receive constructive and honest feedback on work-related matters.
>
> We will openly acknowledge mistakes and errors and make efforts to learn from them.
>
> We will seek input on decisions from those people who will be affected by the decisions.
>
> We will work as a team to support each other and be ever conscious of the organization's mission and priorities in relationship to our own.

the Executive Director, a healthy, productive environment is the result, and the Executive Director is less likely to experience that "lonely at the top" syndrome that is so prevalent in the position. When your staff believes in you and respects you, they support your decisions and work with you to meet the goals of the organization.

HOW DOES AN EXECUTIVE DIRECTOR ENCOURAGE POSITIVE RELATIONSHIPS AND ESTABLISH A HEALTHY CULTURE AMONG STAFF AND VOLUNTEERS?

The Executive Director serves as a role model for staff in building positive relationships. This is just the beginning to creating a healthy culture for all.

Max De Pree, in *Leading Without Power,* describes the essentials of a vital organization. He explains that vital organizations exude health, energy, and enthusiasm. In other words, they have a culture that is robust, where people are working together productively to further the mission of the nonprofit and build its potential.

To paraphrase Max De Pree, some of the essentials that produce and maintain positive relationships among staff and volunteers are nourishment, justice, respect, confidence, transparency, and accountability. In the following list, we provide our translations of these powerful concepts. You can use these ideas to think about what is in place in your organization, and what you need to strengthen.

- *Nourishment:* An environment where people are constantly learning through taking on new tasks and participating in professional development activities, and are able to learn from making mistakes because they do not fear punishment.

- *Justice:* A culture that treats all staff and volunteers equally and fairly in terms of compensation, workload, and opportunities for promotion.

- *Respect:* An environment where staff and volunteers know their voices are heard and valued, and where good manners prevail.

- *Confidence:* A mind-set where every person in the organization believes that they and those served by the nonprofit will enjoy a brighter future, and that their commitment to their cause is making a significant difference in society.

- *Transparency:* Communication that is clear, honest, and travels upwards, downwards, and across all departments. Secrets and gossip are not tolerated.

- *Accountability:* A culture where all staff and volunteers know what is expected of them and are recognized and rewarded for their good work.

When these essentials are in place, relationships are more likely to be strong and the people active in the nonprofit to be working productively. It is also important for you, as Executive Director, to know that creating positive relationships and a healthy culture is not your job alone. It is everyone's job to create a healthy culture. If few of these essentials are in place, you may need to encourage and support managers to develop new practices. Mentoring them is one way to provide support, as is supporting professional development that develops communication and relationship-building skills.

Occasionally, a newly hired Executive Director walks into a culture that is lacking in trust and respect among staff. Because of this unhealthy culture, the Executive Director is immediately targeted as someone who should not be trusted or respected. If things blow up in your face before you've had a chance to do anything to set them off, it is very important to understand that the situation is not personal to you—it has probably been in place for some time. Any culture where you find people spending more time complaining about or blaming and shaming each other than being productive is a culture that needs to be changed. It is generally the job of the Executive Director to take the lead, but it is everyone's job to do the hard work of gaining trust and respect for one another.

For instance, if you find that staff have fallen into a habitual trap of negativity, resisting feedback, fighting new ideas, feeding unproductive rumor mills, and spending significant time talking about one another in negative tones, it's likely that they will almost immediately voice concerns about you as well. In that case, it's important to start changing this slowly by asking people to talk about their working environment and the overall culture of the nonprofit. Invite everyone to openly discuss what they like about working at the nonprofit, what originally brought them to it, what is frustrating, what is needed to create a more harmonious environment, and other such questions.

While you will probably notice resistance, we think you will also get some very good information to help shape a new culture. Also, if you are genuinely interested in the feedback you are receiving and demonstrate your interest, trust will begin to build for you and your position. Talk to staff about what you are finding and how the culture is not a productive or healthy one for anyone working there, and work with them to make changes toward a more positive environment. Some of the exercises in Chapter Four (on nonprofit culture) and Chapter Five (organizational values) may be useful here.

Quickly identifying cultural issues and explaining them to everyone helps staff see the Executive Director as someone who can be objective. Making changes to create a healthy culture helps everyone see that you are interested in their having a positive work experience. It's also a good idea to set some clear ground rules with staff. These might include maintaining zero tolerance for negative comments about fellow staff and volunteers and talking directly to fellow staff you have conflicts with rather than talking about them behind their backs. The following story from the field illustrates how one Executive Director showed leadership in changing a very volatile organizational culture.

Sarah learned within three weeks of starting her job as Executive Director at an environmental organization that her seven-member staff group was very dissatisfied with the organization and did not trust that the Board had made a good decision in hiring her. Rather than taking this somewhat blatantly stated reaction personally, Sarah moved quickly to set up meetings with each staff person and with her five-member Board. She suspected that there were tensions between Board members and staff—and she was right. As Sarah dug a little deeper, she discovered that nobody was very happy. The Board Chair finally explained to her that she was hired with an expectation that she could use her strong communication skills to build better relationships between Board and staff, and in doing so, create a more positive organizational culture.

Sarah started her daunting task of changing this harmful culture by meeting individually with all staff. Through her meetings with everyone, she learned that the previous Executive Director had created a culture where threats and intimidation were the norm, people were encouraged to work separately and in competition for resources, and led to believe that if something was wrong, it was the Board's fault. After her individual meetings, Sarah sat down with all the staff together to describe what she had found out in her individual meetings, and to explain why the culture of distrust and disrespect was going to hurt the organization's ability to achieve its mission. She also gave examples of healthy cultures she had worked in and laid out a vision of what she wanted to see at this nonprofit. She held a similarly frank discussion with the Board of Directors.

At first, Sarah found a lot of resistance from the staff to change the culture, and even some Board members voiced concern about changes. This organization had become so attached to its unhealthy culture that it found it difficult to let go. Some of the most vocal staff tried to get Sarah fired. They wrote a letter to the Board describing Sarah's poor management style and her inability to communicate well. Sarah was very discouraged but found support from the Board members and some of the staff who felt that her ideas were refreshing and needed in this nonprofit.

Several months into her tenure as ED, Sarah was finally able to form a joint Board-staff task force to work with her on short-term and longer-term strategies to build trust and engage everyone in fulfilling the mission together. They started by establishing ground rules for working together and planned a Board-staff retreat for later in the year so they could work together on team building as well as setting some long-term goals.

Sarah made it clear to everyone that changing organizational culture takes a long time, and that it is everyone's responsibility to achieve the vision they created of a healthier nonprofit where everyone worked together well, shared values, and had clear roles and responsibilities.

WHAT ARE WAYS TO BUILD LEADERSHIP AND MANAGEMENT SKILLS AMONG PAID AND UNPAID STAFF?

To be successful in the caretaking role of Executive Director, you must encourage and develop leaders and managers in your nonprofit. These are the people who will work closely with you while you are there as the ED and will stay after your departure to sustain the organization over the long haul.

As a leader and a manager, the Executive Director should serve as a role model for staff who are in these roles already, or who may be interested in taking them on. The supporter role is also an important one for Executive Directors to take in developing managers and leaders. Providing encouragement, resources, and coaching to persons motivated to grow in their positions and take on more responsibility and authority is essential to this supporter role.

Here are some ways an Executive Director can develop management and leadership skills among the staff:

- Hire people who have the skills, or the potential to develop the skills, to serve as leaders and managers.

- Understand that creating and nurturing leaders and managers in the organization is in no way a threat to the Executive Director's position. Instead, having others who lead and manage makes this position more doable.

- Encourage staff who are in management positions or who demonstrate leadership qualities to get more training and increase their skills in these areas so they are continually developing themselves.

- Empower staff to make their own decisions, or at least to suggest options and help select the best one, so as to build confidence among current and potential managers.

- Allow staff to make mistakes and turn them into learning experiences. It is far better to have a discussion on what could have worked better and what was learned from the mistake than to spend time and energy on warnings, reprimands, or demotions.

This last point might make some Executive Directors uncomfortable, because it suggests that mistakes are okay to make. In general, this is true: everybody makes them, and if you banish everyone who ever made a mistake you won't have an occupied office in the organization, including your own. It's worth restating: *build on mistakes, and don't let them tear things apart.* But draw the line at actions that intentionally harm the organization—they do need to be handled swiftly and will require some form of reprimand or dismissal. Everyone should be held accountable for their actions and be praised when they do well, given performance improvement plans when they are making mistakes or faltering, and let go if they are unable to improve or if they choose to do something that is harmful to the organization.

The first point is also important. Finding smart people with good management and leadership potential is not always easy, especially if your organization's salary structure is lower than that of comparable organizations. As you begin your search, it's important to be very clear about what skills and qualities you're looking for in any person you are hiring. If the pool of résumés isn't giving you what you need, then sometimes it's necessary to recruit people from other organizations. Look beyond nonprofits doing similar work as yours, and even beyond the nonprofit sector. Sometimes the best person for your open position is working in a different job altogether but has the right skills and management potential to fit well into your organization. Oftentimes it takes awhile to find the right fit, and remaining patient during the search is crucial. An Executive Director may feel pressured by the fact that others are taking on extra tasks to fill in for someone who has recently left, but in the long run, it is best for everyone if the new hire can do the job well.

It is important for Executive Directors to encourage staff to grow into their own management and leadership styles. This might mean sending staff to management workshops or conferences. They could also find online courses or other resources to gain new knowledge. There are also organizations such as Coro (offices in San Francisco, New York City, Pittsburgh, and Los Angeles) that provide more intensive fellowships and training for tomorrow's leaders. Remember that managers and leaders are not born—they are developed over time. To do this, staff should be supported to develop themselves professionally, given tasks that challenge them (but not overly so), and allowed to take risks that don't jeopardize the organization. They can develop leadership skills on the job and become confident in their own levels of expertise.

HOW DOES AN EXECUTIVE DIRECTOR WORK ACROSS THE GENERATIONS TO HAVE STAFF WORK PRODUCTIVELY TOGETHER?

If you look at the age range of staff in many nonprofits these days, you will see three generations: the Baby Boomers (born 1946–1964); Generation X (born 1965–1979); and the Millennials (born 1980–2000). Each generation brings its own unique style and identification into the workplace, and providing leadership across these generations is challenging. While it is wrong to stereotype anyone based simply on age, the three generations tend to display certain general characteristics that, if understood, can help an Executive Director manage communication flow, motivate everyone, and help resolve conflicts. To get everyone working together, you need to understand the unique strengths and weaknesses of each generation and identify the points of friction among them on how they tend to view the world.

Exhibit 13.2 provides an overview of the three generations and how each is best motivated, its members' work ethic and preferred work environment, and best ways to communicate with them. Executive Directors may find this chart helpful as they lead, manage, and support their staff.

A generation is shaped by the events and circumstances its members experience at certain phases in life, beginning with childhood. Generational personas are formed by a number of factors including the cultural norms for child rearing at the time, the perceptions of the world as the generation starts to come of age, and the common experiences of the generation.

As individuals, the Boomers have experienced successes and learned from their failures. They grew up in the 1960s and 1970s when activism and the talk of social revolution was everywhere. Many were also part of the growing

Exhibit 13.2
Characteristics of the Generations

Area of Comparison	Baby Boomer	Generation X	Early Millennials
Birth range	1946–1964	1965–1979	1980–2000
Important motivators	Promotions Pay raises Fighting for the rights of others Being managers and leaders; being in charge Building community	Independent projects measuring productivity Project ownership Honest feedback Making a difference for others Challenging work Shared power	Acknowledgment Socially responsible employers Making a difference for others Strong-focused leadership Adequate pay to enjoy life
Work ethic	Live to work Long tenures at organizations Respect for bosses and superiors is assumed Commitment to organization Do what asked to do Face-time with bosses is important	Work to live Short tenure (three to five years) Respect is earned, not based on position Commitment to work Entrepreneurial Prefer self-management Enjoy family-like feeling	Work to live Work time must be meaningful and productive Open, constant communication with boss Adequate and positive supervision important Focus on task completion
Work environment	Competitive Political	Flex-time crucial Transparent structure and communication	Collaborative decision-making Best technology used for everything

	Planning time frame based on future	Planning time frame is short-term	Planning time frame based on immediate
	Teamwork critical to success	Multiple options: plans A-D for everything	Mentorship is norm
	Number of hours worked = productivity	Technology is used to manage and control work	Up-front investment for jobs
	Hierarchical decision making	Participatory decision making	Transparent structure and communication
	Can overlook younger generations' skills and abilities to lead		Safe learning environment
Communication style	Telephone	Cell phone	Blogs
	Face-to-face	E-mail	Texting
	E-mail	Facebook	Twitter

middle class—blue-collar workers that joined unions, became highly political, and were unsatisfied with the status quo. The Boomers are community builders and can galvanize a force of their own at the drop of a hat. And they have vision.

In spite of the fact that Boomers are beginning to reach the traditional retirement age of sixty-five, many of them are delaying their retirement due to the need to earn more money, and also because many Baby Boomers "live to work" and are not ready for retirement. While they continue in the workforce, the Boomers inhabit the most powerful leadership positions throughout organizations in both the for-profit and nonprofit arenas. They also retain much of the experiential, technical, institutional, and political knowledge in the workplace. They have the industry connections, networks, and inside scoop to get things done. For some, Boomer culture tends to emphasize competitiveness, self-importance, and youthfulness—qualities that may make it hard for Boomers to grasp their responsibility to mentor and prepare their successors.

Unlike the communal Baby Boomers, Xers tend to be modular people, dealing with each situation on its own terms, in their own way. They are the realists, and also the first generation to view society more globally due to the advance of the Internet and other technologies. They are visionaries too, but are grounded in a realistic viewpoint that believes the world is not secure, and neither is the workplace. They hold few illusions that they will be cared for by the institutions in their lives, and few look forward to company retirement programs, Social Security, or Medicare benefits. The marketplace conditions experienced by many Gen Xers have helped to fashion a self-adept workforce, but one that tends to be skeptical of company promises and grand policy visions.

Generation X workers endeavor to create autonomous, grounded, and satisfying ways to take care of themselves and their families. Responding to the cultural climate, they tend to seek private solutions to public issues, relying upon their own inventiveness rather than their capacity to motivate and organize others. This is the generation that embraced Social Entrepreneurship and has made it an important part of our global society.

Many Xers believe family time is so important that they are less willing to sell their souls to the 24/7 devil and often put work-life balance ahead of income and career advancement. This means opportunities for flextime, part-time work, and telecommuting are very appealing to them.

Independent, pragmatic, and technologically resourceful, Xers have become some of the most sought-after employees in the workplace. Despite their competence, however, many tend to avoid the long-term allegiances and political relationships required to climb the management ranks. Indeed, studies indicate that most Gen Xers would rather own their own businesses than become corporate CEOs, and would rather be an entrepreneur than hold a top job in government—by a ratio of four to one. But they also want leadership roles in nonprofit organizations. Executive Directors can ease their own sense of being overwhelmed by finding ways to include the Generation X staff in positions of responsibility and leadership. Many are eager and willing for the challenge.

The first-born Millennials are turning thirty (as of 2009), and they are potentially the highest-performing generation in history because its members are entering the workplace with more information, greater technological skill, and higher expectations of themselves and others than prior generations.

They may require a lot of management, but they're worth the effort. Statistically, Millennials are the most pluralistic, integrated, high-tech generation in American history—traits that make them ideally suited to our increasingly demanding, diverse, and dispersed global workplace. They demand fast-track career positioning, greater work-life balance, positive feedback, training, and cutting-edge technology. By challenging workforce conventions, the Millennials offer us a long-overdue reality check on the American workplace that may ultimately change it for the better.

One of the Millennials' greatest strengths is their technological sophistication. Digital communication is their birthright. Members grew up in an on-demand world where access to information is immediate. Technology has been and remains an integral part of their daily lives, including their relationships. Thus they possess the tools and savvy needed to work with the information systems running companies today and to address the challenges of working in virtual teams on complex problems. In addition, they have been raised by their Boomer parents to be team players and are well suited for collaborative work environments.

So how do the nonprofit leaders of today help these complex generations work together productively? Using the descriptions suggested here can help create communication systems that will reach all three effectively. Boomers want more meetings, and Millennials might be happy to join them. Boomers will be, and should be, great mentors for the Xers and Millennials in their workplace and they should be encouraged to form teams and work together. But Xers need their independence at work and will be more productive if their projects intersect with others but are not completely dependent on them. Executive Directors may need to spend more time with Xers explaining the necessities of working across departments to complete projects and setting up structures to help them do so effectively.

Executive Directors will also likely need to explain to their Generation X and Millennial employees the big-picture purpose of the organization and how their role serves that purpose. Involving them heavily in organization-wide strategic thinking sessions will be invaluable for them and for your nonprofit. Two of the strongest common denominators across all three generations are the importance of having vision, and the importance of stated values. Executive Directors who keep their nonprofit's vision and values at the forefront, and who are open to applying them in ways that motivate and satisfy the different generations, will generally have a healthy organizational culture.

Another very important common denominator of the generations is the desire for responsibility and leadership. If you are an Executive Director in an organization full of Generation X and Millennial employees, we highly recommend you find opportunities for leadership for those who want them. They are the leaders of the future, and giving them this role in a supportive and learning environment will contribute to their own success as well as that of the nonprofits they lead.

WHAT ARE STRATEGIES FOR ESTABLISHING STRONG LINES OF COMMUNICATION WITH STAFF?

The focus on one-to-one conversations with staff and establishing a values statement mentioned earlier are two strategies that open up good lines of communication. Some other strategies are useful to consider as well.

Good communication involves understanding that you need to communicate effectively throughout all levels of your nonprofit. Too many Executive Directors discuss important issues with their management team, and then let them pass the information on to others. Inevitably the information gets reworded as it moves through the organization, and the intended message becomes distorted or even lost. It's like Post Office—the game children play of whispering something in someone's ear, who then whispers it in the next person's ear, and on down the line to the last person, who has to say what the first person originally whispered. The person at the end of the line always says something radically different from what the first person said!

If you have something important to say to your staff and volunteers, say it to everyone. Using this approach allows you to answer questions immediately, dispel fears and rumors, and show people you genuinely respect them. In turn, they will most likely respect and support you.

While providing good information to staff is important, perhaps the greatest gift of all to everyone is your ability to listen well. We encourage all Executive Directors to spend time every day just listening to staff in the organization, and being clear that every voice in the nonprofit is important.

Here are some other strategies to encourage good communication in your nonprofit:

- Use a variety of techniques to communicate. Some people take in information by reading it, others want to hear it.

- Encourage people to listen and to hold real dialogues with one another.

- Be clear about who needs to know what. While everyone should know about decisions, events, changes, and other happenings at the nonprofit, not everyone needs to know every detail. You want to include a high level of detail for people who are affected directly by the information or who may need to give explanations to others outside the organization. Others just need to know that something new has taken place.

- Encourage feedback. Find ways to make it easy for staff and volunteers to make suggestions for improvement, such as a suggestion box or special meetings with you to just brainstorm new ways of working at your organization.

- Create an evaluation system that involves input from a variety of people close to the person being evaluated. This representative feedback system from all levels of the organization provides specific feedback against specific goals. To keep the workload down, the staff person being evaluated and the supervisor doing the evaluation each identifies three to five people to provide input.

- Practice self-management when someone criticizes or disagrees with you. Remember it is that person's perspective, and work together to determine what is at the source of the critical view or perspective.

- Create a zero-tolerance environment for staff and volunteers who come to you with complaints about others when they have not tried to work out their complaints with the individuals involved.

As Executive Director, you should support effective conflict resolution between staff and volunteers—not step in and do it yourself and deprive them of the opportunity. The first step is to have individuals talk to each other about problems they have with one another. Offer suggestions, role-play ways to work out conflicts, mediate if you need to, but don't ever take matters into your own hands until those in conflict have tried to work out their differences.

HOW CAN TECHNOLOGY AID RELATIONSHIPS AND BE USED AS AN EFFECTIVE COMMUNICATION TOOL WITH STAFF?

As nonprofits become more and more savvy about technology and it becomes more affordable to have all staff linked with it, communication patterns in nonprofits are changing. One of the earlier examples of new technology communication tools is e-mail. It is unusual now to find any nonprofit, small or large, that does not rely heavily on e-mail for communication. This is both good and bad.

E-mail is great for getting those quick announcements out to people, to tell them about visitors coming to the organization, new grant money received, upcoming staff meetings, and the like.

Where e-mail fails miserably is in communicating anything that evokes divergent viewpoints that need to be expressed and discussed. For example, one Executive Director communicated everything by e-mail. He recognized individuals for their good work via e-mail. He offered constructive criticism via e-mail. He gave notice of his decisions to everyone using e-mail. When asked why, he explained that it saved an enormous amount of time to send out an e-mail message, rather than hunt around for an individual or call a meeting. That was true enough, but what he failed to recognize was that his communication was all one-way, leaving staff feeling remote, cut off, and with little input or connection. The organization was suffering in terms of both communication with and respect for the Executive Director. However, it isn't just Executive Directors who fall into this trap of communication exclusively through e-mail. Staff people can find it easier to use e-mail to engage in conflicts with other staff members or make critical comments to others about them. Of course, this is a very destructive use of e-mail—and the problem applies to all other broadcast technology such as texting and Twitter.

Today's technology also means staff can work at home and either connect remotely with their computer in the office or use an older technology of taking flashdrives home with them with files and documents. Developing communication strategies that allow staff to phone in to meetings, and even be there on a computer screen, help create a more flexible work environment. However, telecommuting also requires more frequent communication between the Executive Director or staff supervisor of the person who is sitting at home working. It is important for staff to have specific tasks with benchmarks and time lines so that the supervisor and work-at-home staffer are satisfied with the level of productivity.

Being connected 24/7 to your nonprofit can be comforting for an Executive Director, but it also can mean there is no real relief from the pressures of work. Are you an Executive Director who checks e-mail day and night, or never turns off the cell phone so that no calls or text messages are missed? If so, we guarantee you will burn out at your job faster than the ED who sets boundaries by closing more than the office door at the end of the day. Executive Directors should also respect their staff by not expecting them to receive and respond to messages sent outside of work hours. It's a good idea to make sure everyone has a posted schedule of when they are at work, and not. By not communicating with staff when they are not at work, Executive Directors and others in the organization are showing respect for the need for a life outside work.

HOW DOES AN EXECUTIVE DIRECTOR OFFER AND RECEIVE SUPPORT FROM STAFF AND VOLUNTEERS WHILE KEEPING AN ARM'S-LENGTH RELATIONSHIP?

The implication in this question is that there must be an arm's-length relationship rather than friendship or anything more intimate between the Executive Director and staff. We agree with this basic premise; leading and managing friends or loved ones is a tricky and very difficult job for an Executive Director. Boundaries become fuzzy, resentment builds, and the Executive Director's credibility can fade.

This does not mean that an Executive Director should not have personal interactions with staff. As a matter of fact, we encourage some level of personal interaction as a way to build a strong staff team. Executive Directors all need to create their own boundaries regarding these personal interactions. The following guidelines may help in establishing such boundaries:

- Keep your very personal (intimate) life outside the organization. If you are having problems with a loved one, leave those at home.

- Be open about your interests, food cravings, and favorite things to do.

- If anyone on the staff tries to get you to serve as therapist, help them move their attention to a trained professional in this field. (Even if you are a trained professional, help them find someone else.)

- If you find a friendship developing with a staff person, be clear that your primary responsibility in the friendship is to the nonprofit where you both work, and the friendship will always come second.

- Never, ever engage in an intimate relationship with one of your staff (paid or unpaid).

- If you have a Facebook or MySpace page, remember that it is not only your friends who can chat with you there. Your staff may be able to read your messages there too. Transparent communication is good, but transparency has its limits.

This does not mean that Executive Directors should not seek out staff or volunteers for support. You can and should turn to trusted individuals in your organization, people whose opinions you value, for the purpose of bouncing ideas off them, getting needed input before making decisions, or just having some fun. Just draw the line—and never cross it—at seeking out staff to vent frustrations, talk about other staff or Board members, or complain about how miserable life is at that moment. These are topics that are better handled outside the organization with friends, family, a coach, or anyone who is not directly involved in the organization.

TIPS FOR SUCCESS

- Get to know what your staff thinks about working in your organization—their joys and frustrations—and also what they expect from you.

- Communicate clearly and often with your staff and let them know you expect the same from them.

- Your staff may consist of multiple generations that have different needs and desires. Pay attention to the differences.

- One of your roles as ED is to build management and leadership skills in those staff interested in developing them. Find out who is interested and give them opportunities to manage and lead while also mentoring them.

Following the Founder

*Founder's Syndrome occurs when an organization operates according
to the personality of the most prominent person in the organization
rather than working toward its overall mission. This prominent
person may be the Founder, Board Chair or Executive
Director. The syndrome is primarily an organizational
issue, not simply the fault of the person of prominence.*

—Carter McNamara

Organizations are usually started by someone with an incredible vision and strong passion to address a pressing need or to initiate change. In the early days of an organization, the Founder keeps the vision alive with personal energy, passion, gutsiness, and quite often financial resources as well.

While the term *Founder* originally referred to the person who began an organization, it has since been expanded to apply to anyone with long-term prominence and authority in an organization, such as the first Executive Director or anyone whose identity has become tied closely to that of the organization for a long period of time.

193

Just as moving through adolescence with a child is frequently a highly emotional time, so too we find that a mix of emotions emerges as Founders watch their nonprofits grow up. There is joy for the success of the nonprofit. There is sadness for leaving the good old days. And often, there is some fear of letting go of the attention that being the focal point for the organization has afforded the Founder.

Releasing the responsibilities seems to be the easier part. Giving up authority, visibility, and leadership is more challenging—not only for the Founder but also for others in the organization who will have to change their comfortable ways of doing things.

This chapter addresses the following issues that typically arise for a new Executive Director dealing with a Founder who still wants to be engaged in a nonprofit:

- Why do relationships with Founders in transition tend to be so complicated?

- What is the best way for an Executive Director to work with a Founder who is still a member of the Board of Directors?

- What does the Executive Director do if the Founder is causing serious problems for the organization?

- What are the pros and cons of having the Founder stay on as a staff person or consultant?

WHY DO RELATIONSHIPS WITH FOUNDERS IN TRANSITION TEND TO BE SO COMPLICATED?

Eventually, the Founder discovers that the nonprofit is taking on a life of its own. This usually happens when the Board has grown beyond being just the friends of the Founder, or when the first Executive Director (beyond the Founder) is hired, or when a funder has taken a special interest in the organization and has significantly increased funding for programs, which then intensifies demands for accountability.

In organizational life cycle terms, the nonprofit finds it must grow from its start-up, entrepreneurial roots into a well-managed organization with systems, policies, and planning. Board members must move beyond their mostly reactive engagement with the Founder's individual style toward a more proactive, consensus-oriented model of decision making. In other words, the organization experiences a major cultural shift.

Organizational culture emerges to become more visible and critical during periods of Founder transition. Before successors can begin to understand or adapt the culture toward their own personal leadership style, they must understand its roots, the factors that led to its development, and how this all influences the organization's thoughts and actions.

When an organization hires its first Executive Director to step into the activities once done by a Founder, tensions related to the Founder's process of letting go—as well as that of the rest of the organization—often emerge. They need to be addressed early in this new developing relationship. The incoming Executive Director wonders what to do with this amazing person who started the nonprofit and poured years of life into it. The staff and Board are sometimes torn between their allegiance to the Founder and to the newly hired ED whose success they hope for. The Founder grapples with the desire to delegate day-to-day responsibilities in the face of continuing passion and love of the visibility and authority of the Founder identity.

Shifts in a Founder's role and authority ripple throughout the entire organization, and sometimes into the external community as well. The visibility and strength that the Founder brings to the organization start to become a hindrance as individuals—and sometimes the Founder as well—have trouble letting go of the old ways.

WHAT IS THE BEST WAY FOR AN EXECUTIVE DIRECTOR TO WORK WITH A FOUNDER WHO IS STILL A MEMBER OF THE BOARD OF DIRECTORS?

The Founder as Board member works well if that person understands that the position carries the same responsibilities as that of other Board members and an equal voice—no more and no less. This is a big if. Usually the transition from a Founder-driven Board to a Board led by a strong Executive Director is challenging. More and more organizations allow, suggest, or request that their Founder take a well-deserved break for a year or so. This allows the Founder's vision and work to evolve under the new ED's leadership.

Suppose you are the first Executive Director of a nonprofit where the Founder has always worn the hats of Board member, Board Chair, and Executive Director.

On one hand you see the opportunity to work with someone who has incredible passion for the nonprofit. On the other hand, you may notice that the Founder has a tendency to micromanage your work to ensure that everything continues as it should—at least in the Founder's eyes. Building a trusting relationship with the Founder necessitates constant communication, reassurance, and some frank discussions about your ED role relative to the Founder's new role. As new staff members (paid and unpaid) are added to the organization, you may also need to hold meetings with the full Board to further define the changing roles of the Founder, the Executive Director, and others.

A Founder often retains a Board position but frequently chooses not to be a key officer. This can be tricky to manage. On one hand, the Founder wants others to take on leadership roles. However, when disagreeing with a decision, the Founder may quite actively struggle to take the reins away from the new leaders. When this happens, the Board Chair must step in to gently remind the Founder that Board members can legitimately disagree on issues, but when a decision is made, it is a Board decision and all must accept it.

It can be very helpful for everyone to define a particular Board task for a Founder that channels all that passion and energy in a valuable direction. For example, we have seen Founders asked to develop a written history of the organization and to periodically provide stories to Board members to help everyone understand an organization's roots. We have also seen Founders become major fundraisers because of their charisma and energy.

Another Board member role for the Founder is as an emeritus. Emeritus status elevates Founders to honorary membership on the Board, allowing them to attend meetings whenever interested and give wise advice when asked. An emeritus Board member often does not have voting rights but is able to have a voice at the table whenever needed or desired.

WHAT DOES THE EXECUTIVE DIRECTOR DO IF THE FOUNDER IS CAUSING SERIOUS PROBLEMS FOR THE ORGANIZATION?

In our years of working with nonprofits we have encountered a few situations where the Founder was seriously hindering the progress and success of an organization. A clear indicator of such a circumstance is that everyone in the nonprofit is unhappy most of the time—including the Founder, who often does not understand the source of the problems.

If you as Executive Director find yourself facing this kind of situation, proceed with caution and allow the mission rather than the personalities to be your guide. First, make sure you are not projecting your misery with the Founder onto everyone else. In other words, see if the Board and other staff members are seeing the issues in the same light. Often they share your concern that the Founder is creating problems for the organization but don't know how to initiate the conversation, let alone resolve it. Work with the Board to help its members take the initiative and lead the process. Gather concrete examples of what the Founder is doing that is harmful. Then have the Board Chair or Executive Committee meet with you and the Founder to discuss the problems openly and candidly.

It is very important that the conversation with the Founder be conducted with compassion and respect. This is not a discussion to have when hot tempers are fully engaged. Remember, and make reference to, all the wonderful work the Founder has done. Reinforce for everyone the common vision and passion for the organization that you all share. Then describe very specifically and concretely the actions of the Founder that are hurting the organization. If you describe these actions in the context of the nonprofit growing to a new level where success requires meeting new and different needs, rather than putting the Founder's efforts down, you and the Board stand a better chance of making your point effectively.

Expect anger, tears, silence, denial, and a wide range of other unhappy emotions. Remember too that when emotions are allowed expression in an atmosphere of respect and compassion, energy is often freed up and everyone can more easily share new perspectives. This is the nature of difficult conversations. If the Founder is truly hampering an organization, not having this conversation is more than likely to prolong the unhealthy behaviors that can eventually damage both the Founder and the organization's reputation.

There may be room for negotiation in this meeting. If the issue is one of divided loyalty, staff and stakeholders need to have their support redirected toward the organization so they're no longer torn between allegiances to either the Founder or ED. Perhaps the Founder can take on a goodwill ambassador role outside the nonprofit. Don't close the door on the possibility of an ongoing relationship. But if it is clear that there is no possibility for such a relationship, then your Board or Executive Committee members should gently but firmly let the Founder know that the nonprofit no longer has a role for the Founder to assume.

WHAT ARE THE PROS AND CONS OF HAVING THE FOUNDER STAY ON AS A STAFF PERSON OR CONSULTANT?

When a nonprofit is making the transition from an all-volunteer group in which the Founder has taken the responsibilities of both Chair and ED to hiring its first paid Executive Director, the Founder sometimes chooses to take the paid position. There are many pros to this move. The Founder knows the organization and everyone knows the Founder. Often the Founder is the nonprofit and that transfers to the new position very smoothly. Basically, the programs or services of the organization proceed without disruption and this is a major plus. Having the incredible vision, passion, and energy of the Founder leading the organization on a daily basis is of course an extraordinary benefit.

But having the Founder become the first paid ED does bring some challenges. It is complex to define and set boundaries between the leadership roles of the Executive Director, the Founder, and the Board.

STORY FROM THE FIELD

In a recent Board meeting, Bob, who is the Founder and Executive Director of the organization, and who had formerly been the Board Chair, was running the meeting and making decisions while Board members simply nodded their heads in agreement. The consultant observing this made comments after the meeting to the Board Chair and Bob about the need for a close partnership but separate duties. Bob was not in favor of this and made it clear to the consultant and Board Chair that he saw no reason for changes to be made. The consultant spent several weeks talking to Bob, giving examples of organizations that had struggled without the proposed separation of duties, as well as examples of organizations that had thrived when Board and ED had clear but separate responsibilities. Finally, Bob agreed to give it a try. The two leaders worked with the consultant to draft a new job description that strengthened the Board Chair's role, and took it to the next Board meeting. Presented with the rationale for separation of authority between Board Chair and Executive Director, everyone thought this was a good idea and agreed to move forward quickly to strengthen the Chair's authority and leadership role. It looked like the group would move into its next stage smoothly, but Bob continued to make all the decisions, and the partnership between the Board and the Bob began deteriorating as resentment grew among Board members.

To better understand the friction, the consultant met with Board members individually and asked questions regarding each person's ideas for a better partnership. Then the consultant met with Bob to explain what she had heard and to relay how the Founder's need to control the organization was actually harmful. Bob had had no idea that the rest of the Board was upset, and he agreed something should be done to correct the situation.

The Executive Committee met with Bob and began the slow process of transition from Founder-led organization to a stronger Board-ED partnership. New roles and responsibilities were defined as well as clear lines of authority for decisions. Board members discussed their interests and skills and began taking on some of the tasks Bob had originally done. All these changes led to a much better partnership, and to a healthier culture for this nonprofit.

If you are an Executive Director who founded your organization and also used to be the Board Chair, watch out for the natural tendency to keep both roles. Take time to determine if you are building a healthy relationship with your Chair and Board members.

Sometimes a Founder will want to remain in a staff position in the organization, but not as the Executive Director. One of the pros to this is the knowledge the Founder brings to the organization. Another is that Founders who make this choice usually want a staff role congruent with their gifts and skills, thus eliminating the potential to fill the position with an unqualified individual.

The most important potential con to hiring the Founder in a staff role lies in the sheer difficulty of stepping out of a position of authority, working in partnership with someone who now holds that authority, and reporting to the Board through new lines of communication. A truly great-hearted Founder can do this, especially if the environment stays reasonably consistent for a few years after the transition. If things don't work out, however, the new Executive Director is in an almost untenable position. Imagine yourself with a Founder on staff who disagrees with your vision and leadership of the organization. The Founder can do some serious damage to your credibility by going to friendly Board members and making disparaging remarks about you. While these might be grounds for termination from a strict personnel management viewpoint, can you do this if the Board is supporting the Founder's position?

It is this scenario—which has repeated itself countless times in our experience—that leads us to the conclusion that Founders should not be hired as staff, other than as the Executive Director. The risk of harming the progress and success of the organization is too great.

Founders can and should be engaged as consultants in their area of expertise. The obvious benefit is that you get a consultant who already knows your organization well and has a lot of loyalty to your mission. Also, as the client to the Founder-consultant, you set the project parameters and define the criteria for success. Since projects are time limited, the Founder-consultant can do a specific job and then move on to something else.

No matter what position the Founder takes in your organization, the responsibilities have to be very clear so the Founder fully understands and accepts the new role. Boundaries on decision making (what decisions the Founder can make now) and clarity on what you hold the Founder accountable for should also be stated up front. Remember also that the more specific the project for a Founder, the more likely that person will be successful, and the more likely there will be a good relationship between the Executive Director and Founder.

TIPS FOR SUCCESS

- The departure of a Founder is often a tipping point in any nonprofit. It is a good idea to find ways to honor and respect the Founder's contributions while also making it clear that new opportunities lie ahead.

- If the Founder is stepping aside as ED but wants to remain involved in the organization, make sure the new roles, responsibilities, and accountability are clearly defined.

- If a Founder is causing friction either inside or outside the organization, take the time to sit down with the individual and explain the harm that is being done to the mission and vision first set by the Founder.

PART FIVE

Executive Director as Community Creator

The leaders of all institutions will have to learn that it is not enough for them to lead their own institutions ... they will also have to learn to become leaders in the community. In fact, they will have to learn to create community.

—Peter Drucker

Nonprofit organizations and their leaders increasingly play a dual role, furthering their own mission by working collaboratively with other organizations and within their own communities. These collaborative approaches are built on mutual benefit, and they reward the individuals involved, their nonprofit organizations, and the broader community. Thus the term *community creator* is used when describing this critical ED role.

Technology now plays center stage in most nonprofits, particularly in reaching out to and drawing in the community. Executive Directors and others in organizations are finding new and more efficient ways to reach others with their mission, vision, values, plans, and needs. What was once fairly easily defined by time and financial constraints has evolved into broader, less defined communities where new collaborations, partnerships, and advocacy efforts are happening. Take for instance an organization wanting to complete a regional trail system that spans three states, multiple jurisdictions, and uncountable stakeholders. Today, Executive Directors can use blogs, online surveys, Facebook pages, e-mail, Internet research, and a host of other tools to communicate quickly and effectively to engage stakeholders across all boundaries. While becoming a community creator has been made easier with the use of technology, it has also become more difficult because the term *community* has become less well defined.

To help the Executive Director and others in the organization with creating community, this section of the book examines relationship building beyond the walls of the organization. Chapter Fifteen explores the rewards of informal relationships with a variety of stakeholders, and Chapter Sixteen focuses on more long-term, strategic partnerships such as collaboration and strategic alliances. Both chapters give nonprofit leaders information to think about their organization in a larger, more holistic way.

Engaging External Stakeholders

You cannot build relationships without having an understanding of your potential partners, and you cannot achieve that understanding without a special form of communication that goes beyond ordinary conversation. In other words, you need to engage in dialogue.

—Daniel Yankelovich, *The Magic of Dialogue*

Nonprofits thrive when they have a committed group of external stakeholders ready to provide support through advocacy, funding, and furthering the mission. These stakeholders give added passion and commitment to your cause and create a strong voice in the community. Generally, the more external stakeholders an organization has, the more influence and visibility it has in serving and advocating on behalf of those in need. At the same time, the more visible an organization is through its marketing and public relations, the more easily it can attract new stakeholders.

203

The term *stakeholders* is widely used in our nonprofit vocabulary, yet many outside the sector are caught off-guard by its common reference and broad use. In the nonprofit sector, the term has come to define any individual or group that has, or should have, an interest or stake in an organization's mission, vision, and accomplishments. Although businesses typically define stakeholders narrowly as direct customers and investors, nonprofits regard a complex matrix of individuals and groups who bring a broad range of resources as well as expectations as legitimate stakeholders in their affairs.

In addition to being a source of visibility and resources for nonprofits and support for the Executive Director, stakeholders can present challenges and barriers when they are overlooked or misunderstood. Thus we have dedicated a chapter to helping you answer the following questions:

- Who are an organization's external stakeholders?
- How can the Executive Director develop and nurture relationships with key stakeholders?
- How does an Executive Director rally stakeholders for advocacy?

WHO ARE AN ORGANIZATION'S EXTERNAL STAKEHOLDERS?

Preceding chapters discuss four of the most visible internal stakeholders in any nonprofit: the Board, staff, volunteers (or unpaid staff), and the Founder. But the discussion can't stop there. You also need to look beyond the organization's walls for ideas, insights, trends, and needs in your community. Every organization should be asking itself who the individuals and groups are that it should be nurturing or exploring. We encourage you to do this by taking time as part of your strategic planning process or annual goal-setting to evaluate the importance of identifying all those people who are interested in your organization's ability to achieve its mission. These are your stakeholders, and they will be critical to helping you reach your stated goals, as well as to dealing with those who might hinder your work.

We have found that most nonprofit organizations have two general groups of external stakeholders. The first group is often very obvious to everyone because they touch your organization on a regular basis. The second group can be easy to overlook without some forethought about how they connect with your nonprofit, or should connect.

Most Obvious Stakeholders

- Your clients or customers
- Prospective clients or customers
- Families of clients or customers
- Individual donors
- Foundation and corporate funders
- Government funders
- Prospective funders
- Regulatory agencies
- Vendors you contract with or buy from

Less Obvious and Sometimes Overlooked

- Community leaders
- Local, regional, and national politicians and their staff
- Neighbors near your facilities or offices
- Your landlord or property owner
- Any community person who has contacted your organization for information, made a donation, or signed up for e-newsletters or updates
- Former Board members or advisory board participants
- Former clients, staff, and volunteers
- Nonprofit organizations with similar or competing programs
- Businesses with complementary or competing programs or products used by your clients
- The media
- Companies whose employees benefit from your mission or services
- Nonprofit management support organizations

This list should help you in developing your own targeted list of individuals or groups that you already have a relationship with but need to nurture, and those where new relationships may be critical to your organization's mission or future plans. Remember to look outside the geographic boundaries of your community to find important stakeholders.

Exhibit 15.1 presents one exercise you can use to determine your range of stakeholders, from most obvious to least obvious.

As we describe the communication techniques that can be used with external stakeholders, it is valuable to consider using the more effective personalized communication techniques with the most obvious stakeholders because those are the people you may rely on more than others out in the community.

HOW CAN THE EXECUTIVE DIRECTOR DEVELOP AND NURTURE RELATIONSHIPS WITH KEY STAKEHOLDERS?

Getting the word out about the needs in your community and how your non-profit is responding to those needs is important to your success in achieving your vision and fulfilling your mission. One great way to get the word out is to be accessible to the media, government officials, and opinion leaders who are interested in and sensitive to your mission. They can be excellent resources

---

Exhibit 15.1
Discovering Your Stakeholders

Gather a group of interested staff, volunteers, Board members, and community members for a one- or two-hour session of defining your range of stakeholders. Divide the group into smaller ones and provide each of them with a large piece of paper and some markers.

Ask the groups to draw four concentric circles on the sheet, making the outermost circle as large as the sheet will hold. Tell everyone to write the most obvious stakeholders in the middle circle and to begin working outwards in the circles, putting the least obvious stakeholders in the outermost one.

After about thirty minutes of work, bring everyone back together to share and explain why they placed stakeholders in their chosen circles. There will be differences of opinion but ultimately the Executive Director will have a good list of stakeholders and how they are perceived by the organization.

---

or spokespersons. Current and future external stakeholders need constant reminders of your organization's accomplishments, and of your values and purpose. This builds commitment to your mission and creates a small army of dedicated individuals.

Day-to-day demands often take up so much attention that an Executive Director becomes isolated from the rest of the world. It takes planning and initiative to reach beyond the boundaries of your organization to be reminded of the bigger community perspective and your broader civic responsibility.

The key to building and maintaining any relationship is dialogue and understanding what is important to the other party. For example, you probably already have communications tools in place for your clients that describe or market your programs. But do you really know who your customers are, where they come from, and what they value about your services? Your donors send you a check and you respond with an acknowledgment or thank-you. But do you know why they give to you or their connection with your mission?

What these questions point to is that the underlying principle of working with stakeholders is to develop a healthy pattern of two-way communication. The first step is to listen—get to know them, their current or potential interest in your organization, what they expect of you and your organization, and how they subjectively or objectively evaluate the outcomes or satisfaction. The second step is to educate, inform, and ask for their feedback, insight, and support.

While a face-to-face meeting is often the most personal way to engage in dialogue, it isn't a very efficient form of communication when you have large groups of stakeholders. The communication ladder illustrated in Exhibit 15.2 has been adapted over the years as the Internet has grown, blogs have developed, and Twitter has gained recognition. It lists the various forms of communication from the most personal to least personal way to engage in dialogue (listen, inform, educate, and ask for feedback and support), and from the least efficient to most efficient ways to reach your target audience. Some may debate the effectiveness of e-mail versus "snail mail" for a personal letter depending on where you live, but the ladder does help you to think about the efficiency versus personal trade-off in identifying the most appropriate tools for your specific message to stakeholders.

As you develop your stakeholder strategy, make sure to include your Board and staff. Board members may already have a relationship and credibility with

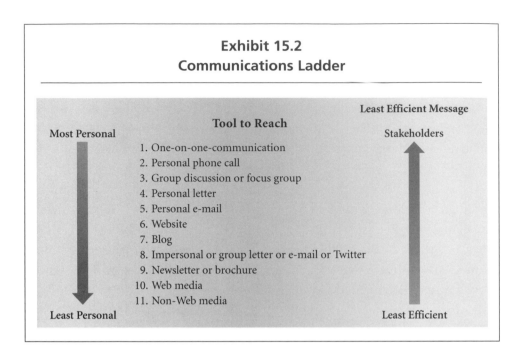

Exhibit 15.2
Communications Ladder

Least Efficient Message

Tool to Reach

Most Personal

Stakeholders

1. One-on-one-communication
2. Personal phone call
3. Group discussion or focus group
4. Personal letter
5. Personal e-mail
6. Website
7. Blog
8. Impersonal or group letter or e-mail or Twitter
9. Newsletter or brochure
10. Web media
11. Non-Web media

Least Personal

Least Efficient

a specific individual or group stakeholder. Funders and regulatory agencies may want to hear directly from key management in the programs or on the front lines.

Executive Directors and others involved in external stakeholder communications need a plan to reach out and engage their communities. Exhibit 15.3 provides an example of a plan that has been used by several groups to decide on the most effective and efficient ways to reach their stakeholders. The following story from the field explains how one group used the plan in their organization.

STORY FROM THE FIELD

Following two years of troubled Board and staff leadership that had left it on the verge of financial crisis, a mental health organization hired Patricia, a seasoned Executive Director, from outside. The organization was at risk of losing critical government funding, referrals from other agencies, and licenses required by the state government to do its work.

Working with the Board and staff, Patricia helped the group develop the plan shown in Exhibit 15.3 as the first phase of a stakeholder strategy designed to rebuild the organization and its reputation. The plan outlined the use of various communication tools, prioritized the key stakeholders, and clarified what the nonprofit needed to learn (or listen to) as well as the key message it needed to deliver, along with the proposed support it was looking to gain and a plan of ongoing communication.

Exhibit 15.3
Stakeholder Communication Strategy

Stakeholder

- Ten largest major donors
- Regulatory agencies
- Former Board members
- Staff
- Clients
- Other nonprofit agencies that refer clients to us

Key Questions and Listening Points

- For donors: What is your interest in us? What do you feel we are doing well? What could we improve upon? How do you feel we are perceived in the community?

- For regulatory agencies: What are we doing well? What do we need to improve on? How much time do we have to reach compliance? What flexibility can you allow us? How should we be evaluated? How can we rebuild our trust and partnership?

- For former Board members: What is your current level of interest? How can you help?

- For staff: What attracted you to this job and the organization? What has been your greatest accomplishment? What is the greatest barrier to getting your job done? What one thing do you need to be more effective?

(Continued)

- For clients: Does the service we provide you meet your needs? If not, what needs to improve in our service to you? How has our service benefited you? Are there other services within our mission and vision that you'd like us to be providing you?
- For other nonprofits: What are we doing well? Where do we need to improve? How can we best partner to support each other? What are your expectations about how we will serve those you refer to us?

Key Messages

- For donors: We value your support. Share mission, vision, what is working, and turnaround strategy. Ask for specific gift to support turnaround.
- For regulatory agencies: Acknowledge past problems. Ask for support and patience to get back on track. Share mission, vision, what is working, and turnaround strategy.
- For former Board members: We value your past support. Share mission, vision, what is working, and turnaround strategy.
- For staff: We value your dedication, skills, and views. We need your support to turn things around. Change is difficult. Share new strategy and reinforce the mission and vision.
- For clients: We value you as a customer. If necessary, we apologize. We are listening and need your feedback. (Remind customers of mission and vision.)
- For other nonprofits: Thank you for your past support and referrals. We are committed to working with you and providing quality services to those you refer to us.

Initial Communication Strategy

- For donors: Face-to-face meetings with ED and an appropriate Board member with existing relationship.
- For regulatory agencies: Face-to-face meetings with ED, Board members, and key staff member.
- For former Board members: Personal letter from Board Chair inviting them to call with feedback.

- For staff: Individual meetings between supervisors and ED. Group meeting with ED and Board member.
- For clients: Small focus group.
- For other nonprofits: Face-to-face meeting with senior staff.

What Do They Value?

- For donors: Accountability, ongoing communication, feeling that their funds are invested in a healthy organization.
- For regulatory agencies: Quantifiable results. Timely reports. No surprises.
- For former Board members: Being part of an organization they believe in and trust. Feeling valued.
- For staff: Being heard, included, and respected.
- For clients: Our interest in their views. Willingness to work with them to implement suggestions.
- For other nonprofits: Quality programs. Partnership between organizations.

Follow-Up Communication

- For donors: Personal thank-you letter signed by ED and Board member, quarterly newsletter via mail or e-mail depending on preference.
- For regulatory agencies: Weekly or monthly updates on progress. Invitation to tour facility and programs in three months.
- For former Board members: Monthly e-mail updates on progress.
- For staff: Ongoing personal, group, and written updates celebrating small successes and candor on the work that still needs to be done.
- For clients: Bulletin board in all facilities that updates clients. Quarterly newsletter or monthly e-newsletter.
- For other nonprofits: Monthly follow-up meetings to keep lines of communication open and explore joint problem solving.

Creating the plan is only the first step. Implementation of this kind of communication strategy requires

- A realistic but tight time frame
- Leadership and coordination from the ED, Board, and key management staff
- Individuals with the appropriate skills and connections
- A process to integrate responses and feedback so that the key messages are not lost
- Ongoing commitment to listen and communicate with stakeholders, updating them on the situation and accomplishments

Few organizations can reach their true potential by themselves. They need the support and wisdom of key individuals and groups that have or should have a stake in their mission. Take the time to look beyond your organization's walls for those who could be instrumental in helping you achieve your mission, as well as those that might present barriers.

HOW DOES AN EXECUTIVE DIRECTOR RALLY STAKEHOLDERS FOR ADVOCACY?

In most nonprofits, the Executive Director has an important responsibility as chief advocacy organizer. There may be others in the organization who share this responsibility, but it is often the Executive Director who leads advocacy efforts and is a key spokesperson.

Advocacy work is very different from lobbying, which has strict government rules about what can and cannot be done. Advocacy is a "cry for action" that can be a local effort to save an arts program in public schools or an international effort to save a species from extinction. Whenever there is a threat to your organization's ability to achieve its mission and vision, you should be at the forefront of rallying your external stakeholders to make their voice heard to end that threat.

This can be done in many ways. Executive Directors can work with their Web site managers to launch an online petition campaign to educate decision makers to stop an action or make an important change. You can work with your communications staff to send mass e-mail to thousands of supporters calling them to action for a specific cause. A more low-tech advocacy approach can also be effective. We know an Executive Director in a small nonprofit who mailed three hundred personal letters to long-time stakeholders asking them to show up at a city council meeting and speak out against a proposal that would have shut down services to many of this organization's clients. So many stakeholders showed up at the city council meeting and spoke passionately about the need for these services that the city council members quickly backed away from the proposal. The services were saved due to the advocacy work of the ED.

It's important to remember that the stakeholders you are engaging in advocacy work need a clear message to deliver. As the Executive Director, you are undoubtedly the person who knows what needs to be said. Developing talking points for your stakeholder advocates is always a good idea. By doing so, you are educating your stakeholders to what the issue is and what needs to change. They, in turn, can educate others.

Equally important is to make sure there are stakeholders ready to take action when you need them to. Nonprofits that do community organizing as part of their mission have leagues of volunteers working on advocacy and organizing activities. All nonprofits can learn good lessons from these groups about how to bring together many stakeholders, organize them with a clear message, and let them loose to advocate for change.

With today's technology, stakeholders do not need to live or work near your nonprofit to be advocates on your behalf. As mentioned earlier, your community's boundaries are defined less by geography and more by your mission and services. Even the smallest of nonprofits can have a dynamite Web site and Facebook page that attracts visitors from anywhere in the world who will respond to a call for action. While this creates a larger pool of stakeholders who will advocate on behalf of a nonprofit, it can also create some headaches for the Executive Director who cannot manage the message across the Internet. Sometimes a well-meaning advocate will send an e-mail, write a letter, or make a phone call that is an embarrassment. If you are engaging stakeholders for advocacy via your Web site or Facebook activity, be very clear what these good people should say on your organization's behalf. Giving them a few statements that you want them to say is often the best idea. This creates a tone of seriousness but not anger or insult.

Also remember to thank everyone who has rallied to your organization's call for action and provided much-needed support. Stakeholders who feel appreciated will be ready and willing when you need their help again.

TIPS FOR SUCCESS

- A large pool of external stakeholders provides your nonprofit with advocates, cheerleaders, and supporters. They give tremendous added value to any organization.

- Communities no longer have well-defined boundaries. Your external stakeholders may live and work anywhere and be connected to you via the Internet, Twitter, or other broadcast technology.

- Your external stakeholders need attention too. They should be communicated with and get support from those working inside the organization. The more visible you are with them, the more support you will get when you need it.

- Listening to your external stakeholders is as important as talking to them. Use blogs, focus groups, town hall meetings, or whatever is needed to hear what your external stakeholders want to tell you.

Embracing Partnerships and Collaboration

No nonprofit organization can survive and succeed in advancing its mission while living independent of other nonprofits. Organizations gain information, political power, and personal and professional support from and in concert with other nonprofits. Thus close working relationships, partnerships and even joint ventures between nonprofit organizations are a fairly natural occurrence.

—David La Piana

A variety of partnerships from collaborations to mergers are evolving as extensions of an organization's relationships with its stakeholders. Nonprofit leaders are embracing the necessity of leading beyond the walls of each individual organization and developing partnerships that thrive on shared strengths and views. Many

Executive Directors find that through short-term collaborations as well as formal structured strategic alliances they can better fulfill their mission, especially when faced with the breadth and complexity of the changing community needs and increasing competition for donor dollars.

The main difference between simple coordination between nonprofits and a more complex partnership relationship is that in a partnership such as a collaboration, two or more organizations have joined forces to publicly work toward some mutual benefit and have agreed to some distributed or shared power or authority. In contrast, coordination between nonprofits is often casual, the benefits are assumed, and there is no shift in authority or power.

Nonprofits have several options when considering new ways to work more collaboratively with other organizations. Many excellent resources can help guide nonprofits through this organizational change. One of the contributors to the growing knowledge base on the subject for nonprofits is David La Piana. David brings much clarity to the whole field of nonprofit partnerships with his explanation of what he calls the "partnership continuum." The partnership continuum identifies a full range of options, from collaborative relationships that allow each organization a great deal of autonomy to the more fully integrated and permanent relationship formed by a merger, which integrates two or more organizations into one.

In this chapter we explore partnerships as an effective tool in helping nonprofits build their capacity and community. These are the main questions that we address:

- How can Executive Directors assess the values and risks of leading their organizations into partnerships?

- What are ways organizations can work together informally, and how does an Executive Director make this happen?

- What forms of partnership exist beyond collaboration?

- How can Executive Directors prepare their organizations to enter into partnerships?

HOW CAN EXECUTIVE DIRECTORS ASSESS THE VALUES AND RISKS OF LEADING THEIR ORGANIZATIONS INTO PARTNERSHIPS?

Partnerships among nonprofits have intensified in the last decade. The primary driving factor for many of these has been the issues facing our communities—poverty, crime, education, environment, housing, health, to name a few. These issues cannot be tackled effectively by any single organization. In addition, pressures from funders and tough economic realities have driven many collaborations, joint ventures, and mergers.

Some of the most effective partnerships have been started by Executive Directors seeking new solutions to old problems, looking for ways to work more effectively, or desiring economies of scale. These partnerships start simply with an invitation to get together to explore the what-if or why-not issues that are often unspoken.

Through partnerships, a variety of nonprofits have pooled their talent and resources to solve problems, create innovative programs, or simply work in a new and more effective way that increases their own capacity to serve.

Partnerships benefit organizations, communities, and the people that have led them in many ways. Here are a few examples of how partnerships can help support individual, organizational, or community capacity building:

- New leadership, communication, and negotiation skills are developed among the Executive Directors or organizational representatives that make up the group.

- Visibility is increased for the organizations and their representatives as a result of working on a collaborative effort or in another form of partnership.

- New insights with regard to issues, trends, research, opportunities, and challenges emerge from the sharing of perspectives.

- Opportunities to capitalize on the collective strengths of the partners and minimize individual risks or weaknesses often become apparent.

- Economies of scale achieved through collectively undertaking projects such as research, marketing, fundraising, program development, and advocacy benefit everyone.

- Expansion of capacity allows organizations to serve more clients, provide more comprehensive services, or broaden the reach of their services.

While the rewards of reaching beyond your organization's traditional walls are many, there are also inherent barriers. Partnerships require a great deal of time and attention that can pull the ED and staff away from internal priorities. The greatest challenge of forming sustainable partnerships is that they can undermine the individuals and organizations they bring together. The following factors often lead to trouble:

- Lack of adequate resources (time, money, leadership) required to address issues or achieve desired goals

- Egos, self-interests, and political agendas that block effective and candid discussions

- Lack of shared purpose or expectations

- Inability of the partners to clearly establish roles, rights, and responsibilities

- Unwillingness of the partners or their respective organizations to reach consensus or compromise, share power, and jointly accept success and failure

- An unfavorable political or social climate that may not support the collaborative process or outcome

- Partnering for political reasons (other people are doing this, a funder suggests it)

- Lack of understanding or commitment from those not fully engaged in the partnership

- Partnering when interests (mutual and separate) are not specified and shared

- An expectation of egalitarianism among partners when some bring more than others to the partnership

By listing these challenges, our intention is not to deter you but rather to increase your awareness and perhaps allow you to address such issues before problems arise. Forewarned, you have a greater chance of reaching your stated goals.

Collaboration is an incredible tool for organizations to pool their talent and resources in search of a common vision. It takes work, compromise, and vision to overcome inevitable issues of self-interest that keep many groups from sustaining their partnership.

The Executive Directors of a group of domestic violence agencies came together and developed a common goal of building transitional housing for their clients. Through their shared vision and purpose they have successfully overcome a variety of challenges that could easily have resulted in the respective agencies parting ways.

The vision for transitional housing originated as a solo project for one of the agencies. As staff members moved on to leadership roles in neighboring agencies, the project followed them, but it was never able to get off the ground until the political climate shifted in a way that raised the awareness of domestic violence and housing issues locally, lowering the competitive barriers that had traditionally isolated the agencies. As the vision became large and visible, the case for the project took on a life of its own. The project formally became a collaboration that was rewarded with early funding and support from private, community, and government sources.

This success meant more work for the Executive Directors who originally came together. Rather than succumb to the challenges of leading their respective agencies while supporting the growing demands of the collaborative, they recognized that additional resources and skills needed to come to the table. Additional agencies with housing experience were invited to join the collaborative. Fundraising support was also hired to help with a collective campaign.

As the number of players in the collaborative grew, so did need for coordination and compromise. Each agency took turns providing leadership to the partnership and the funding campaign. Support staff in each organization shared the load by taking on clearly defined roles and responsibilities. Policies, procedures, and rights were negotiated and adopted.

Despite the visibility and success of the collaborative, the EDs were still feeling pulled between their own organizational issues and those of the collaborative. Boards began to challenge the time that was going into the collaboration at the expense of their own organizations. Board members had lost sight of the vision and the benefits of transitional housing to their respective missions.

The initial reaction was that the collaboration's success necessitated converting it into a stand-alone nonprofit organization. While this would solve many of the ongoing internal struggles the collaborative faced, funders made it very clear that part of their motivation for support was the unique nature of the collaboration, the collective expertise, and the minimal over-head costs associated with the project. After some self-reflection, the EDs recognized the need to increase communication with and among their Boards. They formed an advisory group with representatives of each participating group's Board. The result was to broaden and secure each organization's continued stake in the project.

So far, the collaborative has raised over $14 million and built two innovative projects that provide housing to more than forty families; it now has a third project under consideration. Struggles and occasional setbacks still occur. But the vision, shared purpose, and visible success have allowed the group to accomplish much more than its members could ever have envisioned individually.

WHAT ARE WAYS ORGANIZATIONS CAN WORK TOGETHER INFORMALLY, AND HOW DOES AN EXECUTIVE DIRECTOR MAKE THIS HAPPEN?

These days, we hear more about nonprofits merging, forming joint partnerships, or adopting some other complex way to share resources and work together. We address some of these partnerships with the next question. But it is also possible for nonprofits to have very informal partnerships that are simple to create but give great added value to everyone involved. Quite often, two or more nonprofits begin collaborating together when staff see advantages for resource and idea sharing. For example, the program manager of an arts program for adults with mental disabilities in one community joined forces with her colleague in a neighboring city to develop an art show for the clients of both organizations. By sharing resources for this event, they gained much greater publicity, more variety of artwork, and a large gathering of stakeholders to enjoy the show. In this example, the Executive Directors of both organizations gave encouragement and support to their program staff so the event would be a success.

Sometimes, it is the Executive Directors who initiate a collaboration. It is very common for one ED to contact another to share information about similar programs and to seek ways they can strengthen their own programs to serve clients more effectively. Or both organizations may be purchasing an expensive product for their clients that could be bought cheaper in bulk. For example, six nonprofit animal shelters cooperated on the purchase of microchips for the dogs and cats they were placing in new homes. Because of the volume being purchased, the microchip producer dropped the price significantly, with considerable benefit to all the organizations.

In another situation, several nonprofits with different services to clients with disabling and chronic illnesses cooperated informally on a regional plan to ensure these frail individuals would be cared for with food, shelter, medical treatment, and other services if there was a major natural disaster in their communities. The nonprofits all signed a mutual aid agreement that will help them work closely and effectively when disaster strikes.

Boards of Directors can also participate in working together informally with other organizations. One nonprofit Board sat down with another to develop a plan to purchase a large building where both organizations would move their offices and programs. In this situation, the nonprofits maintained completely separate operations but were able to afford a nicer space for themselves because they worked together. Since both organizations serve the same clientele but with different programs, their co-location was also a great benefit to their clients, who can now go to both organizations in a single trip.

The key factor in each of these efforts to work together is Executive Directors who embrace the idea of sharing information and resources for mutual benefit. Although there may be competition among their organizations for donor dollars, there is the understanding that nonprofits who participate in joint efforts are more successful in achieving their missions and visions. Executive Directors provide the leadership in their organizations for Board and staff to work cooperatively with others in informal and creative ways.

WHAT FORMS OF PARTNERSHIP EXIST BEYOND COLLABORATION?

The challenge and opportunity facing many nonprofits is to look beyond collaboration to more long-term, formal, or sustainable partnerships that will further both groups' missions and provide a broader foundation upon which they can build their capacity to serve their communities.

As stated earlier in the chapter, a variety of partnership opportunities are available to nonprofits. As illustrated in Exhibit 16.1, each varies in the degree of autonomy, integration, collaboration, and legal restructuring needed by the organizations involved.

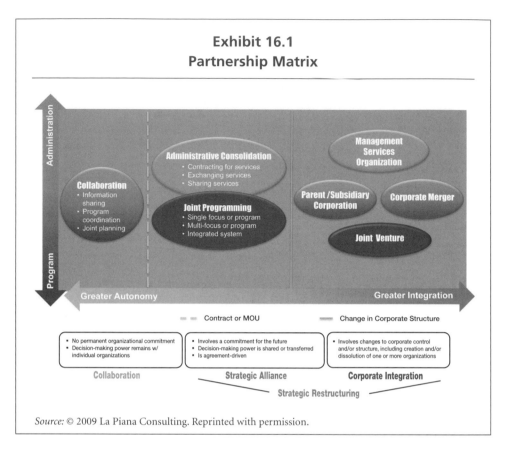

Exhibit 16.1
Partnership Matrix

Source: © 2009 La Piana Consulting. Reprinted with permission.

The following summary lists the three most common ways nonprofits align their programs or integrate their organizations. In our experience many formal arrangements evolve out of highly successful collaborations. All of the following concepts fall into a category known as "strategic restructuring" because they involve a partial or total change in the structure and locus of control of the partners.

Joint Programming or *Joint Venture:* These are widely used terms that can mean anything from program collaboration between several nonprofits to activity that significantly alters a nonprofit's character. The terms are also applied to nonprofits with similar programs that decide to minimize competition by jointly conducting some activities, such as regional fundraising, marketing, or visibility campaigns.

For example, a joint fundraising venture among a group of nonprofits providing home-delivered meal services to local communities lessens competition for foundation grants and individual contributions and thus increases overall capacity to serve their communities. The Executive Directors of the meal delivery programs serve as the Board of Directors of a small subsidiary organization that has its own staff of two. The purpose of the subsidiary is to raise money for all the nonprofits involved, and over the years it has raised hundreds of thousands of dollars.

Another type of nonprofit/for-profit joint venture is emerging, as discussed in Chapter Seven. Corporate leaders are forming nonprofit extensions of their companies to support community philanthropy and initiatives. Nonprofits are forming for-profit services that funnel profits back into the nonprofit.

Administrative Consolidation: The sharing of core administrative functions, usually among nonprofits with similar missions and clients, characterizes a back-office consolidation. The organizations maintain their own Boards and staff and continue to exist as separate entities. However, some or all of their administrative functions are combined, such as payroll and human resource systems, financial and management information systems, and billing systems. There are lots of creative ways to make back-office consolidations work.

For example, suppose two organizations serving homeless individuals determine that, as single entities, they do not have the infrastructure to support program growth. Their administrative costs are soaring. If they combine their finance, human resources, and technology departments, significant advantages in efficiency and cost-effectiveness will result. The nonprofits continue to operate as separate entities, each with its own ED and Board, but with a smoothly functioning, shared administrative department behind the scenes.

Merger: The legal and permanent blending of two or more nonprofits into a single entity is a merger. Rather than driven by the win-lose mentality or takeover approach common to corporate sector mergers, nonprofit mergers are usually driven by win-win opportunities to build on strengths and lessen risk.

Mergers are becoming a common restructuring practice and most communities have already experienced a merger between two nonprofits. Mergers are most successful when both parties agree to forfeit their current identity and establish an entirely new entity. Occasionally, the stronger partner in a nonprofit merger maintains its identity (either legally or symbolically), which results in a consolidation of the smaller nonprofit into the larger one. While consolidations are one good way to restructure, they are not true mergers.

Another term that is sometimes used for a restructuring is *acquisition.* In the nonprofit world, an acquisition is the same as a merger because nonprofit corporations cannot be bought or sold. Their assets must be transferred to a similar nonprofit organization under the close scrutiny of each state's Attorney General's office.

HOW CAN EXECUTIVE DIRECTORS PREPARE THEIR ORGANIZATIONS TO ENTER INTO PARTNERSHIPS?

Entering into any kind of partnership—be it marriage, new job, or organizational collaboration—without first knowing your own strengths and expectations can be dangerous. Thus it makes sense to take time for self-reflection and assessment. What are your motivations for a specific partnership? Is this partner suitable? What are the strengths and weaknesses of your organization? What challenges and opportunities do you face? How much time do you have to form the partnership and do the work?

Executive Directors need to ask themselves, their key staff, and their Board some key questions prior to undertaking a new venture. The following list is not exhaustive, but helps make explicit your motivations, fears, and potential benefits:

- What is driving our interest or desire to enter into this partnership?
- How will our mission be furthered by partnership?
- What do we specifically hope to gain from the partnership?
- What are we willing to contribute or share in terms of staff and Board time, expertise, or financial resources?
- Do Board, staff, and volunteers agree that a collaboration or partnership is beneficial?
- What is our history of working beyond our organization's boundaries?
- Do our potential partners share an environment of collaboration, trust, and mutual support?
- Because it takes more time to finish a project when working in a partnership, do we have the time right now? Or is the deadline so close that we had better do this ourselves?

If you are looking at a long-term strategic alliance or merger, you will want to explore many of the questions we raised regarding partnerships, as well as the following:

- Are we moving forward with restructuring because of desperation or fear, or do we really see advantages?

- What might we gain or lose in terms of our organizational identity and culture?

- Is the partnership being driven by a funder or external stakeholder? If so, what are the implications to our commitment?

In response to the breadth and complexity of the changing nonprofit environment, nonprofits and businesses are exploring new ways of working together. Partnerships of all kinds are being formed to build capacity and better fulfill each group's mission.

TIPS FOR SUCCESS

- Informal and formal partnerships can be of tremendous value to organizations as long as you pay close attention to the compatibility of mission, vision, and priorities.

- Good partnerships take lots of time and energy, just like any relationship. Your time spent on partnerships needs to be considered when deciding on your priorities and annual work plan.

PART SIX

Executive Director as Resource Wizard

The highest use of capital is not to make more money, but to make money do more for the betterment of life.

—Henry Ford

Nonprofit organizations are incredible vehicles that allow communities to show their care and concern for others by giving of their time, talent, and resources. Nonprofit leaders, in turn, transform individual and community philanthropy into responsive programs and services that by law are held to a high level of accountability.

We purposely chose the term *wizard* in the title to reflect the amazing ability of Executive Directors who mix and match dozens of funding streams, each with different expectations, time frames, and reporting requirements, and transform them into innovative programs that make a difference in the lives of those they serve.

Chapter Seventeen addresses the most common concerns EDs raise in managing the financial side of the nonprofit. In Chapter Eighteen, we demystify the process of fundraising and help the ED develop a team-based approach within an organization.

Ensuring Sound Financial Management

By Elizabeth Norton-Schaffer

Your organization is a mission-based business, not a charity.

—Peter Brinckerhoff, *Mission-Based Management*

As an Executive Director, you are constantly balancing the pursuit of the mission and the financial sustainability of your organization. Financial oversight cannot be delegated; it lies at the heart of your accountability to your Board, your stakeholders, and your nonprofit's legal requirement to uphold the public trust.

Your specific financial tasks will vary based on your organization's history, culture, and resources, so it isn't possible to cover all the details. However, this chapter addresses some key financial management activities and questions that Executive Directors typically ask as they work their way through financial details:

- What are the major differences between for-profit and nonprofit finances?
- Who takes the lead in fulfilling the various financial management roles in a nonprofit?

- What financial reports do the Board, staff, and volunteers need to see and how often?

- What is the Board's role in the budgeting process?

- After the Board passes a budget, what authority does the Executive Director have to implement programs or contracts?

- If there is a financial crisis, what does the Executive Director tell the Board and staff?

Before trying to answer these questions, it is helpful to define the key activities of nonprofit financial management: budgeting, implementation, reporting, and analysis.

SOME KEY DEFINITIONS

Budgeting: The budget is simply your plan for the coming year expressed in terms of income and expenses. In many organizations, the budget cycle represents the bulk of the annual planning effort. Budgeting activities include creating an annual program plan, estimating expenses, and forecasting revenue.

Implementation: Once a budget is in place, you'll begin implementing programs, raising and spending money as approved, and recording financial transactions.

Reporting: At the end of each month and quarter, your accounting staff or service will create reports that reflect all of the month's financial activity.

Analysis: Using the reports, you, the Treasurer, and other Board and staff members will monitor financial performance and assess whether the original plan (and budget) is still the best course.

WHAT ARE THE MAJOR DIFFERENCES BETWEEN FOR-PROFIT AND NONPROFIT FINANCES?

Good financial systems and accounting practices in nonprofit organizations are, for the most part, very similar to those used in the for-profit world. Nonetheless, those new to the nonprofit sector—both staff and Board members—often struggle with how nonprofit financial information is presented. The key differences are the classification of net assets, accounting for contributions, recording of functional expenses, and sources of revenue.

Classification of Net Assets

The difference between a nonprofit's assets (property) and liabilities (debt) is known as its *net assets.* Nonprofit accounting conventions require that (audited) financial statements segregate net assets into three categories:

- *Unrestricted net assets:* Net assets that are not subject to donor-imposed restrictions and can be used at the discretion of Board and management.

- *Temporarily restricted net assets:* Net assets that are subject to donor-imposed stipulations that may be met by actions of the organization or will be met by the passage of time. When the restriction expires, temporarily restricted net assets are reclassified as unrestricted. For example, say a foundation gives you a two-year grant (time restriction) targeted to the youth development program (purpose restriction). As you implement the program and spend money hiring staff, creating marketing materials, you will release these funds from restriction.

- *Permanently restricted net assets:* Net assets subject to donor-imposed stipulations that they be maintained permanently by the organization (endowments). The organization can spend the income these assets generate, but cannot dip into the principal sums.

Accounting for Contributions

Nonprofits fund their activities with either earned revenue (client fees, ticket sales, government contracts, and so on) or support (grants and contributions). Accounting for contributions is unique to the nonprofit sector and often misunderstood.

The level of restriction associated with a grant or contribution determines how it is recorded. According to generally accepted accounting principles for nonprofit organizations, support is reported in the following three categories:

- *Unrestricted support:* Grants and contributions given by the donor without reference to a specific purpose or use within a specific time period are recorded when pledged and increase the unrestricted net assets of the organization.

- *Temporarily restricted support:* Grants and contributions that are to be spent for a specific purpose or during a restricted period of time are also recorded when pledged and increase the temporarily restricted net assets. Once any restrictions have been met, the grant or contribution will be released (or transferred) into unrestricted net assets, with a corresponding reduction in temporarily restricted net assets.

- *Permanently restricted support:* These are grants and contributions whose principal is to be invested according to the donor's wishes and are added to the permanently restricted net assets when pledged.

Functional Expenses

As defined by the IRS Form 990 and FASB 117, nonprofits must report their expenses by functional classification: program services and supporting services. Exhibit 17.1 provides a detailed breakout of functional expenses. In general, however, program services are "the activities that result in goods and services

---

Exhibit 17.1
Functional Expense Classifications

Program	Costs resulting in distributing goods and services to clients and fulfilling the mission of the organization
Administration (supporting)	Those costs not identifiable with programs, fundraising, or membership development and indispensable to the organization's existence such as governance (that is, Board-related expenses), finance and accounting, legal, and executive management
Fundraising (supporting)	Costs associated with soliciting contributions from individuals, foundations, and corporations; maintaining donor mailing lists; and conducting fundraising events
Membership development (supporting)	Those costs related to soliciting for prospective members and membership dues, membership relations, and similar activities

---

being distributed to beneficiaries, customers, or members that fulfill the purposes or mission for which the organization exists. Those services are the major output of the organization and often relate to several major programs." Supporting services are "all activities of a not-for-profit organization other than program services. Generally, they include administration, fundraising, and membership development activities."

Revenue Sources

Nonprofit organizations often have more diverse sources of income than for-profit companies. Typical sources of income are contributions from individuals and institutions, earned revenue from clients, government, events, and contracts, and dividends and interest from investments. Nonprofits that rely upon a single source of funding—from an individual donor, a foundation grant, or a government contract—for the majority of their annual income will be more vulnerable than those with diverse sources of income. Further, healthy nonprofits strive to have diversification across income streams—a variety of funding types—and within income streams—a number of sources within a funding type.

WHO TAKES THE LEAD IN FULFILLING THE VARIOUS FINANCIAL MANAGEMENT ROLES IN A NONPROFIT?

Nonprofit financial management is a team process that involves both the Board and staff in planning and implementation, as well as in the reporting and monitoring systems that ensure financial stability and public accountability. While these roles will vary to some degree based on your organization's size, culture, and lines of authority, the chart in Exhibit 17.2 will help guide your organization in determining leadership roles and shared responsibilities. On the staff side, the ED may delegate the responsibility to the appropriate financial or program staff within the organization. On the governance side, the Board often delegates the role to the Treasurer or the Finance Committee. The ED and Board may delegate certain tasks and responsibilities, however, they are still ultimately responsible for the oversight and overall accountability of the organization.

Exhibit 17.2
Fiscal Roles and Responsibilities

Overall: To ensure that the organization has fiscal processes and systems that support appropriate control and oversight.

	Executive Director	Board
Form a Finance Committee.		Lead
Establish meaningful dialogue between Finance, Program, and Development staff and committees.	Share	Share
Establish salary ranges for each job category; ensure that salaries are within approved ranges.	Share	Share
Prepare an annual schedule showing each staff person's category and salary range (for Personnel or Finance Committee).	Lead	

Budgeting and Planning: To ensure that the budget reflects the organization's mission, values, and overall plan.

	Executive Director	Board
Create long-range plan, annual goals, and budgeting parameters.		Lead
Develop annual program plan and estimate costs.	Lead	
Create revenue and fundraising projections.	Share	Share
Propose plan and budget for approval.	Lead	
Approve the plan and budget; give staff authority to make minor changes.		Lead

Record Keeping: To appropriately record all financial transactions and safeguard the assets of the organization.

	Executive Director	Board
Develop a written set of internal policies for handling deposits and payments; follow procedures in spirit as well as to the letter.	Lead	

	Executive Director	Board
Review and approve key accounting policies.		Lead
Authorize bills and invoices for payment; determine expense coding.	Lead	
Determine appropriate revenue coding for deposits.	Lead	

Reporting: To summarize the organization's financial position in an accurate and complete manner, and to comply with all legal and funding requirements.

	Executive Director	Board
Create monthly financial reports within three weeks of month-end.	Lead	
Distribute financial statements before Board and committee meetings.	Lead	
Prepare brief, written narrative analysis to accompany financial reports.	Lead	
Determine whether an audit is required; select the auditor; receive the audit letter directly from the auditor; meet with the auditor with no staff present (at least once per year).		Lead
Ensure that the audit is completed within four months of fiscal year-end; prepare a written response to comments in the management letter.	Lead	
Complete or verify that all legal and funding requirements are completed in an accurate and timely fashion.	Share	Share

Monitoring: To ensure adequate fiscal oversight.

	Executive Director	Board
Carefully review organization's financial information.	Share	Share
Compare actual results to budget; propose revised plan or budget.	Lead	
Propose items for ad hoc investigation.	Share	Share

WHAT FINANCIAL REPORTS DO THE BOARD AND MANAGERS NEED TO SEE AND HOW OFTEN?

The only report that nonprofit organizations are required to file (and then, only those with receipts of more than $25,000) is IRS Form 990. Unfortunately, although satisfying legal requirements is essential, most organizations cannot use the Form 990 as a management tool. Regardless of the organization's income level, Board and staff need other financial information to let them know how things are going. Typically, the Board and staff will want answers to these questions:

- Do we have enough money?
- Are our results consistent with our plan or budget?
- Do we need a new plan?
- What's our cash flow situation?
- Do we have sufficient reserves?

You'll need to be able to answer these questions as frequently as things change in your organization. When you can't locate an answer in your head, it is time to find the answer elsewhere. For most organizations, a small group—such as the staff leadership team or the Board's Finance Committee—reviews data on a monthly basis. Other organizations find that it works well to have a more comprehensive quarterly presentation to the full Board with an update for all staff. Typically, the organization's external constituencies—funders, members, donors, and so on—expect an annual financial update. Most important is to create a schedule and stick to it. When people expect data and don't receive it, they tend to think the worst.

The chart in Exhibit 17.3 provides a list of the reports required in the typical nonprofit organization. The Executive Director's key role in financial reporting is to ensure that everyone—ED, staff leadership, and Board members alike—upholds the public trust. All parties must be educated consumers of financial data and accountable to the organization's stakeholders.

WHAT IS THE BOARD'S ROLE IN THE BUDGETING PROCESS?

The best budgeting process is a partnership between Board and staff. The first and most important step of the budgeting process is for Board and ED to jointly

Exhibit 17.3
Financial Statements for Leaders

Statement of Financial Position	Also known as the balance sheet in the for-profit world, this statement summarizes assets (what the organization has and uses), liabilities (what the organization owes), and net assets (what the organization truly owns) as of a specific date.
Statement of Activity	Also known as the income statement or profit and loss statement in the for-profit world, this statement reports financial activity by function over a period of time.
Budgeted Statement of Activity—Unrestricted	This statement compares the organization's unrestricted financial activity to the budget—see sample statement in Exhibit 17.4.
Statement of Functional Income and Expenses	This report matches income and expense by function—for example, key programs, administration, and fundraising—and is used to evaluate surplus or deficit for each activity.
Restricted Funds Detail	This report includes information on each restricted grant: the amount raised, the amount released from restriction, and the remaining balance available for current and future fiscal years.
Updated Cash Flow Projection	This forecasting tool details the planned cash receipts and disbursements for the coming months.
Updated Projection	This forecasting tool details the year-to-date financial performance and the planned activity for the balance of the fiscal year—see sample projection in Exhibit 17.5, later in this chapter.

Source: Bell, J., and Schaffer, E. *Financial Leadership for Nonprofit Executives: Guiding Your Organization to Long-term Success.* St. Paul, Minn.: Fieldstone Alliance, 2005.

develop a set of overall assumptions about funding and expenses and to clarify fiscal goals for the upcoming year. If you have a strategic plan in place, it may be simple to agree on these goals. Without a strategic plan, developing the annual goals can be a time-consuming and highly iterative process.

Once the Board and Executive Director agree on the overall budgeting direction, the next step is to create program and implementation plans. Next, staff leadership in conjunction with Board committees—Executive, Finance, Program,

Exhibit 17.4
Budgeted Statement of Activity (Unrestricted)

For the Six Months Ending December 31, 2010

	YTD Actual	YTD Budget	Variance B/(W)	Annual Budget	$ Remaining	% Remaining
Contributions	31,477	40,000	(8,523)	80,000	48,523	61%
Fundraising events–net	62,415	67,500	(5,085)	135,000	72,585	54%
Foundation grants	45,000	62,500	(17,500)	125,000	80,000	64%
Total support	138,892	170,000	(31,108)	340,000	201,108	59%
Government contracts	460,887	407,505	53,383	815,009	354,122	43%
Interest and dividends	8,754	5,000	3,754	10,000	1,246	12%
Unrealized gain (loss) on investments	2,251	—	2,251	—	(2,251)	n/a
Total revenue	471,892	412,505	59,388	825,009	353,117	43%
Net assets released from restriction	220,020	225,000	(4,980)	450,000	229,980	51%
Total income	830,804	807,505	23,300	1,615,009	784,205	49%

Shelter services	398,547	401,538	2,991	803,075	404,528	50%
Support groups	194,012	197,098	3,086	394,196	200,184	51%
Administration	98,754	94,913	(3,841)	189,825	91,071	48%
Fundraising	135,214	99,757	(35,457)	199,514	64,300	32%
Total expenses	826,527	793,306	(33,221)	1,586,611	760,084	48%
Change in net assets	4,277	14,199	(9,922)	28,398	24,121	85%
Beginning net assets	298,547	300,000	(-,453)	168,690		
Ending net assets	302,824	314,199	(11,375)	197,088	24,121	12%

Source: Bell & Schaffer (2005).

Exhibit 17.5
Updated Projection—Unrestricted

As of January 20, 2011

	Annual Budget	1st Qtr Actual	2nd Quarter Actual	YTD Actual	3rd Quarter Projected	4th Quarter Projected	Revised Projection	Variance B/(W)
Contributions	80,000	12,540	18,937	31,477	25,741	22,584	79,802	(198)
Fundraising events—net	135,000	21,540	40,875	62,415	–	65,000	127,415	(7,585)
Foundation grants	125,000	15,000	30,000	45,000	32,500	45,000	122,500	(2,500)
Total support	340,000	49,080	89,812	138,892	58,241	132,584	329,717	(10,283)
Government contracts	815,009	204,580	256,307	460,887	180,000	174,122	815,009	–
Interest and dividends	10,000	5,147	3,607	8,754	8,500	8,500	25,754	15,754
Unrealized gain (loss) on investments	–		2,251	2,251	2,500	2,500	7,251	
Total revenue	825,009	209,727	262,165	471,892	191,000	185,122	848,014	23,005
Net assets released from restriction	450,000	95,478	124,542	220,020	125,000	125,000	470,020	20,020
Total income	1,615,009	354,285	476,519	830,804	374,241	442,706	1,647,751	32,742

Shelter services	803,075	201,602	196,945	398,547	201,501	200,154	800,202	2,873
Support groups	394,196	102,547	91,465	194,012	98,541	102,584	395,137	(941)
Administration	189,825	55,140	43,614	93,754	48,521	49,587	196,862	(7,037)
Fundraising	199,514	51,478	83,736	135,214	52,410	48,521	236,145	(36,631)
Total expenses	1,586,611	410,767	415,760	826,527	400,973	400,846	1,628,346	(41,735)
Change in net assets	28,398	(56,482)	60,759	4,277	(26,732)	41,860	19,405	(8,993)
Beginning net assets	300,000	298,547	242,065	298,547	302,824	276,092	298,547	(1,453)
Ending net assets	328,398	242,065	302,824	302,824	276,092	317,952	317,952	(10,446)

Source: Bell & Schaffer.

Notes In the first column of this report, the year-to-date (YTD) financial activity is listed. In the next column , the YTD budget (six months) is listed. The third column calculates the variance, or difference between the two. When the performance is better (B) than planned, for example, government contract revenue is higher than planned, the variance is a positive number. When the performance is worse (W) than planned, for example, the fundraising expenses are higher than planned, then the variance is a negative (bracketed) number. The last two columns calculate the dollars and percentage remaining to meet the goal (income) or stay within budget (expenses).

and Development—develop an initial budget draft with a list of budget assumptions. Then the Board or a designated committee discusses and edits the list, and finally the full Board meets to approve the budget. In approving the budget, the Board is taking the following steps:

- Agreeing to the plan
- Authorizing implementation of that plan
- Expecting that staff will report and analyze financial data to ensure alignment with the plan

Unfortunately, most organizations do not begin the budgeting process by developing or clarifying mutually agreed-upon annual goals. More typically people just look at the numbers. As a result, the Board meeting to review the budget often turns into a heated discussion as participants challenge details and dollars without the structure and support of an underlying plan. This scenario is best avoided by involving the Board and staff members at the beginning of the budgeting process.

As Executive Director, your particular budget tasks will vary based on the size of your organization. If your organization is small, you may be crunching the numbers and linking the spreadsheets yourself. Regardless of organization size, you should be expected to create the underlying operating plan and to validate all assumptions that are made in response to economic and financial trends.

AFTER THE BOARD PASSES A BUDGET, WHAT AUTHORITY DOES THE EXECUTIVE DIRECTOR HAVE TO IMPLEMENT PROGRAMS OR CONTRACTS?

With an approved budget, the Executive Director normally has the authority to execute the plan. You can spend and raise the money represented in the plan—as long as your actions are consistent with the explicit and implicit budget assumptions. For example, this year's budget may include a slot for a new program assistant that is to be funded by a new foundation grant. Although it's not an explicit budget assumption, the Board may expect that you won't fill this position until you receive the grant.

It is common and beneficial to have written policies that clarify the Executive Director's authority and any limitations regarding long-term contracts, approval of payments, and unbudgeted expenses.

As you begin to implement your budget, you'll need to continually verify that your original plan is still valid and that the assumptions still work. If you find that your plan or assumptions need updating, be sure to communicate swiftly and clearly about the changes. You'll probably need to engage jointly—with the Board and key staff—in a planning process to update your goals, your program and development plan, the assumptions, and the budget.

IF THERE IS A FINANCIAL CRISIS, WHAT DOES THE EXECUTIVE DIRECTOR TELL THE BOARD AND STAFF?

When the news spreads that an organization is in financial crisis, what does it mean? It might mean that a significant source of funding was cut, and now the available resources are insufficient to maintain programs. It might mean that the organization is unable to meet its financial obligations. It might mean that someone has defrauded the organization. More often than not, it is one of these scenarios coupled with a lack of information about the financial situation. The best advice in a crisis: whether the news is bad or good, use the same reporting process. Stick to the schedule and keep the information flowing.

Unfortunately, in a crisis, there is typically no data at all. In this case, the sooner you get data, the better. As the Executive Director, you will want to model the best practice of making decisions based on data, not assumptions. And no matter how bad the news, the best practice is to be honest with both Board and staff.

When a financial crisis occurs, first tell the Board Chair and Treasurer, and work with them to lay out a plan for informing the rest of the Board and staff. If there is a Finance Director in the organization, include that individual in the conversation as well. The four of you should be able to come up with a realistic communication plan that can be implemented at the same time the crisis is being resolved. While this communication plan will vary from organization to organization, it should include the following components:

- Clear explanation of what the financial crisis is and why it occurred (program being eliminated because funding slashed, several funders reducing allocations at the same time, stock portfolio significantly reduced with a destabilizing effect—these are examples)
- An outline of the steps being taken to regain financial stability in the organization, including who is taking the steps and a time line

- A process for continued communication with the staff and Board about progress being made

As long as Board and staff can see there is a plan to resolve the financial crisis, they will have confidence in the leadership. They may also have good ideas to offer that can be implemented as part of the action plan.

TIPS FOR SUCCESS

- Look for financial leadership partners on staff and the Board. These may be individuals who already understand nonprofit financial reports or who have an eagerness to learn.
- Set a tone of financial transparency throughout the organization.
- Invest in infrastructure to ensure accurate financial information that is managed well and reported on a timely basis.
- Educate your Board to read, understand, and challenge financial statements.

Sustaining the Organization with Team-Based Fundraising

Of all the factors that contribute to sustained success in fund raising, none may be more important than creating a cohesive and effective development team.

—Kay Sprinkel Grace, *Achieving Excellence in Fundraising*

Raising funds is both a joy and a curse for Executive Directors. The joy comes when you are successful in sharing your passion and vision for the organization with the community, who in turn invest in your mission with a grant, major gift, or some other challenging donation. The curse comes when you feel that your entire job is about fundraising, and things aren't going well.

The reality is that Executive Directors need to know a lot about fundraising, but they don't have sole responsibility for making sure the organization always has enough funds.

This chapter provides insights that will help Executive Directors create a team to raise funds. Our belief is that this all-important task is one that everyone in the nonprofit can be involved in. These are the questions answered here:

- Who has the primary responsibility for raising money in a nonprofit?
- How much of an Executive Director's time should be spent raising money?
- Where do nonprofits find funds for overhead costs of administration and building infrastructure?

Much of the material in this chapter comes from the book *Team-Based Fundraising: Step by Step,* by Mim Carlson.

WHO HAS THE PRIMARY RESPONSIBILITY FOR RAISING MONEY IN A NONPROFIT?

The Executive Director isn't the only person with significant responsibility for fundraising. The Board of Directors shares this responsibility, because it is the Board that ultimately must keep the doors open and programs operating. If Board members are not supporting fundraising in some way, they are not doing their job.

We view fundraising as a team effort between Board members, the Executive Director, and to a lesser extent, others in an organization. Whether you are identifying prospective donors, cultivating them, asking for contributions, or recognizing donor generosity, each person on the team shares the responsibility for making sure that fundraising activities are carried out and that goals are being achieved.

For a team approach to fundraising to work well in any nonprofit, a good understanding of roles among all the members of the team is essential. It is best to develop a brief matrix like the one shown in Exhibit 18.1 to summarize key team member roles in fundraising.

Members of the leadership group have some very specific responsibilities to be aware of. In this context, we're referring to the Board Chair, the chair of the Board's Fundraising Committee, the Executive Director, and the Development Director (if an organization has a paid or unpaid staff person in this role).

Exhibit 18.1
Fundraising Team Responsibilities Matrix

Who	What
Team Leader: Board Chair	• Sets the example for the full Board in terms of performance. • Builds commitment among Board members and makes sure that the skills and experience of Board members are matched to the tasks they perform. • Remains conscious that fundraising is only one of the essential duties of the Board of Directors.
Team Leader: Executive Director	• Sets the example for the rest of the staff in terms of performance. • Demonstrates enthusiasm about the goals, builds commitment among staff to raise funds, and effectively matches skills and experience to the tasks that need to be carried out. • Focuses on the staff's performance. • Manages the process of team selection and ensures effectiveness of the team.
Directors:	• Accept training to increase skills and become more effective. • *Identify:* Provide names of colleagues, businesses, and others who might be prospects for development. • *Cultivate:* Serve on task forces matching interests and skills. • *Ask:* Obtain donations and make donations themselves. • *Recognize:* Thank donors for their generosity. • *Monitor:* Set fundraising policies with staff.
Staff:	• Accept training to increase skills and become more effective. • *Identify:* See every contact as a potential donor; track donor data. • *Cultivate:* Provide information about constituent needs and service quality and about program results that are making a difference in the community; demonstrate those positive results and thus provide a reason for donors to give; communicate to potential and current donors that their nonprofit operates smoothly and is professionally managed. • *Ask:* Visit with donors and prospects to provide details of the organization's work. • *Recognize:* Thank donors they know for their generosity.

(Continued)

Non-Board Volunteers	• Accept training to increase skills and become more effective.
	• *Identify:* Introduce their places of employment to the nonprofit's mission to generate contributions, develop list of contacts for solicitations and maintain the donor database and research prospective donors.
	• *Cultivate:* Serve on task forces according to interest and skills.
	• *Ask:* Solicit friends, family, work colleagues, and neighbors to become donors; organize special events; make financial contributions of their own.
	• *Recognize:* Thank donors they know for their gifts.

This group provides management through planning, monitoring, and implementing. It provides leadership through motivating, supporting, and encouraging the team.

Team members can determine their responsibilities in these four key fundraising areas: identifying donors, cultivating them, asking for contributions, and recognizing donor generosity.

As the chart in the exhibit indicates, everyone has a role in fundraising. It is your leadership, as Executive Director, that creates the culture of a fundraising team and ensures that everyone supports one another as well as meeting their own responsibilities as team members. Strong communication skills and the desire to work through others to raise funds are very important for the busy Executive Director, who cannot possibly do all the fundraising in the nonprofit.

HOW MUCH OF AN EXECUTIVE DIRECTOR'S TIME SHOULD BE SPENT RAISING MONEY?

Although we are asked this question often, it is difficult to answer because circumstances are different in every nonprofit. In all nonprofits, you spend time as a leader providing vision, motivation, and strategic thinking to the task of fundraising. You also raise money and are a leader on the fundraising team. Some organizations, though, have a lesser need for fundraising because of where they are in their life cycle, so it is a lower priority. Others base their existence on raising funds so it is a higher priority.

For instance, as an Executive Director of a land trust, with no other staff, you are going to spend a majority of your time on some aspect of raising funds because that is what fulfills the purpose of the trust (to purchase land or easements for protecting open space). On the other hand, if you are in charge of a large social services agency with many programs and numerous staff, you may spend less time raising money because government contracts pay for most of the services, and you have numerous other demands on your time as you work to fulfill the mission of the organization. Also, a nonprofit early in its life cycle or going through a heavy growth period will need an Executive Director who spends more time finding and building relationships with donors, while an ED leading a nonprofit later in its life cycle may find that those relationships have stabilized and thus demand less time.

But remember that wherever the organization is in its life cycle, the Board, staff, community volunteers, and other key stakeholders are participating too. The Executive Director is a leader and a manager, but not the solo solicitor.

As you work to figure out how much time you should be spending on fundraising, ask yourself the following questions and consider some ideas to manage your time on this task.

- Are there times during the year when you have noticed that more fundraising tasks need to be done? If so, plan ahead and have a team working on some of those tasks so it is not just your job to write those grant proposals, facilitate the direct mail appeal, or go after major gifts.

- Is someone on staff—or perhaps a volunteer—eager to build fundraising skills? Does that person seem to have the capacity to do so? If yes, then mentor them with training and chances to work alongside you.

- Do you find that fundraising is consuming so much of your time that other priorities are not being met? If yes, then it is time for a heart-to-heart with your Board. If the relationship is a healthy partnership, then your Board is there to support and encourage you—and to do their fair share of fundraising.

- Does everyone know what is involved with the task of fundraising at your organization, and how much time it consumes? If not, then it is time to communicate and educate staff, Board, and volunteers about the many facets of raising money. It is also a good idea to talk about fundraising and create a plan to involve more of your organization in the task.

Remember always that your primary job at your organization is to be a leader. This goes for fundraising as well as all other tasks you do.

WHERE DO NONPROFITS FIND FUNDS FOR OVERHEAD COSTS OF ADMINISTRATION AND BUILDING INFRASTRUCTURE?

This question often comes up when Executive Directors are stretched to the limit with providing programs and want some more administrative dollars to build structures to support those programs. The term *unrestricted* is often used to define these funds because it is money that can be used for any purpose in the nonprofit.

The real time to be thinking about finding unrestricted money is before you really need it. The reason for this is that the search for unrestricted funds can be a long one and generally takes the time of everyone in your organization.

Unrestricted funds come primarily from individual donors to your nonprofit. To a much lesser extent, they come from ongoing foundation support, service clubs, small businesses, and groups that have philanthropic dollars to give away. Much has been written on how to raise money from individuals and groups, and you will find our favorite guides in this chapter's section of the resources list at the end of the book.

Instead, the focus here is on ways that you can create a culture in your nonprofit that supports obtaining individual or other donor gifts. This is important because nonprofits that find themselves in need of unrestricted funds have usually relied heavily on grant funds or government contracts that direct the majority of their dollars to specific programs and require different relationships and skills. New systems and skills to target individual donors, track donations, and recognize gifts need to be established.

STORY FROM THE FIELD

Marcia took a new ED position in a stable, mature organization that had always relied on government contracts with minimal foundation grant support. One of her new priorities was to bring in unrestricted funds to increase administrative support. Marcia unwisely agreed to a substantial goal of $100,000 in one year in unrestricted gifts. But wisely, she said that the Board and staff needed to participate in achieving the goal. The Board agreed to this.

Marcia made the assumption that the Board and staff would be interested in raising funds, and that the organization had a database of potential donors, as well as systems for tracking gifts, communicating about progress, and the like. But the organization had never seen the need to have that sort of database or systems, nor had anyone in it any experience in asking for money, so there was, in fact, nothing in place.

Rather than setting herself up to fail with a $100,000 goal and no way to achieve it, Marcia went back to her Board with an analysis of the situation and a proposal. She outlined what it would take financially and in terms of time to move the organization to being able to reach the Board's original goal. The Board accepted Marcia's proposal and learned about the realities of switching to a culture of raising unrestricted funds.

The lesson here is to set funding goals that match your capacity to achieve them. To raise unrestricted gifts, you need, at a minimum, to have individuals, groups, and businesses to solicit and to have them listed in an easily accessible and up-to-date database. You also need a plan for soliciting and people to carry out the plan. Are you going to use events, face-to-face requests, fundraising letters, phone calls, or what? You also need a good system to track the gifts when they come in, and a recognition strategy to ensure that everyone gets thanked regardless of the size of their gift.

This is a lot to put in place if you are a busy Executive Director with many other matters to attend to, so the team concept of fundraising is what makes the most difference here. It should not be your job to set up a database, track donors, solicit them, recognize them, communicate with them regularly about your organization's accomplishments, and all the other things that need to happen in a solid unrestricted gift program. The chart in Exhibit 18.2, from *Team-Based Fundraising: Step by Step*, identifies ways others in the organization can turn your dream of getting unrestricted gifts into a reality. We recommend that Executive Directors share this survey with Board and staff and begin to build a team on the interests expressed by each person.

Exhibit 18.2
Team Involvement in Unrestricted Gifts

Team Member Name _____

Team Goal: To obtain unrestricted gifts

Objective	Task	Will Do	Maybe— Ask	I'd like to learn how
Systems Development	• Design or modify a database to track unrestricted gifts			
	• Develop a plan for obtaining donations			
	• Create evaluation tools to monitor progress			
Identify Donors	• Provide lists of names			
	• Research current donors			
	• Input data into the database			
	• Assist with database management			
Cultivation	• Talk to other groups about our organization			
	• Work on a newsletter task force			
	• Develop the agency case statement			
	• Visit prospects			
	• Work on a legislative task force			
	• Recruit new volunteers			
Solicitations	• Organize a major donor drive.			
	• Recruit volunteer solicitors.			
	• Solicit people and groups.			
	• Conduct a phone-a-thon.			
	• Organize a direct mail campaign.			
	• Work on a direct mail campaign.			
	• Help plan special events.			
	• Lead an events committee.			
	• Work at the event.			

Objective	Task	Will Do	Maybe— Ask	I'd like to learn how
Recognize Donors	• Develop recognition events for donors. • Write and send donor thank you letters.			

Note: This survey is not all-inclusive. Your team will want to add and subtract tasks depending on your needs.

To use the chart in the exhibit effectively, ask everyone who is part of the fundraising team to fill it out individually. Then the team leadership can compile the information and create an unrestricted donations plan that allows people to do what best matches their skills and interests.

Fundraising can be fun and rewarding for Executive Directors and for everyone in the organization who participates. Since this is the critical task that keeps the doors open and the programs operating, it needs to be a shared responsibility to be truly successful.

TIPS FOR SUCCESS

- It is important for your organization to operate in a fundraising culture that has Board, staff, and volunteers involved in finding funds. Fundraising is not just the Executive Director's job.

- Finding unrestricted funds to support overhead costs requires special systems to be in place that help to identify and track donor contributions and ensure good recognition of their gifts. If your organization has always been grant dependent, time is needed to shift systems to support asking for and receiving individual donations.

- Never abdicate fundraising leadership to others in the organization. While you may not be the only person raising funds, you must still take a leadership role if fundraising is to be successful.

PART SEVEN

Leadership in Transition

*Through attention to leader transitions, succession planning,
and leader development, we will demystify the path
to a more leaderful and effective organization.*

—Tom Adams,
*The Nonprofit Leadership Transition and Development Guide:
Proven Paths for Leaders and Organizations*

No one has a job for life, especially not in the nonprofit sector. If you are an accomplished Executive Director or have a senior staff member with a long tenure, it is easy for your organization to lose sight of the fact that one of you will move on at some point. Remember, as a nonprofit leader, you are serving as a temporary caretaker of the mission.

It is common for leaders to outgrow the organizations they lead, and some organizations outgrow the skill set of their current leadership. Some leaders need new or different challenges, others find themselves in an organization whose values or culture are not in line with their own. Career transitions are a natural progression but an often forgotten or uncomfortable topic for many Executive Directors and their Boards.

Part Seven brings this topic out into the open and provides Executive Directors and their Boards with tools and insight to plan for and manage healthy and productive leadership transitions. We purposely use the term *transition*, because it better defines the planning and process versus the outcome of changes in leadership.

Transition, as described by William Bridges, is the psychological and emotional process the ED, the organization, and stakeholders go through in order to come to terms with change. Some move through this process smoothly and with relative ease; others, particularly those with a strong culture built on long-term relationships, find transition difficult, complex, and emotional. They need time to feel their emotions, reflect upon what the change means to them personally, and come to terms with the professional impact of the change.

In Chapter Nineteen we provide insights into how nonprofits can plan for leadership succession. We offer tools and support to help both Executive Directors and organizations plan for and manage planned and emergency transitions as well as ensure the continuity of mission-critical information. Chapter Twenty explores the Executive Director's own transition. Rather than viewing leadership turnover as a challenge, we encourage you to look at this transition as a time of growth and reflection for you and your organization.

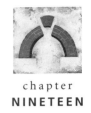

Planning for Healthy Transitions of Leadership

Boards will navigate chief executive leadership transitions more successfully by anticipating a continuum of steps embedded in the succession planning process.

—Nancy Axelrod, *Chief Executive Succession Planning*

The question isn't whether you or members of your management team will ever leave your current organization, but when. The goal of succession planning is not to encourage turnover but rather to acknowledge the need for ongoing planning to inform the direction and leadership needs of the organization. This chapter considers the challenge of how to translate an often intangible concern about succession and the continuity needs of an organization—"I know we should be doing something"—into a tangible plan. Incorporating the topic of succession planning into existing planning and management systems reduces staff and Board anxiety and expedites the move to new leadership when the time comes. This chapter addresses the following questions.

- Why is succession planning important?
- How can an Executive Director integrate practices that support succession planning throughout the organization?
- Where does continuity or knowledge management fit within the framework of succession planning?
- What does an emergency succession plan look like?

WHY IS SUCCESSION PLANNING IMPORTANT?

Several national and regional studies have raised the visibility and importance of succession planning among nonprofit organizations, given that a majority of Executive Directors plan to leave their current position in the next five years. The sustainability of many community-based nonprofits can be tied directly to their ability to ensure the efficient and effective transfer of leadership, as well as of the critical operational knowledge and stakeholder relationships tied to the ED position.

Over the past decade, both empirical and anecdotal findings indicate that organizations that thoughtfully embrace succession planning and address continuity and transition issues proactively find that they

- Are more open and better prepared to respond to organizational change at many levels.

- Benefit from a more open and candid Board-ED partnership, which is often reflected throughout the management chain.

- Sharpen their vision and direction in ways that that influence the selection of incoming leadership.

- Have stronger management infrastructure and systems that can be sustained during either an emergency or planned transition.

- Are better able to manage the risks and amplify the opportunities of the change in leadership.
- Ensure continuity of programs, services, funding streams, and stakeholder relationships critical to the mission and future of the organization.

For most nonprofit organizations, the term *succession planning* should no longer be limited to grooming a select individual to fill a key position. Few organizations are large enough to have that depth of expertise on staff. Rather, a more systematic approach to nonprofit succession planning, often referred to as *leadership planning,* has emerged. (See Exhibit 19.1.) This approach addresses the topic in a way that ensures that key staff are identified and prepared to provide continuity in planned and emergency staff transitions. It also systematizes critical knowledge, relationships, and processes.

Exhibit 19.1
Leadership (Succession) Planning

The following have been found to be critical elements to successful succession planning:

1. Key staff and Board leadership must be part of the initial planning and implementation so that discussions can happen openly and honestly under an umbrella of mutual trust. Leadership needs to have ownership of the process and a vision of the benefits.

2. Planning needs to balance the reliance on an individual's skills and expertise with the need for sustainable systems that allow organizational continuity of information, process, and relationships when a key leader leaves.

3. Given the competing demands on organizational time and attention, it is often difficult to make succession planning a priority, let alone justify the time and resources required to build and maintain the systems necessary to support succession planning. By integrating goals and outcomes into existing organizational or personnel performance systems and training, the organization benefits from the truth of the maxim, "That which is monitored and rewarded gets done."

HOW CAN AN EXECUTIVE DIRECTOR INTEGRATE PRACTICES THAT SUPPORT LEADERSHIP SUCCESSION WITHIN THE FRAMEWORK OF EXISTING STRATEGIC PLANNING AND MANAGEMENT STRUCTURES?

While the concept of thinking strategically about leadership and succession planning isn't new, making it a priority and putting it into operation can be difficult for organizations with limited resources. The following practices provide insight into how an organization can integrate succession planning practices into existing planning and management processes.

Strategic Planning and Direction

Succession planning is a natural yet often overlooked extension of strategic planning. While most strategic plans clearly addresses resource and program implications, succession planning goes a step further and focuses on identifying the skills and experience leadership will need in the future.

The foundation of succession planning starts with two critical pieces: an organization's mission and vision and its values. Given the organization's program, funding, and management structure, the greater the clarity the Board and key leadership have about the organization's desired community impact, mission, focus, priorities, definitions of success, and boundaries (that is, what is regarded as outside the scope of the mission), the greater the probability of attracting and retaining leadership with the right mix of skills, attributes, and sustainability.

The other area that is critical for success, and is often overlooked, is a clearly articulated and written set of core values. These values help define the culture, behavior, and philosophy of how you approach your programs, clients, and community.

Once a strategic vision, priorities, and values are defined, the Board and key leadership can engage in some objective gap analysis of current versus future skills and experience the organization will need in its key leadership positions. By documenting current skills and experience and comparing to the evolving needs of the organization—by position, not current incumbent—plans can be developed that allow the ED to

- Identify and as needed invest in the development of existing positions to ensure the incumbents have the skills necessary to drive evolving strategic priorities.

- Backfill with new or restructured positions and skills.
- As needed, update job descriptions (roles and responsibilities) along with candidate profiles to help inform future hiring needs. These should be viewed as planning tools, since the actual job and candidate profile must be informed by situation and leadership at the time of hiring.

Governance

Leadership and succession planning extend to the Board as well as staff leadership. Board members individually and collectively often hold much of the organization's history and relationships. The following are steps that Boards can take to ensure their own succession and continuity:

- Board member recruitment should follow the same gap analysis following any changes in vision or strategic priorities. What skills, expertise, access, connections, and leadership attributes are needed in addition to those currently present?
- Board member roles, authority, responsibilities, expectations, and conflict-of-interest guidelines should be clearly defined in writing and discussed as part of an orientation.
- The by-laws or policies of the Board should identify an emergency succession plan for key officers such as Board President, Executive Director, and Treasurer for starters in case of a sudden or unplanned departure.
- Term limits for Board members and officers ensure a constant flow of new ideas and energy into the organization and reduce the potential for stagnation and burnout.
- The Board should annually evaluate the staff and Board's succession planning and resources and make recommendations for improvement.

Human Resources

Human Resources is often the gatekeeper for succession planning efforts since this department is a partner with managers during transitions. Organizations have a variety of opportunities to strengthen succession and continuity through human resources policies and practices:

- New staff orientation for key leadership should go beyond traditional human resources and administrative details to include some historical context, vision, mission, strategic direction, and values that help align the organization.

- Job descriptions of key leadership positions should be revisited following updates or changes to strategic priorities and goals, every two years, or as positions turn over. This is an opportunity to revisit the basic functions, skills, experience, and attributes needed in key positions to most effectively support the organization's evolving priorities and goals.

- Recruitment and screening processes for key leadership should focus not only on the skills and experience needed but also the underlying values and style candidates bring to the position.

- Compensation and benefit packages should be competitive with the marketplace to both attract and retain the skills and talent necessary to achieve your strategic goals and mission. This is especially true for a growing percentage of EDs who are approaching retirement age and have dedicated their life work to organizations that have made little or no contribution to their retirement. Some of these dedicated nonprofit leaders have not planned adequately for retirement, and they may wind up spending their "golden years" as clients of the organizations they once led.

- HR policies should help define the organization's expectations for key leaders' participation in planning and also inform the offer letter or contract that sets expectations for exit strategies. (That is, how many weeks' notice is reasonable and expected, sustainability of systems, knowledge and management transfer. . . .)

- Performance reviews should include reviews and updates of emergency transition plans and continuity planning documents.

WHERE DOES CONTINUITY OR KNOWLEDGE MANAGEMENT FIT WITHIN THE FRAMEWORK OF SUCCESSION PLANNING?

The primary goal of both succession and continuity planning is to allow for the efficient and effective transfer of leadership, especially mission-critical operational knowledge and relationships the incumbents hold. What organization hasn't experienced a loss of productivity, increase of employee or client frustration, and reduction in efficiency as the result of staff turnover? If a departing employee fills a critical position in a smaller organization—a long-term Board member, Executive Director, fundraiser, or finance manager—the impact can be significant.

The rewards of systematically capturing and retaining critical knowledge about systems, processes, and relationships are extremely powerful in speeding up the learning curve of new leaders. The process to capture key information can be as simple or complex as your organization will allow. Following sections list some of the more obvious places to start:

Governance

- Board members should be asked to document key financial, political, or programmatic relationships they have in the community that can or should be important to the mission.

- Critical governance and operations documents created or maintained by individual Board members at their home or office should also be backed up within the organization.

- Long-term or retiring Board members should be asked to share and document key historical milestones, decisions, and challenges to ensure that this history can benefit and inform future leadership.

Fund Development

Much of fundraising is built upon sustainable relationships; thus the development and maintenance of donor records and relationships is key. Common practices:

- Donor records should not only track giving histories clearly, they should also document information about the donor's connection to the organization. (The latter information is often held personally by Board members, the Executive Director, or other key staff, and therefore in particular danger of being lost in a sudden transition.)

- More than one staff member should be trained in the operations and management functions of the donor data base.

- Files and records of current and pending grant requests and awards should be cross-filed with the appropriate program or appropriate operations or financial department. This will assist tracking and oversight and also help make sure that key deadlines and opportunities are not missed.

Finance

Transparency and accountability are central to nonprofit and public sector financial management, so much so that continuity issues are often already mandated by a funder or government entity. Typical recommendations:

- All accounting procedures and practices should be clearly documented, reviewed, and updated regularly.

- More than one person (internal staff or external consultant or contractor) should be trained in the essential operations and reporting functions:

    a. Financial and data management systems and software

    b. Payroll systems

    c. Budgeting and forecasting systems and scenarios

    d. Debt acquisition and management

    e. Program- or grant-specific accounting and reporting needs

- The Treasurer and Finance Committee should have adequate knowledge and informed oversight of the organization's key financial indicators, dashboard, and trends.

- Budgets, forecasts, scenarios, and financial reports should include an overview of key assumptions or risks that are behind the numbers or trends.

Programs and Services

It is helpful to discuss and capture the following insights for each program, service, or line of business to provide context and focus for incoming staff. This information is often integrated in strategic planning or a program review.

- How does each program support or further your mission? (List specific examples.) Is it seen as central to the mission or auxiliary to your work? In other words, what would be the implications to the organization if you were to discontinue it?

- How does each program complement or compete with other programs or services in the community and what are the competitive advantages or barriers?

- Who are the program's strategic partners or collaborators?

- What are each program's funding streams by source and approximate percentage?

- What program assessments or evaluations have been completed in the last two or three years?

Technology

Technology can be an area of high staff turnover in many nonprofit organizations, and in others it is volunteer led or contracted out—both conditions that make it an area of continuity risk. The more technology an organization incorporates into its work, the more critical this area is to the sustainability of services and programs. Opportunities for continuity planning in this area vary greatly, but might include

- Pre-researched or vetted names and contact information for technology firms or consultants that have knowledge or experience with your systems

- Internet service provider including name, contact info, and specific information about the plan or Internet service you've signed up for

- Web hosting company information (often this is also your e-mail host): name, contact info, and your login info for the hosting site or control panel

- Domain registrar, contact info, and your login info for the domain Web site

- Specifics of your organization's internal network

- Login information for various databases, individual workstations, and any tools or services that are accessed on the Web

- Inventory of all equipment, its location, and as appropriate, restrictions to a particular program or grant

- Any technology plans or assessments that have been completed in the last two or three years

- License and registration information for all hardware and software used in your organization

The following story from the field helps illustrate how one organization pulled all this information together.

STORY FROM THE FIELD

A transition consultant was working with a large community development organization that had been mandated by one of its funders to engage in some succession and continuity planning as part of a larger capacity development grant. Despite early enthusiasm for the project, the time line was continually pushed back by more urgent issues.

After several months of delays, the consultant asked if she could have thirty minutes at each meeting of the management team for the next few months. The plan was to help the key leadership of the organization identify critical knowledge and relationships within the organization and personally connect to the benefits of the planning. One week she asked the team, "If you were asked to fill in for the Executive Director for three months and only had an hour with her before she left, what information would be most critical to your success?" The group quickly brainstormed and narrowed the list down to fifteen questions or documents they felt would be most helpful. The Executive Director spent a few hours the following week pulling the information together in both a binder and electronic file.

The process continued with each member of the management team documenting information that was identified by their peers—and in less than four months they had documented the most important. The management team shared the exercise with their staff teams, and within six months all key staff positions had made significant progress in documenting key information, systems, and relationships critical to their positions. When the Fund Development Director left with only two weeks' notice, he was able to efficiently transfer responsibilities and relationships and his replacement was able to step into the job and hit the ground running.

As you can see, effective succession planning is not simply a stand-alone project or plan focused solely on leadership. It can and should touch nearly every part of the organization to ensure the continuity not just of the leadership but also of the systems, knowledge, and relationships that are critical to your mission.

WHAT DOES AN EMERGENCY SUCCESSION PLAN LOOK LIKE?

Last but not least, organizations all need an emergency plan to cover the possibility of the sudden and unexpected absence of the Executive Director or leadership staff. While such an absence is uncommon and certainly undesirable, some simple planning will ensure continuity in leadership, relationships, and service delivery. An emergency plan builds on the succession planning and continuity management work we have already discussed. The added element is identifying the individuals best qualified to step into the role in an emergency, and allowing for the cross-training and knowledge transfer necessary to prepare the backup staff to cover the leadership functions. Though the process and the eventual plans differ greatly along with the size and structure of each organization, the following list highlights some of the key elements of emergency succession plans:

- Emergency succession planning is often led by staff but approved by the Board, and can easily fit within strategic planning.

- Plans can range from informal verbal agreements to formal binders of information—there's no one-size-fits-all solution.

- Responsibilities of key positions are spelled out, either in the job description or in supplementary documentation.

- The plan identifies one or two key staff members or volunteers who could be brought into action with short notice.

- There is a training plan to ensure that staff or volunteers identified as emergency stand-ins have the skills and experience to take on the acting role effectively.

- Where possible, staff have opportunities to practice in leadership roles during vacations and absences. It is important for these staff to be given not only responsibility but also authority to make key decisions and take action as needed.

- These are documents that it is helpful to have in one location, specified in the plan:
  - Staff rosters and job descriptions.
  - Committee rosters and work plans.
  - Strategic plan or annual goals and accomplishments to date.
  - List of vendors, task forces, or collaborative organizations that the position has the primary responsibility for. Include contact information and schedule of meetings if possible.

- Deadlines for reports to funders, stakeholders, community leaders.
- Voice mail, computer, e-mail, cell phone, bank, alarm system instructions, account numbers and passwords, location of keys.

  Note: All the information in this bullet point should be stored in a secure file drawer in an office that is locked when not occupied. One or two staff should have access to that office and file drawer.
- Brief summary of a typical week and month in terms of time spent with the Board, staff, clients, reports, and administration, and key seasonal issues that impact the role.
- Communication plans in case you need to activate the emergency succession plan—and who has the authority to activate it. Typically the Board President will activate in the case of the Executive Director and the Executive Director for staff.
- The plan includes a process to quickly review and update its contents and associated documents once a year or as needed.

TIPS FOR SUCCESS

- Incorporating the topic of succession planning into existing planning and management systems reduces staff and Board anxiety about Executive Director and management turnover and expedites the move to new leadership when the time comes.
- Key staff and Board leadership must be part of the initial succession and leadership planning and implementation so that discussions can happen openly and honestly under an umbrella of mutual trust.
- It is often difficult to make succession planning and continuity management a priority. By integrating goals and outcomes into existing organizational or personnel performance systems and training, the organization improves its chances that the planning will get done.
- A key element to emergency succession plans is identifying the individuals best qualified to step into to the role with little notice, and allowing for the cross-training and knowledge management necessary to ensure these individuals are prepared.

Moving On
Making Your Own Career Transition

*The departing executive's final two leadership tasks
are the leadership of letting go and the
leadership of preparing the way.*

—Tim Wolfred, CompassPoint,
Managing Executive Transitions

Executive Directors are widely regarded as champions of change
in organizations, yet relatively few welcome or spend much
time considering their own process of exiting an organization. This
chapter considers the opportunities and challenges imposed on
you and your organization during an Executive Director transition

and offers guidance to both the ED and the Board in managing the process. The chapter addresses the following questions:

- How will I know it is time for a career move?
- Why is the decision to leave so difficult for the Executive Director and the organization?
- How can the departing Executive Director make the leadership transition run smoothly?
- What are some typical career paths for former Executive Directors?

HOW WILL I KNOW IT IS TIME FOR A CAREER MOVE?

There is never an ideal time to leave an organization or change jobs. You will always see opportunities or challenges you'd like to address before leaving your organization. The decision to consider a change may be driven by external opportunities or by internal reflections on staying inspired by the thought process that we discuss in Chapter Two.

In addition to examining barriers to your inspiration, consider your responses to the questions in Exhibit 20.1. These same questions are also helpful in coaching a member of your management team who is struggling with job performance toward making a difficult choice to move on or seek the support and development needed to thrive.

Often the decision to move on is driven by new career opportunities. Other times it will come from internal reflection about your life goals and how your job as an ED complements them or competes with them. However, having already engaged in the succession and continuity planning recommended in Chapter Nineteen will not only help to ease your departure anxieties and those of your organization, it can also transform your departure into an opportunity for growth and change instead of a crisis.

Once you decide to leave, remember that there are a wealth of books, workshops, career counselors, and Web sites that promote career planning and transition. You'll find a few starting points listed among the resources for this chapter at the back of the book. In addition, colleagues, mentors, family, and, when appropriate, your Board can provide you with invaluable feedback and guidance.

Exhibit 20.1
The Decision to Stay or Go

- Would a new position provide new or different opportunities that would challenge or develop your skills in new ways?
- Do you still love the work you are doing and the organization you are working for?
- Are you still passionate about the mission?
- Do you enjoy going to work and interacting with your staff, Board, volunteers, and clients?
- Do you believe you are making a difference?
- Do you receive supportive or appreciative feedback from your Board, staff, and stakeholders?
- Are your leadership and management skills appropriate to the stage of development that your organization is moving through?
- Do your career and personal goals complement each other?

    If your answers to these questions are mostly no or hesitantly yes, it may be time to seriously reflect on your skills and your career and life goals. Are you simply in the wrong agency or in the wrong field? If your answers are mostly yes and you still wonder about your job commitment, answer these questions:

- Would additional support or coaching help you deal with the opportunities and challenges at hand? Chapter Two may offer some additional insight into ways coaching can help.
- Have you ever taken more than one week of vacation? If so, how recently and how did it affect you?
- Is it time to take a sabbatical? That is, a real break—a month or even a six-month inspirational vacation. As one close friend told us after a sabbatical, "The boulders now look more like pebbles and I have a more absorbent wall to bang my head against."
- Is retirement or partial retirement an option? Have you adequately planned and saved for retirement?

It is advisable for Executive Directors to give a minimum of four to six weeks' notice and not uncommon for longer-term EDs to start planning their transition one to two years before it is publicly shared with the staff and community.

WHY IS THE DECISION TO LEAVE SO DIFFICULT FOR THE EXECUTIVE DIRECTOR AND THE ORGANIZATION?

There is more to leaving your position as Executive Director than simply writing a letter of resignation, cleaning out your desk, wrapping up loose ends, and celebrating your accomplishments with colleagues. For many long-time nonprofit leaders, their professional identity and personal passions are interwoven into the organization they lead. Despite your best intentions, your departure may be met with caution, even fear, and sometimes resentment.

Why? Because your transition involves more than the simple departure of one key staff member and the subsequent hiring of another. Your departure thrusts both you and your entire organization into a significant period of cultural change. In addition to dealing with your own reactions, you must also deal with the organization's reaction to the loss of a friend, colleague, and leader. Remember the lesson of Chapter One: you are only a temporary caretaker of the organization's mission. Part of your transition role is to help the organization you have led accept that change is healthy, and the next person will do things differently.

While the decision to leave an organization is not an easy one for most Executive Directors, the fact that you have made the choice to move on provides you with a sense of control. By contrast, your organization finds itself unexpectedly having to deal with the emotional loss of a colleague and the demanding process of filling the leadership void. The longer you have been with the organization, the harder the transition may be. It takes time for staff, volunteers, and Board members to envision the organization without you. Celebrations that recognize your legacy and give you an opportunity to say thank-you and good-bye are a critical part both of your term's ending and of a healthy foundation for the next ED's term.

HOW CAN THE DEPARTING EXECUTIVE DIRECTOR MAKE THE LEADERSHIP TRANSITION RUN SMOOTHLY?

As noted, the ending you orchestrate for your leadership term creates the foundation on which the next Executive Director will begin to build. This goes beyond celebrations; in the context of Board leadership and in consideration of the elements of change discussed in Chapter Ten, the steps discussed in this section will help guide you to a good ending for yourself while the Board focuses on a new beginning for the organization. There are some similarities in the steps, but the focus here is on you and your ability to let go and move on.

Step One: Take care of yourself. With honesty and clarity, identify your reasons for leaving. Set a definite time line for your departure and avoid the temptation to delay your departure in response to anxieties expressed by your staff or Board members. Sometimes it is difficult to set a departure date because of uncertainty about your future plans. If this is the case, set a date to leave and decide to develop your future plans after you're on your own.

If you are a Founder or have been with the organization for many years, your identification with the organizational culture may be so strong as to make it especially difficult for people to envision moving forward without you. It is both challenging and essential to find a balance between your strong leadership legacy and an objective evaluation of the organization's strengths, weaknesses, opportunities, and barriers to success. Without burning bridges, you must pass the authority to lead the organization forward on to your successor.

Step Two: Work with the Board to draft a departure communication and transition plan. Who needs to know what and when? Sit down with your Board Chair or Executive Committee and discuss how to share the news of your departure and the plan for a smooth transition with the rest of the Board, staff, volunteers, and stakeholders. If your departure is months away, keep your circle of confidentiality close. If your departure is imminent—say, two months or less—the sooner people know, the sooner the personal and organizational transitions can begin.

The checklist in Exhibit 20.2 is designed to help guide the Board through their leadership roles in the event of a transition. (A similar checklist to help guide the ED through the management issues of a transition can be found in Exhibit 20.3.)

If you are able to give longer notice, six months to a year, it is important to guide your Board through the pros and cons of having a lame-duck leader and a prolonged transition period. As departing ED, you are often delegated to deal with day-to-day management issues rather than those that affect the organization's future direction.

Once plans for announcing your departure are determined and made public, encourage your Board leadership to put those plans into writing—summarizing your tenure, accomplishments, future plans, recognition event, time line, and preliminary plans for continuity of leadership. Having a continuity plan already in place will of course make this much easier.

Exhibit 20.2
Board Leadership Transition Checklist

In the event of an ED transition, the Board should consider the following list to guide their work:

Task	Purpose	✓
Form transition committee.	• Evaluate interim management needs. • Develop a plan to manage transition issues.	
Create a communication plan.	• Communicate the transition to internal and external stakeholders in a timely manner. • Provide reassurance of a plan and leadership for a smooth transition.	
Plan celebration for departing ED.	• Recognize and celebrate ED's legacy.	
Develop interim leadership plan.	• Maintain ongoing operations. • Ensure communications channels between Board and staff and volunteers. • Support processing of emotional and psychological transition issues.	
Evaluate need for outside expertise to guide the Board through the ED search process.	• Ensure adequate process and resources are in place for an effective and timely transition.	

Task	Purpose	✓
Assess organizational strengths, challenges, opportunities, and threats.	• Accurately determine skills and experience needed in new ED.	
Revisit strategic plan for clarification of shifts in organizational focus.	• Represent organization accurately.	
Prioritize the essential skills and experience needed in the new ED.	• Ensure a good fit, improving chances of longer tenure.	
Determine recruitment and selection strategy, including implementation steps.	• Develop a strong pool of qualified candidates.	
Plan new ED orientation.	• Welcome, educate, and support new ED. • Clarify roles, responsibilities, and authority.	
Establish three-month ED performance expectations.	• Clarify priorities and expectations between Board and ED.	
Set first-year schedule for ED quarterly reviews.	• Provide feedback and support to clarify priorities and expectations.	

Step Three: Support but do not lead the search process. Do not feel that you need to identify or recruit your successor, lead the search process, or even serve on the search committee. This is the Board's responsibility and not one they can delegate. They are more likely to fully support and engage with a leader of their choice. Your role is to encourage them to adopt an efficient and effective transition and search strategy, and to identify resources and assistance to support them in the process.

Step Four: Transfer leadership. It is time to transfer the leadership reins to the Board. From the moment you announce your intention to leave, you relinquish long-term leadership of the organization and, by default, move into the role of interim ED. It is important to remember that your Board will not start to lead the transition process until you let go of the reins. Now is not the time to commit the organization to the details of a new strategic vision that you will not be around to implement, or to launch a new program based on your connections and skills.

Your priority is to continue the day-to-day management of the organization, focusing on the transfer of knowledge, responsibilities, and relationships. You will need to negotiate clear boundaries with the Board for your transitional role, transfer responsibilities for long-range projects to others, and clarify your level of authority on major issues that will affect the organization beyond your tenure.

If you and the Board anticipate a gap of three months or more between your departure and the arrival of the next Executive Director, the Board may want to consider hiring someone act as an interim ED. While this may be a new concept for some communities, more and more nationally affiliated and local management support organizations are recruiting and developing seasoned nonprofit professionals to serve in interim management roles so that organizations and Boards have the necessary time to do a comprehensive search and accomplish a smooth leadership transition.

This interval can be especially valuable when Board and staff are dealing with the more intense emotional and organizational issues associated with ending a lengthy relationship with their Executive Director.

Step Five: Celebrate your legacy. Finally, you get to step back and celebrate your legacy—embrace the relationships you have formed and candidly acknowledge the opportunities and challenges you are passing on to your successor. Then let go. Assuming everyone has paid attention to the details of this transition, the new Executive Director will be able to move into the job with a couple of days of orientation and a few phone calls or meetings a month or so down the road.

Lengthy overlap with the new ED is usually not necessary and can create awkward dual leadership issues for Board and staff. Also, avoid the invitation to join the Board or consult, at least initially. While the intent is good, the offer is often a sign of reluctance to let go or accept change. Your tenure is complete and it is now time for your successor to establish a new pattern of identity, authority, and visibility in the organization and the community. The organization should be ready to explore its vision, opportunities, and challenges through new eyes. The next ED will probably approach the organization much differently than you did and that can be very healthy.

Exhibit 20.3 provides a checklist for Executive Directors to orchestrate good endings and help track the many management tasks that need to be done during the transition time. There are suggested steps to guide both longer- and

Exhibit 20.3 ED Transition Management Checklist	
Task	✓
If transition is approximately eight months or longer away:	
• Maintain a small circle of confidentiality.	
• Strengthen Board leadership.	
• Implement or update succession and continuity plans.	
• Revisit your strategic direction (not full-scale strategic planning) for	
• Clarity and agreement about the organization's direction	
• Candor about the challenges	
• Definition of the values and culture of the organization	
• Build the management team.	
• Move the stakeholders and funders closer to staff and Board.	
• Delegate, delegate, delegate.	
If your transition is four months away or closer:	
• Compile list of pending projects and assignments.	
• Meet with Executive or Transition Committee to set priorities and determine delegation procedures.	
• Set up a transition or continuity file to include	
• Board roster, job descriptions, and biographies.	
• Volunteer committee structure and membership.	
• Staff roster and job descriptions.	
• Organization chart.	
• Board and volunteer committee rosters.	
• Strategic plan or annual goals and accomplishments to date.	
• Employee handbook.	
(Continued)	

Task	✓

- Most recent budget, financial statements, cash flow statements, and audit.
- By-laws and policies, procedures, or practices not documented elsewhere.
- List of vendors, task forces, or collaboratives for which you have primary responsibility. Include contact info and meeting schedules.
- Staff, Board, volunteer, and community challenges or threats (in conjunction with Executive Committee).
- Brief summary of your typical week and month in terms of Board, staff, clients, reports and administration, community connections, and key seasonal issues that affect your role.
- List of deadlines for reports to funders, stakeholders, community leaders.
- Critical info pertaining to voice mail, e-mail, pager, cell phone, bank, alarm systems, account numbers, and passwords.

  Note: All the information in this bullet point should be stored in a secure file drawer in an office that is locked when not occupied. One or two staff should have access to that office and file drawer.
- Complete outstanding employee evaluations and document deficiencies or warnings.
- Develop a schedule of pending reviews and how they are to be handled.
- Make the following contacts:
  - Inform the auditor of the transition and see if you need to set down anything for next year's audit that only you may know.

Task	✓
• Change signature authority with all banks and payroll services. • Inform external stakeholders of the transition and assure them that the organization will be in good hands. Transfer your relationship to others in conjunction with the Board communication plan.	

near-term transitions. Above all, be clear about your decision to leave. Once you have made that decision, leave with integrity in a time-sensitive manner. Your ultimate legacy and years of hard work will be framed in your ability to make a clean transition.

The actions proposed in Exhibit 20.3 and the information compiled as a result of using it become part of your parting legacy to the organization and form a welcoming foundation for the interim or incoming ED. The new Executive Director's initial success will help put the organization on track for years to come, so the effort is well worthwhile.

How you leave the leadership of an organization is as important as how you enter it. Do it well and it contributes to your legacy and the well-being of those that follow. Do it poorly and your years of accomplishments can be quickly forgotten. Career transitions are never easy to anticipate, but like wills and memorial services, are part of the natural progression of life. The following story from the field shows how one Executive Director made a difficult but successful transition from his job.

STORY FROM THE FIELD

Every spring when it came time for Tom's review, he would find himself burned-out and defensive given the stress of the last several months. When he met with his Board Chair for his review, Tom would privately announce that he was anticipating retiring in the near future. At the same time, many members of the Board were beginning to voice concerns about Tom's performance and lack of enthusiasm for the organization's new direction. Given that Tom would be leaving soon, and no one on the Board wanted to rock the boat, the feedback about these concerns was less than candid.

Two years later, Tom was still in the role of the Executive Director, the organization had made little progress in achieving its new strategic direction, and tension between the Board and Tom had reached an all-time high. When it came time for his review, the new Board Chair took Tom to lunch and through a series of coaching questions helped Tom to realize that the tensions were organizational rather than personal. The organization valued his many contributions, but its survival hinged on this new direction and a different set of skills. Tom became less defensive and reflected on his strengths and how they could be put to work in possible new career paths. A few months later he announced that he was moving to a partner organization in a newly created position that allowed him to focus on program delivery. He left the organization on a high note and made room for a new leader to be successful.

WHAT ARE SOME TYPICAL CAREER PATHS FOR FORMER EXECUTIVE DIRECTORS?

In our twenty-five years' experience in the field, we have observed some common paths that many former EDs pursue, assuming they are not attracted to leading another organization. The following ideas may help you match your interests and skills to a new career strategy.

Program specialist or director: If you find yourself driven by your organization's mission and love working closely with clients and their issues, consider stepping into a program role. Program management allows you to focus your energy and skills more directly on the heart of the mission rather than on balancing management and leadership roles.

Development director: Great fundraisers are great matchmakers. They have a special gift for matching community needs or an organization's vision with the investment resources of donors and community leaders. If you enjoy building and nurturing relationships with donors, designing outreach and community events, and are detail-oriented in the context of tracking and recognizing donations, this may be the next job for you. Salaries for fundraisers with a proven track record in capital campaigns or planned giving are often comparable to those of Executive Directors.

Nonprofit consultant: As a consultant, you can apply your skills and expertise toward helping a variety of organizations. You can work independently or through a consulting firm. Consulting can provide great flexibility, but that flexibility may be counterbalanced by a lack of funds to sustain you as you build a practice, irregular paychecks, and fewer benefits. This field demands great time management and communication skills.

Interim ED: Often organizations find themselves in need of an Executive Director or specialist to help with day-to-day management during staff transitions or sabbaticals. The primary differences between interim management and permanent positions are the length of service (usually a few months) and the scope of work (mostly internal and focused more on maintenance and support than innovation). You need to be able to hit the ground running, to quickly form relationships, and to gain the trust of the staff and the Board.

Government or public sector: The public and government sectors are similar to the nonprofit sector in the types of work done, accountability requirements, and work with Boards. In addition, this work normally includes night and weekend meetings and events. This may be a career opportunity if you are strong at consensus building and find the political arena intriguing. The benefits and retirement packages also tend to be very attractive.

Foundations: Your knowledge of the nonprofit sector and your experience raising funds can be transferred to the opportunities and challenges of grant making. Giving money isn't as easy as it may sound. Whether you are a program officer in a large foundation or a director of a family fund, you need to be able to clearly define and articulate the organization's priorities while screening and prioritizing a multitude of requests and proposals. Many of these positions tend to be heavy on administration, while others are more externally focused.

Corporate sector, community affairs officer: Many corporations feel strongly about their corporate responsibility to support the community in which they operate. Your experience in the nonprofit arena and understanding of how to meet broader community needs are often directly transferable to a liaison post with a major corporation.

The message of this book is to support and sustain you in your career choice of Executive Director. While we hope that your current career is fulfilling, you may eventually want to redirect the incredible array of skills and relationships you have built into a new organization or even career path. Whatever your path, let your values and vision guide you to work that you love.

TIPS FOR SUCCESS

- The decision to leave an Executive Director position may be driven by external opportunities, but more often it is informed by internal reflection about your life goals and how your job as an ED complements them or competes with them.

- You will need to negotiate clear boundaries with the Board for your transitional role, transfer responsibilities for long-range projects to others, and clarify your level of authority on major issues that will affect the organization beyond your tenure.

- If you are a Founder or have been with the organization for many years, it is essential to find a balance between your strong leadership legacy and ensuring that the organization engages in an objective evaluation of their strengths, weaknesses, opportunities, and barriers to success as part of your transition.

- How you leave the leadership of an organization is as important as how you enter it. Do it well and it contributes to your legacy and the well-being of those that follow. Do it poorly and your years of accomplishments can be quickly forgotten.

- Celebrations that recognize a departing Executive Director's legacy and give you an opportunity to say thank-you and good-bye are a critical part of your term's ending. Doing them well establishes a healthy foundation for the next ED to build on.

CONCLUSION

As you have surmised from this book, the role of an Executive Director is one of the biggest and most challenging jobs anyone can ever love. While the work itself is normally straightforward, the issues, relationships, competing priorities, and environment constantly change, and the constant scarcity of resources demands incredible passion, focus, and leadership. It is not a career choice to be made lightly. Once entered, the job of Executive Director is exciting and rewarding, as well as frustrating. If you are committed to staying awhile longer in this incredible position, we commend you. We need you. Our hope is that *The Executive Director's Guide to Thriving as a Nonprofit Leader* gives you new perspective and new tools for your leadership.

And if you are feeling ready to move on to a new career, we thank you for bringing your passion to the profession. This book was inspired by those Executive Directors who have put passion before profit to make our neighborhoods, communities, and world a better place for all.

CHAPTER ONE (UNDERSTANDING THIS BIG JOB)

Books and Articles

Brinckerhoff, P. C. *Mission-Based Management: Leading Your Not-for-Profit into the 21st Century.* (3rd ed.) Hoboken, N.J.: Wiley, 2009.

CompassPoint and The Meyer Foundation. Daring To Lead 2006. San Francisco: CompassPoint, 2006. Available at www.compasspoint.org/daringtolead2006.

Connors, T. D. (ed.). *The Nonprofit Handbook: Management.* (3rd ed.) Hoboken, N.J.: Wiley, 2001.

De Pree, M. *Leading Without Power.* San Francisco: Jossey-Bass, 2003.

Drucker, P. *Managing the Non-Profit Organization.* New York: HarperCollins, 2006.

Greenleaf, R. *Servant Leadership: A Journey into the Nature of Legitimate Power & Greatness.* Mahwah, N.J.: Paulist Press, 2002.

Herman, R. D. (ed.). *The Jossey-Bass Handbook of Nonprofit Leadership and Management.* (2nd ed.) San Francisco: Jossey-Bass, 2004.

Hesselbein, F., Goldsmith, M., and Beckhard, R. (eds.). *Leader of the Future 2.* San Francisco: Jossey-Bass, 2006.

Kouzes, J., and Posner, B. *A Leader's Legacy.* San Francisco: Jossey-Bass, 2006.

Kouzes, J., and Posner, B. *The Leadership Challenge.* (4th ed.) San Francisco: Jossey-Bass, 2008.

Lewis, R. L. *Effective Nonprofit Management: Essential Lessons for Executive Directors.* New York: Aspen, 2001.

McGee-Cooper, A., and Looper, G. *The Essentials of Servant-Leadership: Principles in Practice.* Waltham, Mass.: Pegasus Communications, 2001.

Perry, J. (ed.). *The Jossey-Bass Reader on Nonprofit and Public Leadership.* San Francisco: Jossey-Bass, 2009.

Spears, L., and Lawrence, M. *Practicing Servant Leadership: Succeeding Through Trust, Bravery, and Forgiveness.* San Francisco: Jossey-Bass, 2004.

Periodicals

The Leadership Quarterly. Published quarterly by Elsevier. For more information go to www.elsevier.com/.

Leader to Leader. Published quarterly by the Leader to Leader Institute and Jossey-Bass. Phone 888-481-2665 or e-mail jbsubs@jbp.com for more information.

Nonprofit Quarterly. Published by Third Sector New England of Boston, Massachusetts. Phone 800-281-7770 or check www.nonprofitquarterly.org/ for more information.

NonProfit Times. Published by The NonProfit Times, Parsippany, New Jersey. Phone 973-394-1800 or fax 973-394-2888 for more information; order online at www.nptimes.com/.

Nonprofit World. Published by the Society of Nonprofit Organizations, Canton, Michigan. Phone 734-451-3582 or fax 734-451-5935 for more information; order and read online at www.snpo.org/.

Online Resources

Note that Web sites and other online resources are subject to frequent change. All the URLs given here and in subsequent sections were active as of November 10, 2009, but may not remain active, or the links may be broken. If the URLs do not take you to the expected site, try searching for the organization or publication name in a search engine before assuming it does not exist.

Action Without Borders Nonprofit FAQ. Available at www.idealist.org/if/idealist/en/ FAQ/ Nonprofit/Home/default.

Charity Channel Forums. Available at www.charitychannel.com/forums/discussion-lists .aspx.

Free Management Library. Available at http://managementhelp.org/. (Note: This is a good and helpful Web site for all aspects of nonprofit management.)

Leader to Leader Institute. Available at www.leadertoleader.org/.

U.S. Small Business Administration (SBA): Small Business Planner. Available at www.sba .gov/smallbusinessplanner/manage/lead/serv_twodiffani.html.

CHAPTER TWO (DEVELOPING AS AN EXECUTIVE DIRECTOR)

Books and Articles

Bennis, W. *On Becoming a Leader.* (4th ed.) New York: Basic Books, 2009.

Bennis, W., and Goldsmith, J. *Learning to Lead: A Workbook on Becoming a Leader.* New York: Basic Books, 2003.

DePree, M. *Leadership Jazz.* (revised ed.) New York: Doubleday, 2008.

Kouzes, J. *Credibility: How Leaders Gain and Lose It, Why People Demand It.* (rev. ed.) San Francisco: Jossey-Bass, 2003.

Kouzes, J., and Posner, B. *Leadership Practices Inventory: A Self-Assessment and Analysis.* San Francisco: Jossey-Bass, 2003.

Kouzes, J., and Posner, B. *The Leadership Challenge: How to Keep Getting Extraordinary Things Done in Organizations.* (4th ed.) San Francisco: Jossey-Bass, 2007.

Linnell, D., Radosavich, Z., and Spack, J. *The Executive Director's Guide: Better Leaders, Better Nonprofits, Better World.* Boston, Mass.: Third Sector Press, 2002.

Organizations

The following organizations provide management support to nonprofits. This is only a sample of organizations in each region that provide consulting, training, information resources, or any combination of the three. For additional referrals, contact the Alliance for Nonprofit Management at www.allianceonline.org/ or your local United Way, Community Fund, or volunteer center. Any of the groups listed in the following sections may also be able to provide useful referrals.

West

Center for Excellence in Nonprofits, San Jose, Calif.; www.cen.org/.

Center for Nonprofit Management in Southern California, Los Angeles, Calif.; www.cnmsocal.org/.

Center for Volunteer and Nonprofit Leadership, Marin County, Calif.; www.cvnl.org/.

Colorado Nonprofit Development Center, Denver, Colo.; www.cndc.org/.

CompassPoint Nonprofit Services, San Francisco, Calif.; www.compasspoint.org/.

The CBO Center, Oakland, Calif.; www.cbocenter.org/cms/index.php.

Nonprofit Resource Center, Sacramento, Calif.; www.nprcenter.org/.

Nonprofit Support Center of Santa Barbara County, Santa Barbara, Calif.; www.nscsb.org/.

Sierra Nonprofit Support Center, Sonora, Calif.; www.sierranonprofit.org/.

Southwest

Arizona State University Lodestar Center for Philanthropy and Nonprofit Innovation, Phoenix, Ariz.; www.asu.edu/copp/nonprofit.

Center for Community Based and Nonprofit Organizations, Austin, Tex.; www.nonprofitaustin.org/.

Center for Nonprofit Excellence, Albuquerque, N.M.; www.centerfornonprofitexcellence.org/.

Center for Nonprofit Excellence, Colorado Springs, Colo.; www.cnecoloradosprings.org.

Center for Nonprofit Management, Dallas, Tex.; www.cnmdallas.org/.

Nonprofit Management Center of the Permian Basin, Midland, Tex.; www.nmc-pb.org/.

Nonprofit Center, Tacoma, Wash.; www.npcenter.org/.

Nonprofit Management Center of Wichita Falls, Wichita Falls, Tex.; www.nonprofitcenterwf.org/.

Nonprofit Resource Center of Texas, San Antonio; www.nprc.org/.

Santa Fe Community Foundation, Santa Fe, N.M.; www.santafecf.org/.

Texas Nonprofit Management Assistance Network, San Antonio; www.txnetwork.org/.

Midwest

Center for Nonprofit Excellence, Akron, Ohio; www.cfnpe.org/.

Center for Nonprofit Management, Minneapolis, Minn.; www.stthomas.edu/business/centers/nonprofit.

Center for Nonprofits, Oklahoma City, Okla.; www.oklahomacenterfornonprofits.org/.

Indiana Nonprofit Resource Network, Elkhart, Muncie, and Indianapolis, Ind.; www.inm.org/.

Iowa Nonprofit Resource Center, University of Iowa; http://nonprofit.law.uiowa.edu/.

Management Assistance Program for Nonprofits, St. Paul, Minn.; www.mapfornonprofits.org/.

Mandel Center for Nonprofit Organizations, Cleveland, Ohio; www.cwru.edu/mandelcenter.

Michigan Nonprofit Association, Lansing, Mich.; www.mnaonline.org/.

Midwest Center for Nonprofit Leadership, Kansas City, Mo.; www.mcnl.org/.

Minnesota Council of Nonprofits, St. Paul, Minn.; www.mncn.org/.

Nonprofit Alliance, Michigan; www.nonprofitalliance.org/.

Nonprofit Center of Milwaukee, Milwaukee, Wisc.; www.nonprofitcentermilwaukee.org/.

University of Michigan—Nonprofit & Public Management Center, Ann Arbor, Mich.; www.ssw.umich.edu/underoneroof.

Northeast

Bayer Center for Nonprofit Management, Pittsburgh, Penn.; www.rmu.edu/bcnm.

BoardSource, Washington, D.C.; www.boardsource.org/.

LaSalle University Nonprofit Center, Philadelphia, Penn.; www.lasallenonprofitcenter.org/.

Leader to Leader Institute, New York; www.leadertoleader.org/.

Maryland Association of Nonprofit Organizations, Baltimore and Silver Spring, Md.; www.mdnonprofit.org/.

National Council of Nonprofit Associations, Washington, D.C.; www.councilofnonprofits.org/.

New Hampshire Center for Nonprofits, Concord, N.H.; www.nhnonprofits.org/.

Nonprofit Support Center, Worcester, Mass.; www.greaterworcester.org/services/NSC.htm.

Not For Profit Resource Center, Buffalo, N.Y.; www.uwbec.org/.

Support Center for Nonprofit Management, New York; www.supportcenteronline.org/.

Third Sector New England, Boston, Mass.; www.tsne.org/.

Southeast

C-One, Center on Nonprofit Effectiveness, Miami, Fla.; www.c-one-miami.org/.

Center for Nonprofit Excellence, Louisville, Ky.; www.cnpe.org/.

Center for Nonprofit Management, Nashville, Tenn.; www.cnm.org/.

Center for Nonprofits, Chattanooga, Tenn.; www.cnpchatt.org/.

Georgia Center for Nonprofits, Atlanta, Ga.; www.gcn.org/.

Greater New Orleans Nonprofit Knowledge Works, New Orleans, La.; www.nkw.org/.

Mississippi Center for Nonprofits, Jackson, Miss.; www.msnonprofits.org/.

Nonprofit Center of Northeast Florida, Jacksonville, Fla.; www.nonprofitctr.org/.

Nonprofit Resource Center, Sarasota, Fla.; www.cfsarasota.org/.

Nonprofit Resource Center of Alabama, Birmingham, Ala.; www.nrca.info.

North Carolina Center for Nonprofits, Raleigh, N.C.; www.ncnonprofits.org/.

South Carolina Association of Nonprofit Organizations, Columbia, S.C.; www.scanpo .org/.

Periodicals

Fast Company. Published by Gruner + Jahr USA Publishing. Phone 800-542-6029 or check www.fastcompany.com/ for more information.

Stanford Social Innovation Review. Published by Stanford University. Phone 888-488-6596 or check www.ssireview.org/ for more information.

Online Resources

Centerpoint for Leaders Online Leadership Assessment and Development Program. Available at www.centerpointforleaders.org/.

Coaches Training Institute. Available at www.thecoaches.com/.

Directory of Life Coaches. Available at www.lifecoachguide.com/.

Free Management Library, an online resource hosted by The Management Assistance Program, St. Paul, Minn. Available at www.managementhelp.org/; phone 651-647-1216.

Institute for Professional Empowerment Coaching. Available at www.ipeccoaching.com/.

International Coaches Federation. Available at www.coachfederation.org/.

W.K. Kellogg Foundation, "Community Partnership Toolkit, Section Three, Leadership Development." Available at www.wkkf.org/Pubs/CustomPubs/CPtoolkit/cptoolkit/ Sec3-LeadershipDev.htm.

Zimmerman Lehman Associates, "Eight Characteristics of Leadership, 2007." Available at www.zimmerman-lehman.com/leadership.htm.

CHAPTER THREE (FINDING BALANCE IN THE ROLE OF EXECUTIVE DIRECTOR)

Books and Articles

"A New Way To Capacity: Executive Coaching." *Irvine Quarterly,* 2005, 4(4).

Blanchard, K., and McBride, M. *The Fourth Secret of the One Minute Manager: A Powerful Way to Make Things Better.* New York: HarperCollins, 2008.

Chambre, S. M. "Burnout: What to Do When You're at the End of Your Rope." *Volunteer Leadership,* July-Sept. 1998, pp. 23–24.

CompassPoint Nonprofit Services, *Executive Coaching Project: Evaluation of Findings.* San Francisco: CompassPoint Nonprofit Services, 2003.

Corrigan, M. "Burnout: How to Spot It and Protect Yourself Against It." *Journal of Volunteer Administration,* 1994, *12,* 24–31.

Covey, S. *The 7 Habits of Highly Effective People.* New York: Simon & Schuster, 2004.

Covey, S. *The 8th Habit: From Effectiveness to Greatness.* New York: Free Press, 2005.

Firedman, S. *Be a Better Leader, Have a Richer Life.* Boston: Harvard Business Press, 2008.

Friedman, S. D., and Greenhaus, J. H. *Work-Family: Allies or Enemies?* Oxford, England: Oxford University PR on Demand, 2000.

Harari, O. *Leadership Secrets of Colin Powell.* Columbus, Ohio: McGraw-Hill, 2002.

Jenson, D. "In Search of the Balanced Leader." *Nonprofit World,* Nov.-Dec. 1998, *16,* 48–50.

Kofodimos, J. *Balancing Act: How Managers Can Integrate Successful Careers and Fulfilling Personal Lives.* San Francisco: Jossey-Bass, 1993.

Kofodimos, J. *Your Executive Coaching Solution: Getting Maximum Results from the Coaching Experience.* Palo Alto, Calif.: Davies-Black, 2008.

Marcus-Newhall, A., Halpern, D. F., and Tan, S. J. *The Changing Realities of Work and Family.* Hoboken, N.J.: Wiley-Blackwell, 2008.

Oncken, W., Jr., and Burrows, H. *The One Minute Manager Meets the Monkey.* New York: Morrow, 1989.

Solomon, J., and Sandahl, Y. "Stepping Up or Stepping Out." Washington, D.C.: Young Nonprofits Professional Network (YNPN), 2007. Visit www.ynpn.org/ for copy of report.

Weiss, A. *Life Balance: How to Convert Professional Success into Personal Happiness.* San Francisco: Jossey-Bass/Pfeiffer, 2003.

Online Resources

Balancing Act, an electronic newsletter discussing the blending of life, work, and relationships. Edited by Alan Weiss, Ph.D.; subscribe at balancingact@summitconsulting.com.

Barr Foundation. Available at www.barrfoundation.org/.

The California Wellness Foundation. Available at www.tcwf.org/.

Durfee Foundation, www.durfee.org/.

The Free Management Library, hosted by the Management Assistance Program of St. Paul, Minn. (see "Online Resources" for Chapter Two), has a Personal Wellness Page at www.managementhelp.org/prsn_wll/wrk_life.htm.

Foundations Offering Sabbaticals for Nonprofit Executives Alston/Bannerman Program. Available at www.alstonbannerman.org/.

Virginia Piper Charitable Trust. Available at www.pipertrust.org/.

Windcall Resident Program. Available at www.commoncounsel.org/.

CHAPTER FOUR (UNDERSTANDING NONPROFIT ORGANIZATIONAL CULTURE)

Books and Articles

Bridges, W. *The Character of Organizations.* Palo Alto, Calif.: Davies-Black, 2000.

Cameron, K. S., and Quinn, R. E. *Diagnosing and Changing Organizational Culture: Based on the Competing Values Framework.* San Francisco: Jossey-Bass, 2005.

Driskill, G. W., and Brenton, A. L. *Organizational Culture in Action: A Cultural Analysis Workbook.* Thousand Oaks: Sage, 2005.

Gallos, Joan V. *Organization Development: A Jossey-Bass Reader.* San Francisco: Jossey-Bass, 2006.

Harrison, R., and Stokes, H. *Diagnosing Organizational Culture.* San Francisco: Jossey-Bass, 1992.

Heskctt, J. L., and Schlesinger, L. "Leaders Who Shape and Keep Performance-Oriented Culture," in F. Hesselbein, M. Goldsmith, and R. Beckhard, (eds.), *Leader of the Future.* San Francisco: Jossey-Bass, 1996.

Lee, S.K.J., and Yu, K. "Corporate Culture and Organizational Performance." *Journal of Management Psychology,* 2004, *19*(4), 340.

Lund, D. B. "Organizational Culture and Job Satisfaction." *Journal of Business & Industrial Marketing,* 2003, *18*(2/3), 219-236.

Martin, J. *Organizational Culture, Mapping the Terrain.* Thousand Oaks, Calif.: Sage, 2002.

Schabracq, M. *Changing Organization Culture: The Change Agent's Guidebook.* Hoboken, N.J.: Wiley, 2007.

Schein, E. *Organizational Culture and Leadership.* (3rd ed.) San Francisco: Jossey-Bass, 2003.

Schein, E. *The Corporate Culture Survival Guide, New and Revised Edition.* San Francisco: Jossey-Bass, 2009.

Online Resources

McNamara, C. "Organizational Culture." Available at www.managementhelp.org/org_thry/culture/culture.htm.

Management Strategies, Visionomics Quarterly Newsletter. Available at www.visionomics.com/.

The Organizational Culture Web site. Available at www.organizational-culture.com/.

Toolpack Consulting—various articles. Available at www.toolpack.com/.

Other articles and newsletters can be found at www.leadershipadvantage.com/.

CHAPTER FIVE (EMBRACING YOUR ORGANIZATION'S VALUES)

Books and Articles

Barrett, R. *Building a Values-Driven Organization: A Whole Systems Approach to Cultural Transformation.* Burlington, Mass.: Elsevier, 2006.

Hampden-Turner, C., and Trompenaars, F. *Building Cross-Cultural Competence: How to Create Wealth from Connecting Values.* New Haven, Conn.: Yale University Press, 2000.

Rothman, J. *Cultural Competency in Process and Practice: Building Bridges.* Upper Saddle River, N.J.: Allyn & Bacon, 2007.

Schokley-Zalabak, P. *Fundamentals of Organizational Communication: Knowledge, Sensitivity, Skills, and Values.* (7th ed.) Upper Saddle River, N.J.: Allyn & Bacon, 2008.

St. Onge, P. *Embracing Cultural Competency.* St. Paul, Minn.: Fieldstone Alliance, 2009.

Whiteley, A., and J. *Core Values and Organizational Change: Theory and Practice.* Hackensack, N.J.: World Scientific, 2006.

Williams, M. A., and Clifton, D. O. *The 10 Lenses: Your Guide to Living and Working in a Multicultural World.* Herndon, Va.: Capital Books, 2001.

Online Resources

About.com: Human Resources. "Build an Organization Based on Values," by Susan Heathfield. Available at http://Humanresources.about.com/od/strategicplanning1/a/organizvalues.

Alliance for Nonprofit Management: Cultural Competency Initiative. Available at www.allianceonline.org/.

"Cultural Competence." En.wikipedia.org.

Olson, L., Bhattacharya, J., and Scharf, A. "Cultural Competency: What It Is and Why It Matters." Published by California Tomorrow, 2006. Available at www.lpfch.org/informed/culturalcompetency.pdf.

CHAPTER SIX (CREATING A VISION AND PLAN)

Books and Articles

Allison, M., and Kaye, J. *Strategic Planning for Nonprofit Organizations.* (2nd ed.) Hoboken, N.J.: Wiley, 2003.

Barry, B. W. *The Strategic Planning Workbook for Nonprofit Organizations.* (2nd ed.) St. Paul, Minn.: Amherst H. Wilder Foundation, 2000.

Bryson, J. *Strategic Planning for Public and Nonprofit Organizations.* (3rd ed.) San Francisco: Jossey-Bass, 2003.

Bryson, J. and Alston, F. *Creating and Implementing Your Strategic Plan: A Workbook for Public and Nonprofit Organizations.* San Francisco, Jossey-Bass, 2004.

De Pree, M. *Leadership Is an Art.* New York: Doubleday, 1989.

Gross, S. *Seven Turning Points: Leading Through Pivotal Transition in Organization Life.* St. Paul, Minn.: Fieldstone Alliance, 2009.

Kouzes, J., and Posner, B. *The Leadership Challenge.* San Francisco: Jossey-Bass, 2006.

La Piana, D. *Play to Win: The Nonprofit Guide to Competitive Strategy.* San Francisco: Jossey-Bass, 2004.

La Piana, D. *Nonprofit Strategy Revolution: Real-Time Strategic Planning in a Rapid-Response World.* St. Paul, Minn.: Fieldstone Alliance, 2009.

Lindgren M., and Bandhold, H. *Scenario Planning—Revised and Updated Edition: The Link Between Future and Strategy.* New York: Palgrave-McMillan, 2009.

Nanus, B. *Visionary Leadership.* San Francisco: Jossey-Bass, 1995.

Nanus, B. *Leaders Who Make a Difference: Essential Strategies for Meeting the Nonprofit Challenge.* San Francisco: Jossey-Bass, 1999.

Schwartz, P. *The Art of the Long View: Planning for the Future in an Uncertain World.* New York: Doubleday, 1997.

Waechter, S. *Driving Strategic Planning.* Washington, D.C.: Board Source, 2010.

Wilson, I., and Ralston, B. *Scenario Planning Handbook: Developing Strategies in Uncertain Times.* Boerne, Tex.: Southwestern Educational, 2006.

Online Resources

McNamara, C. "Developing Your Strategic Plan." Available at managementhelp.org/np_progs/sp_mod/str_plan.htm.

NonprofitExpert.com. "Strategic Planning." Available at www.nonprofitexpert.com/strategic_planning.htm.

Whatcom Council of Nonprofits. "Best Practices for Nonprofits: Strategic Planning." Available at www.wcnwebsite.org/practices/strategic.htm.

CHAPTER SEVEN (DETERMINING ORGANIZATIONAL EFFECTIVENESS)

Books and Articles

Carman, J. G., and Fredericks, K. A. *Nonprofits and Evaluation.* New Directions for Evaluation, no. 119. San Francisco, Jossey-Bass, 2008.

Carver, J. *The Policy Governance Model and the Role of the Board Member, A Carver Policy Governance Guide. Volume 5, Evaluating CEO and Board Performance, Revised and Updated Edition.* San Francisco: Jossey-Bass, 2009.

Collins, J. *Good to Great and the Social Sectors: A Monograph to Accompany Good to Great.* New York: HarperCollins, 2005.

Crutchfield, L., and McLeod-Grant, H. *Forces for Good: The Six Practices of High-Impact Nonprofits.* San Francisco: Jossey-Bass, 2008.

Dees, J. G., Emerson, J., and Economy, P. *Strategic Tools for Social Entrepreneurs: Enhancing the Performance of Your Enterprising Nonprofit.* Hoboken, N.J.: Wiley, 2002.

Drucker, P. F. *The Effective Executive.* (2nd ed.) Oxford: Butterworth-Heinemann, 2007.

Dubois, A. "Is It Time for an Organizational Assessment?" *Nonprofit World,* 1995, *13,* 40, 42.

Fitz-Gibbon, C. T. *How to Design a Program Evaluation.* Thousand Oaks, Calif.: Sage, 1987.

Galer, D. "Achieving Quality in Nonprofits." *Nonprofit World,* 1988, *6,* 22–24.

Gray, S. T. *Evaluation with Power: A New Approach to Organizational Effectiveness, Empowerment, and Excellence.* San Francisco: Jossey-Bass, 1998.

Kettner, P., Martin, L., and Moroney, R. *Designing and Managing Programs: An Effectiveness-Based Approach.* Thousand Oaks, Calif.: Sage, 2007.

Owen, J., and Rogers, P. *Program Evaluation: Forms and Approaches.* (3rd ed.) St. Leanords, NSW, Australia: Allen & Unwin, 2006.

Saul, J. *Benchmarking for Nonprofits: How to Measure, Manage, and Improve Performance.* St. Paul, Minn.: Fieldstone Alliance, 2004.

Stern, G. *The Drucker Foundation Self-Assessment Tool.* San Francisco: Jossey-Bass, 1999.

York, P. *Funder's Guide to Evaluation: Leveraging Evaluation to Improve Nonprofit Effectiveness.* St. Paul, Minn.: Fieldstone Alliance, 2005.

Online Resources

Eight Steps to Success. Available at www.liveunited.org/outcomes/.

Examples of Outcomes and Indicators. Available at www.liveunited.org/outcomes/.

Glossary of Outcome Measurement Terms. Available at www.liveunited.org/outcomes/.

Introduction to Outcome Measurement. Available at www.liveunited.org/outcomes/.

McNamara, C. "Basic Guide to Outcomes-Based Evaluation for Nonprofit Organizations with Very Limited Resources." Available at http://managementhelp.org/evaluatn/outcomes.htm.

Program Outcome Model. Available at www.liveunited.org/outcomes/.

United Way of America Outcome Measurement: What, Why, and How? Excerpts from Measuring Program Outcomes: A Practical Approach. Available at www.liveunited.org/outcomes/.

Why Measure Outcomes? Available at
Agency Uses of Outcome Information. Available at www.liveunited.org/outcomes/.

CHAPTER EIGHT (EMBRACING A CHANGING NONPROFIT ENVIRONMENT)

Books and Articles

Borrup, T. C. *Creative Community Builder's Handbook: How to Transform Communities Using Local Assets, Arts, and Culture.* St. Paul, Minn.: Fieldstone Alliance, 2006.

Cavanagh, R., and Drucker, P. *Emerging Partnership: New Ways in a New World.* Available at Leader to Leader Institute Web Site, http://leadertoleader.org/forms/partners.pdf.

Dees, J. G., Economy, P., Emerson, J., and Johnston, R. *Enterprising Nonprofits: A Toolkit for Social Entrepreneurs.* Hoboken, N.J.: Wiley, 2001.

Drucker, P. F. *The Five Most Important Questions You Will Ever Ask About Your Organization.* San Francisco: Jossey-Bass, 2008.

Frumkin, P. "On Being Nonprofit: The Bigger Picture." *Harvard Business School Working Knowledge,* Sept. 9, 2002. Available at http://leadertoleader.org/forms/4-99news.pdf.

Hart, T. R., Greenfield, J. M., MacLaughlin, S., and Geier, P. H. *Nonprofit Internet Management: Strategies, Tools & Trade Secrets.* Hoboken, N.J.: Wiley, in press.

"Insights from All Three Sectors." *Drucker Foundation News,* April 1999. Available at leadertoleader.org/forms/4-99news.pdf.

Jackson, P. M., and Fogarty, T. E. *Sarbanes-Oxley and Nonprofit Management: Skills, Techniques, and Methods.* Hoboken, N.J.: Wiley, 2006.

"Job or Vocation." *Nonprofit Quarterly,* Feb. 2001, entire issue.

Light, P. *Making Nonprofits Work: A Report on the Tides Nonprofit Management Reform.* Washington, D.C.: Brookings Institution Press, 2000.

Linzer, R., and Linzer, A. *The Cash Flow Solution: The Nonprofit Board Member's Guide to Financial Success and Cash Flow Strategies.* San Francisco: Jossey-Bass, 2008.

O'Neil, M. *Nonprofit Nation: A New Look at the Third America.* San Francisco: Jossey-Bass, 2002.

Pietersen, W. *Strategic Learning: How to Be Smarter Than Your Competition and Turn Key Insights into Competitive Advantage.* Hoboken, N.J.: Wiley: in press.

Ross, H. (ed.). *Managing Technology to Meet Your Mission: A Strategic Guide for Nonprofit Leaders.* San Francisco: Jossey-Bass, 2009.

Sagawa, S. *The Charismatic Organization: Eight Ways to Grow a Nonprofit that Builds Buzz, Delights Donors, and Energizes Employees.* San Francisco: Jossey-Bass, 2008.

"Sector at Work: Identity Under Construction." *Nonprofit Quarterly,* July 2001, entire issue.

Welytok, J. G. *Nonprofit Law & Governance for Dummies.* Hoboken, N.J.: Wiley, 2007.

Online Resources

About.com, Nonprofit Charitable Orgs. Available at http://nonprofit.about.com/.

Blue Avocado. Available at www.blueavocado.org/.

NonProfit Times. Available at www.nptimes.com/.

CHAPTER NINE (UNDERSTANDING CHANGING LIFE CYCLE STAGES IN NONPROFITS)

Books and Articles

Burns, M. "Act Your Age! The Organizational Lifecycle and How It Affects Your Board." *Nonprofit Quarterly,* Summer 1997. Available online: http://216.65.35.60/pdf/actyourage.pdf.

Connolly, P. M. *Navigating the Organizational Lifecycle: A Capacity-Building Guide for Nonprofit Leaders,* Washington D.C.: BoardSource, 2006.

Greiner, L. "Evolution and Revolution as Organizations Grow." *Harvard Business Review,* May-June 1998, pp. 55–68. (Originally published in the Jul.-Aug. 1972 issue.)

Gross, S. *Seven Turning Points: Leading Through Pivotal Transitions in Organizational Life.* St. Paul, Minn.: Fieldstone Alliance, 2009.

Hernandez, C. M., and Leslie, D. R. "Charismatic Leadership: The Aftermath." *Nonprofit Management & Leadership,* 2001, *11,* 493–497.

McLaughlin, T. A. "Where Is Your Agency? The Life Cycle of Nonprofit Organizations." *NonProfit Times,* 1996, *10,* 27.

Miller, L. *Barbarians to Bureaucrats.* New York: Potter, 1989.

Simon, J. S., and Donovan, J. T. *The Five Life Stages of Nonprofit Organizations.* Saint Paul, Minn.: Amherst H. Wilder Foundation, 2001.

Stevens, S. K. Nonprofit Lifecycles: Stage-based Wisdom for Nonprofit Capacity. Long Lake, Minn.: Stagewise Enterprises, 2002.

Online Resources

Fieldstone Alliance. "The Nonprofit Life Stage Assessment." Available at http://surveys .wilder.org/fieldstone/lifestages/.

CHAPTER TEN (LEADING ORGANIZATIONAL CHANGE)

Books and Articles

Adams, T. *The Nonprofit Leadership Transition and Development Guide: Proven Paths for Leaders and Organizations.* San Francisco: Jossey-Bass, in press.

Black, J. S., and Gregersen, H. B. *Leading Strategic Change.* Upper Saddle River, N.J.: Prentice Hall, 2002.

Dolny, H. *Banking On Change.* London: Viking Press, 2001.

Duck, J. D. *The Change Monster.* New York: Random House, 2001.

Dyck, B. "The Role of Crises and Opportunities in Organizational Change: A Look at a Nonprofit Religious College." *Nonprofit and Voluntary Sector Quarterly,* 1996, *25,* 321–346.

Fullan, M. *Leading in a Culture of Change.* San Francisco: Jossey-Bass, 2001.

Fullan, M. *Change Leader: Learning to Do What Matters Most.* San Francisco: Jossey-Bass, in press.

Galaskiewicz, J., and Bielefeld, W. *Nonprofit Organizations in an Age of Uncertainty: A Study of Organizational Change.* Hawthorne, N.Y.: Aldine de Gruyter, 1998.

Grobman, G. M. *Improving Quality and Performance in Your Non-Profit Organization: An Introduction to Change Management Strategies for the 21st Century.* Harrisburg, Penn.: White Hat Communications, 1999.

Johnson, S. *Who Moved My Cheese?* New York: Putnam, 1998.

Kotter, J. P. "Winning at Change." *Leader to Leader,* 1998, *10,* 27–33.

Letts, C. *High Performance Nonprofit Organizations: Managing Upstream for Greater Impact.* Hoboken, N.J.: Wiley, 1998.

Online Resources

The HRD Group Ltd., Nottingham, England. Available at www.organisationalchange .co.uk.

Interchange International, Dallas, Tex.; phone 800-878-8422. Available at www.change-cycle.com/.

Maurer & Associates; phone 703-525-7074. Available at www.beyondresistance.com/.

CHAPTERS ELEVEN AND TWELVE (NURTURING A RELATIONSHIP WITH THE BOARD; DEVELOPING RELATIONSHIPS WITH INDIVIDUAL BOARD MEMBERS)

Books and Articles

American Bar Association. *Guide to Nonprofit Corporate Governance in the Wake of Sarbanes-Oxley.* Chicago: American Bar Association, 2006.

Bell, P. D. *Fulfilling the Public's Trust: Ten Ways to Help Nonprofit Boards Maintain Accountability.* Washington, D.C.: National Center For Nonprofit Boards, 1993.

BoardSource. *The Handbook of Nonprofit Board Governance.* Washington, D.C.: BoardSource, in press.

BoardSource. *The Nonprofit Board Answer Book: A Practical Guide for Board Members and Chief Executives.* (2nd ed.) Washington, D.C.: BoardSource, 2009.

BoardSource. *Board Self-Assessment: Assess to Advance.* Washington, D.C.: BoardSource, 2009.

BoardSource. *The Source: Twelve Principles of Governance That Power Exceptional Boards.* Washington, D.C.: BoardSource, 2005.

BoardSource. *Exceptional Board Practices: The Source in Action.* Washington, D.C.: BoardSource, 2007.

BoardSource. *Principles Workbook: Steering Your Board Towards Good Governance and Ethical Practice.* Washington, D.C.: BoardSource, 2009.

Carver, J. *Boards That Make a Difference.* San Francisco: Jossey-Bass, 2006.

Carver, J. *The Policy Governance Model and the Role of the Board Member, A Carver Policy Governance Guide, Set.* (Six Booklets for Board Members.) San Francisco: Jossey-Bass, 2009.

Chait, R. P. *How to Help Your Board Govern More and Manage Less.* (2nd ed.) Washington D.C.: National Center For Nonprofit Boards, 2003.

Chait, R. P. *Governance as Leadership: Reframing the Work of Nonprofit Boards.* Hoboken, N.J.: Wiley, 2004.

Connor, J. A., and Kadel-Taras, S. "Governing Outside: Bringing the Board into the Community." *Board Member,* 2000, *9,* 6–7.

Hughes, S., Lakey, B., and Bobowick, M. *The Board Building Cycle: Nine Steps to Finding, Recruiting, and Engaging Nonprofit Board Members.* Washington, D.C.: BoardSource, 2000.

Independent Sector. *Principles of Good Governance and Ethical Practice.* Washington, D.C.: Independent Sector, 2007.

Jackson, D. K., and Holland, T. P. "Measuring the Effectiveness of Nonprofit Boards." *Nonprofit and Voluntary Sector Quarterly,* 1998, *27.*

Lakey, B. *The Board Building Cycle: Nine Steps to Finding, Recruiting and Engaging Nonprofit Board Members.* Washington, D.C.: National Center for Nonprofit Boards, 2007.

Masaoka, J. *Best of the Board Café.* St. Paul, Minn.: Fieldstone Alliance, 2009.

Moyers, Richard L. *The Nonprofit Chief Executive's Ten Basic Responsibilities.* Washington, D.C.: BoardSource, 2006.

O'Connell, B. *Board Overboard: Laughs and Lessons for All but the Perfect Nonprofit.* San Francisco: Jossey-Bass, 1995.

Souccar, M. K. "Lunching Ladies Meet Hip-Hop: A Charity Finds New Donors, Vitality." *Crain's New York Business,* May 2002, *18.*

Taylor, B. E., Chait, R. P., and Holland, T. P. "The New Work of the Nonprofit Board." *Harvard Business Review,* Sept.-Oct. 1996. Reprint #96509.

Walsh, J. A. "Nonprofit Boards: Eight Leadership Development Stories." *Nonprofit World,* 2002, *20*(1), 11–17.

Williams, S., and McGinnis, K. *Getting The Best From Your Board.* Washington, D.C.: BoardSource, 2007.

Wood, M. N. (ed.). *Nonprofit Boards and Leadership: Cases on Governance, Change, and Board-Staff Dynamics.* San Francisco: Jossey-Bass, 1996.

Organizations

BoardSource, Washington, D.C.; phone 800-883-6262; www.boardsource.org/.

Independent Sector, Washington, D.C.: phone 202-467-6100: www.independentsector.org.

Trustee Leadership Development, Indianapolis, Ind.; phone 877-564-6853; www.tld.org/.

Periodicals

Board Leadership: Policy Governance in Action, edited by J. Carver. Published bimonthly by Jossey-Bass. Phone 888-378-2537 for more information.

Board Member. Published bimonthly by BoardSource. Phone 800-883-6262 or check www.boardsource.org/ for more information.

CHAPTER THIRTEEN (ESTABLISHING PRODUCTIVE STAFF RELATIONSHIPS)

Books and Articles

Armstrong, S., and Mitchell, B. *The Essential HR Handbook.* Franklin Lakes, N.J.: Career Press, 2008.

Brinckerhoff, P. C. *Generations: The Challenge of a Lifetime for Your Nonprofit.* St. Paul, Minn.: Fieldstone Alliance.

De Pree, M. *Leading Without Power.* (paperback ed.) San Francisco: Jossey-Bass, 2003.

Hacker, C. A. *The High Cost of Low Morale.* Boca Raton, Fla.: Saint Lucie Press, 1997.

Kouzes, J., and Posner, B. *Credibility: How Leaders Gain and Lose It.* San Francisco: Jossey-Bass, 2003.

Kouzes, J., and Posner, B. *Encouraging the Heart.* San Francisco: Jossey-Bass, 2003.

Kunreuther, F., Kim, H., and Rodriguez, R. *Working Across Generations.* San Francisco: Jossey-Bass, 2009.

Mathis, R., and Jackson, J. *Human Resource Management.* Mason, Ohio: Thompson Learning Academic Resource Center, 2008.

Messmer, M. *Human Resources Kit for Dummies.* Foster City, Calif.: IDG Books Worldwide, 1999.

Rees, F. *Teamwork from Start to Finish.* San Francisco: Jossey-Bass/Pfeiffer, 1997.

Senge, P. *The Fifth Discipline: The Art and Practice of the Learning Organization.* New York: Doubleday, 1990.

Weisbord, M. *Productive Workplaces Revisited: Dignity, Meaning, and Community in the 21st Century.* San Francisco: Pfeiffer, 2004.

Wilson, J., and Gislason, M. *Coaching Skills for Nonprofit Managers and Leaders: Developing People to Achieve Your Mission.* San Francisco: Jossey-Bass, 2009.

Online Resources

Gelston, S. "Gen Y, Gen X and the Baby Boomers: Workplace Generation Wars," CIO. com, 2008. Available at www.cio.com/article/178050/Gen_Y_Gen_X_and_the_Baby_ Boomers_Workplace_Generation_Wars?page=1.

Gilburg, D. "Management Techniques for Bringing Out the Best in Generation Y," CIO. com, 2007. Available at www.cio.com/article/149053/Management_Techniques_for_ Bringing_Out_the_Best_in_Generation_Y?source=artrel_top.

Gilburg, D. "Generation X: Stepping Up to the Leadership Plate," CIO.com, 2007. Available at www.cio.com/article/28475/Generation_X_Stepping_Up_to_the_Leadership_ Plate?source=artrel_top.

CHAPTER FOURTEEN (FOLLOWING THE FOUNDER)

Books and Articles

Adams, T. *The Nonprofit Leadership Transition and Development Guide: Proven Paths for Leaders and Organizations.* San Francisco: Jossey-Bass, 2010.

Adams, T. "Departing? Arriving? Surviving and Thriving Lessons for Executives." *Nonprofit Quarterly,* Winter 2003, p. 6.

Block, S. *Why Nonprofits Fail: Overcoming Founder's Syndrome, Fundphobia and Other Obstacles to Success.* San Francisco: Jossey-Bass, 2003.

Block, S., and Rosenburg, S. "Toward an Understanding of Founder's Syndrome." *Nonprofit Management and Leadership,* Summer 2002, p. 353.

Clampa, D., and Watkins, M. "The Successor's Dilemma." *Harvard Business Review,* Nov.-Dec. 1999.

Kunreuther, F. *Working Across Generations: Defining the Future of Nonprofit Leadership.* San Francisco: Jossey-Bass, 2009.

Lewis, H. "Founder's Syndrome: An Affliction for Which There Is Rarely Immunity." Development Consultant Associates, 2006, www.fianationalnetwork.org/viewfile .cfv?id=1474.

McNamara, C. *Founder's Syndrome: How Corporations Suffer and Can Recover.* St. Paul, Minn.: Management Assistance Program for Nonprofits, 1999, www.managementhelp.org/misc/founders.htm.

Rechtman, J. "Legacy and Letting Go: A Framework for Leadership Transfer." *BoardSource,* April 2000, p. 8.

Redington, E., and Vickers, D. *Following the Leaders: A Guide for Planning Founding Director Transition.* Columbus, Ohio: Academy for Leadership and Governance, 2001.

CHAPTER FIFTEEN (ENGAGING EXTERNAL STAKEHOLDERS)

Books and Articles

Avner, M. *Lobbying and Advocacy Handbook for Nonprofit Organizations: Shaping Public Policy at the State and Local Level.* St. Paul, Minn.: Fieldstone Alliance, 2002.

Bonk, K., Griggs, H., and Tynes, E. *The Jossey-Bass Guide to Strategic Communications for Nonprofits.* (2nd ed.) San Francisco: Jossey-Bass, 2008.

Bray, R. *SPIN Works!* San Francisco: Independent Media Institute, 2000.

Drucker, P. F. *The Five Most Important Questions You Will Ever Ask About Your Organization.* San Francisco: Jossey-Bass, 2008.

Elberg, G., and Phillips, J. "The Art of Community Building in Light of R. Putnam's *Bowling Alone.*" *Journal of Volunteer Administration,* 2001, *19*(3), 33.

Etling, A. "Evaluability Assessment Clarifies Complex Programs." *Journal of Volunteer Administration,* 1990, *8*(3), 21–28.

Leet, R. K. *Message Matters: Succeeding at the Crossroads of Mission and Market.* St. Paul, Minn.: Fieldstone Alliance, 2007.

Mattessich, P. W., Monsey, B. R., and Roy, C. *Community Building: What Makes It Work—A Review of Factors Influencing Successful Community Building.* St. Paul, Minn.: Amherst H. Wilder Foundation, 1997.

Patterson, S. J., and Radtke, J. M. *Strategic Communications for Nonprofit Organization: Seven Steps to Creating a Successful Plan.* (2nd ed.) Hoboken, N.J.: Wiley, 2009.

Sagawa, S., and Jospin, D. *The Charismatic Organization: Eight Ways to Grow a Nonprofit that Builds Buzz, Delights Donors, and Energizes Employees.* San Francisco: Jossey-Bass, 2008.

CHAPTER SIXTEEN (EMBRACING PARTNERSHIPS AND COLLABORATION)

Books and Articles

Arsenault, J. *Forging Nonprofit Alliances.* San Francisco: Jossey-Bass, 1998.

Austin, J. *The Collaboration Challenge.* San Francisco: Jossey-Bass, 2000.

"Building Strategic Partnerships." *Nonprofit Quarterly,* Fall 2001, entire issue.

Golensky, M., and DeRuiter, G. L. "The Urge to Merge: A Multiple-Case Study." *Nonprofit Management & Leadership,* 2002, *13*, 137.

Hoskins, L., and Angelica, E. *Fieldstone Alliance Nonprofit Guide to Forming Alliances: Working Together to Achieve Mutual Goals.* St. Paul, Minn.: Fieldstone Alliance, 2000.

James Irvine Foundation. "Strategic Solutions: Mergers and Acquisitions Nonprofit Style." *Irvine Quarterly,* Summer 2002.

Kohm, A., and La Piana, D. Strategic Restructuring for Nonprofit Organizations. Westport, Conn.: Praeger, 2003.

La Piana, D. *Beyond Collaboration: Strategic Restructuring of Nonprofit Organizations.* Washington D.C.: National Center for Nonprofit Boards, 1997.

La Piana, D. *Nonprofit Mergers Workbook Part I: The Leader's Guide to Considering, Negotiating, and Executing a Merger, Updated Edition.* St. Paul, Minn.: Fieldstone Alliance, 2008.

La Piana, D. *Play to Win.* San Francisco: Jossey-Bass, 2005.

Linden, R. M. *Leading Across Boundaries: Creating Collaborative Agencies in a Networked World, Updated and Expanded Edition.* San Francisco: Jossey-Bass, 2010.

Mattessich, P., Murray-Close, M., and Monsey, B. *Collaboration: What Makes It Work.* (2nd ed.) St. Paul, Minn.: Amherst H. Wilder Foundation, 2001.

McCormick, D. *Nonprofit Mergers: The Power of Successful Partnerships.* Boston: Jones and Bartlett, 2003.

Peter F. Drucker Foundation for Nonprofit Management. *Meeting the Collaboration Challenge Workbook: Developing Strategic Alliances Between Nonprofit Organizations and Businesses.* San Francisco: Jossey-Bass, 2002.

Ray, K., and Winer, M. *Collaboration Handbook: Creating, Sustaining and Enjoying the Journey.* St. Paul, Minn.: Fieldstone Alliance, 1994.

Wheeler, D. "Rethinking Nonprofit Partnerships." *Chronicle of Philanthropy,* June 27, 2002.

Online Resources

"Collaboration: What Makes It Work," workshops from the Leader to Leader Institute. Available at www.leadertoleader.org/.

"Emerging Partnerships: New Ways in a New World," Leader to Leader Institute Reports. Available at www.leadertoleader.org/.

"Meeting the Collaboration," a monthly e-mail newsletter from the Leader to Leader Institute Challenge. Available at www.leadertoleader.org/.

Strategic Solutions for Nonprofits and Foundations. Available at www.lapiana.org/.

CHAPTER SEVENTEEN (ENSURING SOUND FINANCIAL MANAGEMENT)

Books and Articles

Bell, J., and Schaffer, E. *Financial Leadership for Nonprofit Executives: Guiding Your Organization to Long-term Success.* St. Paul, Minn.: Fieldstone Alliance, 2005.

Blazek, J. *Nonprofit Financial Planning Made Easy.* Hoboken, N.J.: Wiley, 2008.

Dropkin, M., and Halpin, J. *Bookkeeping for Nonprofits: A Step-by-Step Guide to Nonprofit Accounting.* San Francisco: Jossey-Bass, 2005.

Dropkin, M., Halpin, J., and LaTouche, B. *The Budget-Building Book for Nonprofits: A Step-by-Step Guide for Managers and Boards.* (2nd ed.) San Francisco: Jossey-Bass, 2007.

"Financial Str(u/i)ctures." *Nonprofit Quarterly,* Spring 2003, entire issue.

Larkin, R. F. *Wiley Not-for-Profit GAAP 2009: Interpretation and Application of Generally Accepted Accounting Principles.* Hoboken, N.J.: Wiley, 2009.

McLaughlin, T. A. *Streetsmart Financial Basics for Nonprofit Managers.* Hoboken, N.J.: Wiley, 2009.

Raymond, S. U. *Nonprofit Finance for Hard Times: Leadership Strategies When Economies Falter.* Hoboken, N.J.: Wiley, 2009.

Ruegg, D., and Venkatrathnam, L. M. *Bookkeeping Basics: What Every Nonprofit Bookkeeper Needs to Know.* St. Paul, Minn.: Fieldstone Alliance, 2003.

Online Resources

Guidestar (an easy-to-use Web site that allows you to search for the Form 990 filed by any nonprofit organization). Available at www2.guidestar.org/.

Nonprofit Finance Fund. Available at www.nonprofitfinancefund.org/.

Resource Directory: Nonprofit Genie (a series of FAQs on finance topics including audit, Form 990, and fiscal sponsorship). Available at www.compasspoint.org/askgenie/index.php.

CHAPTER EIGHTEEN (SUSTAINING THE ORGANIZATION WITH TEAM-BASED FUNDRAISING)

Books and Articles

Bray, I. *Effective Fundraising For Nonprofits.* (2nd ed.) Berkeley, Calif.: Nolo Press, 2008.

Carlson, M. *Team-Based Fundraising: Step by Step.* San Francisco: Jossey-Bass, 2000.

Ciconte, B. and Jacob, J. *Fundraising Basics.* (3rd ed.) Boston: Jones and Bartlett, 2009.

Fredricks, L. *The Ask: How to Ask Anyone for Any Amount for Any Purpose.* San Francisco: Jossey-Bass, 2006.

Grace, K. S. *Beyond Fundraising: New Strategies For Nonprofit Innovation and Investment.* (2nd ed.) Hoboken, N.J.: Wiley, 2005.

Joyaux, S. P. *Strategic Fund Development.* New York: Aspen, 1997.

Klein, K. *Fundraising for Social Change.* (5th ed.) San Francisco: Jossey-Bass, 2006.

Klein, K. *Reliable Fundraising: What Good Causes Need to Know to Survive and Thrive.* San Francisco: Jossey-Bass, 2009.

Rees, F. *25 Activities for Developing Team Leaders.* San Francisco: Jossey-Bass, 2004.

Sargeant, A., and Shang, J. *Fundraising Principles and Practice.* San Francisco: Jossey-Bass, 2010.

Schaff, T., and Schaff, D. *The Fundraising Planner.* San Francisco: Jossey-Bass, 1999.

Tempel, E. R. *Hank Rosso's Achieving Excellence in Fund Raising, 2nd Edition.* San Francisco: Jossey-Bass, 2003.

Warwick, M. *Fundraising When Money Is Tight.* San Francisco: Jossey-Bass, 2009.

Warwick, M. *How to Write Successful Fundraising Letters* (w/CD). (2nd ed.) San Francisco: Jossey-Bass, 2008.

CHAPTER NINETEEN (PLANNING FOR HEALTHY TRANSITIONS OF LEADERSHIP)

Books and Articles

Adams, T. *The Nonprofit Leadership Transition and Development Guide: Proven Paths for Leaders and Organizations.* San Francisco, Jossey-Bass, in press.

Adams, T. "Departing? Arriving? Surviving and Thriving Lessons for Executives." *Nonprofit Quarterly,* Winter 2003, p. 6.

Axelrod, N. *Chief Executive Succession Planning: The Board's Role in Securing Your Organization's Future.* Washington, D.C.: BoardSource, 2002.

Beazley, H., Boenisch, J., and Harden, D. *Continuity Management.* Hoboken, N.J.: Wiley, 2002.

Goldsmith, M. *Succession: Are You Ready?* Cambridge: Harvard Business Press, 2009.

McLaughlin, T. A., and Backlund, A. N. *Moving Beyond Founder's Syndrome to Nonprofit Success.* Washington, D.C.: BoardSouce 2008.

Rechtman, J. *Legacy and Letting Go: A Framework for Leadership Transfer.* Washington, D.C.: National Center for Nonprofit Boards, 2000.

Rothwell, W. *Effective Succession Planning: Ensuring Leadership Continuity and Building Talent from Within.* New York: AMACOM, 2005.

Wolfred, T. *Managing Executive Transitions.* St. Paul, Minn.: Fieldstone Alliance, 2009.

Organizations

Annie E. Casey Foundation Series on leadership transition, www.aecf.org/.

Bridgestar, www.bridgestar.org/.

CompassPoint (www.compasspoint.org)

Transition Guides, www.transitionguides.org/.

Periodicals

Nonprofit Quarterly, www.nonprofitquarterly.org, "Leadership Transitions," Winter 2002.

Nonprofit Quarterly, www.nonprofitquarterly.org, "Powerful Nonprofit Leadership," Spring 2008.

CHAPTER TWENTY (MOVING ON: MAKING YOUR OWN CAREER TRANSITION)

Books and Articles

Albion, M. *Finding Work That Matters* (audiocassette). Louisville, Colo.: Sounds True, 2002.

Bolles, R. N. *What Color Is Your Parachute: A Practical Manual for Job-Hunters and Career-Changers.* Berkeley, CA: Ten Speed Press, 2002.

Bolles, R. N. *What Color Is Your Parachute? for Retirement: Planning Now for the Life You Want.* Berkeley, CA: Ten Speed Press 2007.

Bridges, W. *The Way of Transition: Embracing Life's Most Difficult Moments.* New York: Perseus, 2001.

Bridges, W. *Managing Transitions: Making the Most of Change.* New York: Perseus, 2003.

Cryer, S. *The Nonprofit Career Guide.* St Paul, Minn.: Fieldstone Alliance, 2008.

Depew, N. *Character in Transition: A Guide to Not Burning the Bridge.* Bloomington, Ind.: iUniverse, 2005.

Kouzes, J., and Posner, B. *A Leader's Legacy.* San Francisco: Jossey-Bass. 2006.

McLaughlin, T. A., and Backlund, A. N. *Moving Beyond Founder's Syndrome to Nonprofit Success.* Washington D.C.: BoardSouce, 2008.

Sher, B. *I Could Do Anything If I Only Knew What It Was.* New York: DTP, 1995.

Tebbe, D. *Chief Executive Transitions: How to Hire and Support a Nonprofit CEO.* Washington D.C.: BoardSouce 2008.

Organizations

Annie E. Casey Foundation Series on leadership transition, www.aecf.org/.

Bridgestar, www.bridgestar.org/.

CompassPoint, www.compasspoint.org/.

Transition Guides, www.transitionguides.org/.

Periodicals

Nonprofit Quarterly, www.nonprofitquarterly.org, "Leadership Transitions," Winter 2002.

Nonprofit Quarterly, www.nonprofitquarterly.org, "Powerful Nonprofit Leadership," Spring 2008.

INDEX

Page references followed by *e* indicate an exhibit.

D

De Pree, M., 173, 177, 178

Decision making: background information needed for, 157; Board–ED relationship and, 158–160; Executive Director career transition, 271e–272

Decline and closing stage: description of, 122e; Executive Director skills needed during, 125e

Delegating, learning the art of, 45

Development director, 280

Development stage: description of, 122e; Executive Director skills needed during, 125e

Dobbs, S., 15

Donor records, 263

Drucker, P., 89, 201

Duca, D., 144e

E

E-mail communication, 185e, 189–190

Economic cycles, 111–114

ED Transition Management Checklist, 277e–278e

Effectiveness. *See* Organizational effectiveness

Emergency succession planning, 267–268

Encouraging the Heart (Kouzes and Posner), 65

The Enduring Skills of Change Leaders (Kanter), 127

Executive coaches: caution related to selecting, 25; development facilitation by, 22–23; establishing mutual goals and expectations with, 24; health relationship between a board and, 150–152; personal level of assessing use of, 23; professional level of assessing use of, 24; sharing financial crisis information, 243–244; story on selecting and using, 25–26

Executive Director development: activities for, 21e; competency worksheet for, 17e–18e; executive coaches used for, 22–26; Management Prioritizing Decision Tree for, 19–20e; using peer group or leadership circle for, 26–27; self-reflection on skills and, 16–18; staying inspired to continue with, 27–29; time and opportunities for, 18–22; tips for successful, 29

Executive Director responsibilities: clear communication with board on, 39; of different roles, 4–8; differentiating between board and, 152–155; fiscal, 234e–235e; preparing their nonprofits for partnerships, 224–225; prioritizing time to fulfill, 40–45

Executive Director roles: change agent, 6, 51–52, 105–136, 194–195; community creator, 6–7, 201–225; in embracing organizational change, 128–134; fiscal, 234e–235e; leader versus manager, 8–10e; in mobilizing outside community change, 107–108; resource wizard, 7, 227–253; responsibilities of different, 4–8; tips for successful, 14; visionary role, 5e, 47–102; when to take on specific, 10–14. *See also* Relationship building role

Executive Directors (EDs): action steps to grow into position of, 8; building quick credibility, 174–177; career transition of, 269–281; "fit" between nonprofits and, 53–54; interim, 280; leadership during restructuring process, 101–102; leading a culturally competent organization, 74–76; life cycle stages and skills required by, 123–126; organizational effectiveness examined by, 94–95; organizational effectiveness linked to performance of, 96–98e; as overwhelming position, 3–4; sample job description for, 41e–42e; shared organizational vision lead by, 79–81; staying inspired, 27–29; taking sabbaticals, 28–29; time spent fundraising by, 248–250. *See also* Board–Executive Director partnerships

Executive Director's Guide (Linnell, Radosevich, and Spack), 139

Executive Leadership in Nonprofit Organizations (Herman and Heimovics), 161

Expansion and growth stage: description of, 122e; Executive Director skills needed during, 125e

External stakeholders: communication strategies for, 209e–211e; description of, 204; discovering your, 206e; identifying, 204–206; less obvious and sometimes overlooked, 205; most obvious, 205. *See also* Community; Stakeholders

External stakeholders–ED relationship: Communications Ladder to use for, 208e; rallying stakeholders for advocacy, 212–213; strategies for developing and nurturing, 206–208; tips for success, 214

F

Facebook, 81, 117, 191, 213

Farquharson, P., 137

FASB 117, 232

Leaders: comparing managers to, 8–10e; of culturally competent organization, 74–76; sample task list for, 10e; when Executive Directors take the role of, 10–14. *See also* Managers

Leaders Who Make a Difference (Nanus and Dobbs), 15

Leadership: building staff and volunteer, 181–183; culturally competent organization, 74–76; financial management roles of, 233–235e; organizational change, 127–136; planning for health transitions of, 257–268

The Leadership Challenge (Kouzes and Posner), 78

Leadership circles, 26

Leadership transition: Board Leadership Transition Checklist, 274e–275e; departing Executive Director and smooth, 272–279; ED Transition Management Checklist, 277e–278e; planning succession for, 257–268

Leading Without Power (De Pree), 173, 177

Life balance: definition of, 33–34; learning to delegate to maintain, 45; reflections and setting priorities for, 34e–36; setting boundaries to achieve, 36–40; setting priorities for your time, 40–45; story on creating, 44; tips for successful, 46

Life Balance Reflection Chart: example of a, 35–36; how to create a, 34–35

Life cycle stages: description of individual, 122e; Executive Directors skills needed in each, 123–126; Founder transition during, 194–195; identifying current stage your nonprofit is at, 121–123; organizational culture development during, 51–52; recognizing that nonprofits may have different, 120; tips for success, 126

Light, P., 105

Linnell, D., 139

M

McNamara, C., 193

The Magic of Dialogue (Yankelovich), 203

Management Prioritizing Decision Tree, 19–20e

Managers: comparing leaders to, 8–10e; making financial reports to, 236, 237e; sample task list for, 10e; when Executive Directors take the role of, 10–14. *See also* Leaders

Managing Executive Transitions (Wolfred), 269

Mathiasen, K., III, 119, 142e

Maturity stage: description of, 122e; Executive Director skills needed during, 125e

Measurable outcomes demands, 114–116

Mergers, 223

Millennials: characteristics of, 183, 184e–185e; working with, 186–188

Mission statement, 80

Mission-Based Management (Brinckerhoff), 229

Mistakes, 182

Monitoring fiscal issues, 235e

MySpace, 81, 191

N

Nanus, B., 15

Net assets, 231

Nonprofit consultant, 280

The Nonprofit Leadership Transition and Development Guide (Adams), 257

Nonprofit organizations: accountability demands on, 114–116, 178, 211e; changing environment of, 105–118; collaboration and partnerships of, 66–67, 215–225; creating vision and strategic plans, 77–87; effectiveness of, 89–102; financial practices unique to, 230–233; "fit" between Executive Directors and, 53–54; initial identity established by Founders, 51; leading change in, 127–136; life cycle stages in, 51–52, 119–126, 194–195; organizational culture of, 51–63; Social Entrepreneur objectives for, 109; technological changes impacting, 116–117; "three-legged stool" analogy of government, business, and, 107; values guiding the, 56–59. *See also* Organizations

Nonprofit sector: accountability/measurable outcome demands on, 114–116; change synonymous with identity of, 106–107; Executive Director role in shaping, 110–111; organizational change impacted by changes in, 108–110

Nourishment environment, 178

O

Objectives: board work plan with performance, 156e–157e; ED work plan performance, 38e–39

Organizational change: accountability/ measurable outcome demands leading to,

Organizational change (*Continued*) 114–116; boom-and-bust economic cycles and, 111–114; business and nonprofit sector changes affecting, 108–110; ED, board, staff, and volunteer roles in, 134–135; Executive Director role in mobilizing outside, 107–108; Executive Director's role in embracing, 128–134; leadership challenges during, 127–128; process of, 130*e*–131*e*; technological changes impacting, 116–117; timing of, 135–136; tips for success, 118, 136

Organizational culture: definitions of, 50–51; development of, 51–53; encouraging positive staff relationships and healthy, 177–181; essentials of a healthy, 178; Executive Director's impact and influence on, 55–59; Executive Director's understanding of, 53–55; life cycle stages and development of, 51–52; strategies for shifting, 59–63; tips for success in determining, 63. *See also* Culture

Organizational effectiveness: Executive Director's performance tied to, 96–100; increasing scrutiny of, 89–90; methods of gathering feedback on, 92*e*; questions to ask about, 94; recognizing, 90–94; steps for correcting problems with, 100–102; tips for success, 102; when to measure, 94–95. *See also* Performance

Organizational values: collaboration as, 66–67; compared to ground rules or code of conduct, 71; cultural competence as, 71, 73–74; description and significance of, 65–66; guiding nonprofits, 56–59; how an Executive Director establishes, 71; organizational activities and, 66–71; tips for success, 76; Values Exercise on, 72*e*–73*e*; The Women's Foundation of California Values Chart, 67*e*–70*e*

Organizations: culturally competent, 71, 73–76; financial practices unique to for-profit, 230–233; life cycle stages of, 51–52, 119–126, 194–195. *See also* Nonprofit organizations

Overhead costs, 250

P

Partnership Matrix, 222*e*

Partnerships: ED assessment of values and risks of, 217–220; ED's organizational preparation to enter into, 224–225; importance for nonprofits, 215–216; tips for successful, 225; variety of opportunities for nonprofit, 221–224. *See also* Collaboration; Crisis and restructuring stage

Peer support groups, 26–27

Performance: board work plan objectives for, 156*e*–157*e*; defining measures of, 98*e*; ED work plan objectives for, 38*e*–39; organization effectiveness link to personal, 96–100. *See also* Organizational effectiveness

Permanently restricted net assets, 231

Permanently restricted support, 232

The Philosophy of Andy Warhol (Warhol), 103

Posner, B., 65, 78

Powell, C., 31

Professional Development Activities for Executive Directors, 21*e*

Program specialist/director, 279–281

Programs: implementation of, 230, 242–243; succession planning relationship to, 264–265

R

Radosevich, Z., 139

Relationship building role: with the board, 139–160; description of, 137–138; differentiating between board and ED responsibilities, 152–155; embracing partnership and collaboration, 215–225; engaging external stakeholders, 203–214; establishing productive staff relationships, 173–192; following the Founder, 193–202; healthy Executive Director-Board relationship, 150–152; with individual board members, 161–172; responsibilities of, 6. *See also* Executive Director roles

Renegade board members, 166–169

Reporting: definition of, 230; ED role in, 235*e*; financial information to managers and boards, 236, 237*e*

Resource wizard role: description of, 227–228; ensuring sound financial management, 229–244; responsibilities of, 7; sustaining nonprofit with team-based fundraising, 245–253

Respect, 178, 197

Restructuring. *See* Crisis and restructuring stage

Revenue: accounting for contributions, 231–232; accounting for sources of, 233; covering overhead costs, 250; fundraising, 245–253

Revenue sources, 233

S

Sabbaticals, 28–29

Sarbanes-Oxley Act (2002), 115

Schaffer, E. N., 229

Setting priorities, 34c–36, 44–45

Skoll Foundation Web site, 110

Smith, D. K., 3

Social Entrepreneurs, 109

Social networking technology: blogs, 117; description of, 117; Facebook, 81, 117, 191, 213; MySpace, 81, 191; Twitter, 117. *See also* Technology

Spack, J., 139

Staff: articulated learning of paid and unpaid, 56; assumptions guiding behavior of, 56; building leadership and management skills, 181–183; cultural competence of, 74, 76; fundraising team responsibilities by, 247e; ground rules for, 179; keeping Founders on as, 198–200; nonprofit values shaping and guiding, 56–59; organizational change role by, 134–135; sharing financial crisis information with the, 243–244; shifting organizational culture of, 59–63; telecommuting by, 116–117. *See also* Stakeholders; Volunteers

Staff Expectations Statement, 176–177e

Staff–ED relationships: building quick credibility with staff, 174–177; building staff leadership and management skills, 181–183; encouraging healthy culture and positive, 177–181; establishing appropriate boundaries in, 191–192; establishing strong lines of communication, 188–189; generational differences and, 183–188; importance of establishing, 173–174; tips for success related to, 192

Stakeholder Communication Strategy, 209e–211e

Stakeholders: definition of, 204; nonprofit need for, 203. *See also* External stakeholders; Staff; Volunteers

Start-up stage: description of, 122e; Executive Director skills needed during, 125e

Stories from the Field: building ED–external stakeholder relationship, 208–209; building relationship with board, 146–147; career transition, 279; changing harmful culture, 180–181; ED skills during life cycle stages, 123–124; executive coaching, 25–26; leading organizational change, 132–133; organizational effectiveness, 98–100; partnership value and risks, 219–220; planning organizational vision, 84–85; setting priorities for life balance, 44; shifting nonprofit organizational culture, 60–61; succession planning, 266; surviving poor economy, 112–113; team-based fundraising, 250–251; transition from Founder-led to Board–ED leadership, 198–199; "two-hat theory" on board member actions, 168; on when to take leader vs. supporter role, 12–13

Strategic plans: contents of a, 83e; description of, 82; organizational vision guiding, 82–86; succession planning component of, 260–261. *See also* Work plans

Stress: burnout due to, 31–32; finding a balance to manage, 33–46; of unrealistic expectations and work plans, 32–33

Succession planning: emergency, 267–268; goal of healthy, 257–258; importance of, 258–259e; knowledge management role in, 262–268; organizational structures included in, 260–262; tips for successful, 268

Supporter roles, 10–14

Survey Monkey, 91

T

Team-based fundraising: matrix for responsibilities, 247e–248e; primary responsibility for, 246, 248; tips for successful, 253; unrestricted gifts and role of, 252e–253e

Team-Based Fundraising: Step by Step (Carlson), 246, 251

Technology: effective staff communication using, 189–191; organizational changes due to, 116–117; succession planning and role of, 265. *See also* Social networking technology

Telecommuting, 116–117

Temporarily restricted net assets, 231

Temporarily restricted support, 232

"Three-legged stool" analogy, 107

Tips for success: Board–ED partnerships, 160, 172; collaboration and partnerships, 225; creating organizational vision, 87; ED career transition, 281; Executive Director development, 29; Executive Director roles/responsibilities, 14; external stakeholders–ED relationship, 214; financial management,